THE PRINCE CONSORT

THE PRINCE, AFTER SHOOTING, WITH THE QUEEN AT WINDSOR CASTLE

Reproduced from the painting by Landseer, by gracious permission of His Majesty the King

THE PRINCE CONSORT

BY

ROGER FULFORD

LONDON
MACMILLAN & CO. LTD
1949

COPYRIGHT

KING ALFRED'S COLLEGE
LIBRARY

KING ALFRED'S COLLEGE
WINCHESTER.
942.081
FUL
37952

PRINTED IN GREAT BRITAIN

TO SIBELL

CONTENTS

ILLUSTRATIONS

INTRODUCTION

AFTER the death of the Prince Consort, Queen Victoria decided that a full biography of him should be written. Material for such a book abounded. Ever since he first came to England the Prince had carefully bound all letters and official papers received by him, his memoranda commenting on them and copies of his or the Queen's letters in reply. He kept a brief diary in German, and there was a large correspondence of private letters to members of his family and to Stockmar. The Queen was able to contribute an astonishingly vivid day-to-day journal of their life together. There were also copious reminiscences of the Prince from his private secretaries and personal servants. The choice of the Queen for writing this book eventually fell on Theodore Martin — a comparatively unknown man who was a parliamentary lawyer with a taste for letters and the drama.

The task was formidable, and it was not perhaps made easier for the writer by the knowledge that the Queen was ever peeping over his shoulder. In fact the resulting biography is really a joint production by the Queen and Martin. Not only did she go through every scrap of material with him, but again and again her easy, vivid style springs out at the reader from the more sober language of Martin.

In the result the book, which was finally completed eighteen years after the Prince's death, runs to five heavy volumes bound in a peculiarly gloomy shade of brown. To-day they sit rather heavily on the less accessible shelves of the Library, or in the cheaper trays of the sellers of second-hand books. Even teachers of history — ever the best salesmen of a dull book — fight shy of them, on the ground that they are merely five stodgy volumes of eulogy. Criticism of this biography coupled with cheap gibes against Martin is easy. Nonetheless the book is of the first importance and will only be neglected by students of the nineteenth century at their peril. Certainly no one following in the wake of this leviathan could feel anything but deeply grateful for the patience, accuracy and integrity with which Martin discharged his task.

When Martin's book was published many people, among them some of the Queen's own family, felt that the picture was too detailed, the revelations too personal. The Queen would have none of this criticism and she wrote forcibly to her second daughter, who had voiced it :

> Then you must also remember, that endless false and untrue things have been written and said about us, public and private, and that in these days people will write and will know ; therefore the only way to counteract this is to let the real, full truth be known, and as much be told as can be told with prudence and discretion, and then no harm, but good, will be done. Nothing will help me more than that my people should see what I have lost.

Monumental and exhaustive as was Martin's biography there were two sides of the Prince's life to which, at that time, full justice could not be done. The first — and the most important — was his personal contribution to the increase in the political power of the Crown during the middle years of the nineteenth century. Although the original readers of Martin's book were surprised to find it " brimful of politics ", the half was not told. That story I have attempted to complete.

The second side of his life, which had for obvious reasons to be slurred over, concerned his relations with his wife and children. That likewise I have tried to tell. In reading it some may feel that the book has caught the fashionable standpoint of the Victorian intellectuals that the Prince was everything, the Queen nothing. Splashing the Queen with casual approbation and adulation would plainly be out of place in a book in which she is only the secondary figure, but it has certainly not been my intention to denigrate her. For no one who has been privileged to read her private papers could fail to agree with some words of Lord Morley (by no means tender to monarchical personages) after he had read her letters :

> Queen Victoria stands in the first place, for not only was her rank and station illustrious, but her personality was extraordinary — in its vigour, tenacity, integrity and in the union of all these stubborn qualities with the suppleness and adaptability required from a Sovereign in a constitutional system.

The difficulty is — and no one was more conscious of this than she was — that her personality, at once extraordinary and strong, has to some extent blurred the true character and quality of her husband. Certainly it is true that the Queen, the Prince and their family — high-spirited but deeply affectionate — have nothing to fear from a keener appreciation of the true facts about them. As Mr. Gladstone said in a different connexion, " In the final distribution of posthumous fame they have nothing to forfeit, they have only to receive." Those who seek for skeletons in the cupboard may find them on the cinema screen or behind the footlights but not in the realm of truth.

In the general preparation of this book I want to acknowledge my indebtedness to Mr. Bolitho for his vivacious studies of the Prince and Queen and for his kindness in lending me certain unpublished letters. My obligations to Mr. Lytton Strachey will be obvious ; though here and there I may differ from him, I venture even now — a generation after the publication of his book on Queen Victoria — to acclaim it as still the greatest contribution by one man to a true understanding of a glorious epoch in English history.

With respectful gratitude I acknowledge the gracious permission of His Majesty the King to consult certain papers in the Royal Archives, and in particular the journal of Queen Victoria. In this connexion I wish to thank the Keeper of the

Royal Archives — Sir Alan Lascelles. Like all who have had the privilege of working at Windsor, I shall always remember the warm welcome and steady encouragement given to me by the Recorder, Miss Mary Mackenzie. At every stage of this book I have had the advantage of the sage guidance of the King's Librarian, Sir Owen Morshead ; from the pitfalls of many errors both of fact and judgment he has saved me, and such merits as the book may possess have been magnified by his kindness. The Keeper of the King's Pictures, Mr. Anthony Blunt, most generously gave me the benefit of his advice in the chapter on the artistic side of the Prince's life. I am greatly indebted to Mrs. Peter Loxley for her help with the Index.

ROGER FULFORD

August 1948

CHAPTER I

LEGITIMACY AGAINST LIBERALISM

"WHEN a legitimate King is restored, every sprig of Royalty in Europe becomes more insolent and insufferable." The robust felicity of this language, used by Lord Holland to his confidential crony, Thomas Creevey, reveals something of the splendid swagger of the Whig Aristocracy in England. From the vantage points of an assured income, of a large political influence, of a huge luxurious home, Lord Holland felt that he could afford to despise the legitimate rulers of Europe. In the autumn of 1814, he, and scores of English Whigs like him, watched these despised and exiled sovereigns ascending the thrones of their fathers in the mass restoration which followed the downfall of Napoleon. In Germany, in France, in the Peninsula and in Italy there was a general brushing of ermine robes and a general burnishing of golden crowns as "insolence and insufferability" wrapped themselves once more in the ample garb of royalty. The mystic solemnities of the Divine Right of Kings and the confidential relations — almost one might say the telephonic communications — between the King on earth and God in heaven still cast their spell over the minds of men. Even the guillotine in revolutionary France had not entirely disturbed the magic; and almost the last sounds which reached the ears of King Louis XVI, before the rattle of the blade, were the comforting words "Son of St. Louis, ascend to Heaven". The divinity of monarchy meant nothing to Lord Holland; to him all was insufferable insolence.

Yet, as is perhaps often the case when an Englishman surveys the European scene, vision was blurred by prejudice and by the trick of interpreting European events in terms of English politics. In fact European legitimacy in 1814 was not so much insolent as pathetic, not so much insufferable as merely antiquated. The spectacle of monarchy restored bore some resemblance to the appearance of a Victorian maiden aunt at a cocktail party. For in those triumphant and delirious days of 1814 the scions of the great reigning families found themselves, as it were, lifted out of the long drawer. From the comfortable seclusion of lavender and camphor they were teazed for an airing amid the harsh realities of the modern world. Creeping and hobbling they came — Princes of Savoy to Piedmont, Princes of Nassau to Luxemburg and the *Pays Bas*, Habsburgs to Tuscany, Habsburgs to Parma and Habsburgs to Modena, Bourbons to Naples, Bourbons to Spain and Bourbons to France. The mustiness of ancient days hung heavily about them and they brought their suffering peoples nothing more soothing, nothing more comfortable than the solace of the past. A spectator who saw the triumphant entry of King Victor Emmanuel into Turin wrote many years afterwards, " I can distinctly recall the appearance of the King and his staff. Their dress was old-fashioned, almost grotesque ; for they wore powder, pig-tails and hats dating from the time of Frederick the Great."[1] Frequently their opinions matched their clothes. The Pope, naturally in the van of reaction, shuffled back to the Vatican and immediately abolished all street lighting in Rome. This harmless amenity he castigated as " a revolutionary innovation ".

But it was perhaps the French Bourbons who provided the most astonishing spectacle of putting back the hands of the clock. The Royal Family of France made its triumphal entry into Paris in the early summer of 1814. Parisians in their thousands turned out to welcome the exiles and to prove that they really wanted the extravagance and indulgence of Bourbon government to provide, as it were, a gentlemanly sequel to the coarse glories of

[1] D' Azeglio, *Ricordi*.

Napoleon. The King — Louis XVIII — was now nearly sixty, enormously fat and almost incapable of movement. This respository of all the lustre of le Roi Soleil, of all the elegance of Louis XV, of all the stolidity of Louis XVI, this eighteen-stone son of St. Louis swaying through the streets in an open carriage drawn by eight white horses drew few cheers from the quizzical citizens of Paris. Nor did his travelling companions do much to brighten the picture. In the place of honour by his side sat the Duchess d'Angoulême — the only surviving child of Louis XVI and Marie Antoinette. Napoleon once described her as the only man of the Bourbon family, but returning to the city where her parents and brother had been done to death she naturally appeared lugubrious rather than cheerful, sentimental rather than manly. Opposite the King sat the Prince de Condé and the Duc de Bourbon. As the Prince was in his dotage and took not the slightest notice of anything, the occupants of the back seat could hardly be described as a spirited pair. In addition the King and his family were all wearing old-fashioned clothes and, what was peculiarly odious, of English cut. As a writer of the 1850's observed, "This calèche load of superannuated countenances and costumes did not impress the Parisians".[1]

Indeed the return of the Bourbons to Paris was not so much a restoration as a resurrection. This resurgent quality in the French Royal Family was quickly emphasised by the exhumation and reburial of King Louis XVI and Queen Marie Antoinette. When the vast funeral car, containing the coffins, came lumbering along the streets with its plumed top knocking against the street lamps, ribald cries were heard from the crowd of "A la lanterne."

Simultaneously with this slightly macabre spectacle in Paris, a solemn requiem for the repose of the souls of the King and Queen of France was held in the Cathedral at Vienna, where the rulers of Europe were gathered together for the Congress. All the women attending were in deepest mourning, enveloped in long

[1] Eyre Evans Crowe, *History of Reigns of Louis XVIII and Charles X.*

crepe veils. As eleven o'clock struck, moving in solemn procession to a stand draped entirely in black, walked the Emperor of Austria, the Emperor and Empress of Russia, the King of Prussia, the King and Queen of Bavaria and the King of Denmark. Beneath an enormous canopy over sixty feet high and ornamented with all the insignia of Royalty was a cenotaph surrounded by four colossal statues. One represented France dissolved in tears, another Europe similarly afflicted, the third Hope guiding the soul of the virtuous King to everlasting bliss, and the fourth represented Religion, holding in its hand the King's last will, which made it look more like the family solicitor than a personage from heaven.

Yet oddly enough, in spite of this resurrection and deification of ancient days, Europe was, on the whole, glad to get its Kings again. For notwithstanding a general aura of antiquity and a general lack of nimbleness, and notwithstanding the foibles and fashions of the eighteenth century with which they were encumbered, the sovereigns of Europe were by no means unpopular. This was most clearly shown when, at the beginning of the Congress of Vienna, the three most powerful rulers in Europe — the Emperors of Russia and Austria and the King of Prussia — met outside the city. For long they stood with clasped hands, contemplating the triumphs of the past and enjoying the solemnity of the present. In full dress uniforms the three monarchs then mounted their horses and rode slowly into the city of Vienna amidst the booming of artillery, followed by an infinite number of generals belonging to all the nations of Europe. The sun was sparkling, the crowds were cheering with unfeigned joy, all the bells of Vienna were pealing and the air was filled with the explosion of cannon as they blazed their unceasing *feux de joie*. Hollywood alone could have done justice to the scene.

The explanation of this genuinely warm welcome was not far to seek. Emperors, kings, princes, grand dukes and electors were pledges for the stability of the future. They were to turn the key on war and disturbance. They had brought peace in their wake and they could be relied upon to stifle revolution in the folds of their copious robes. Any extremists who escaped this rich suffocation could be snared by those trusty henchmen of the king — the priests and clergy. As was well said at the time in one of the early debates of the Cambridge Union, " Have they not a black dragoon in every parish, on good pay and rations, horse meat and men's meat, to patrol and battle for these things ? "[1]

There was, of course, a handful of liberals and intellectuals in all countries to whom the restoration was anathema. Of these the English Whigs were typical. To them the revival of monarchy was a disastrous and retrograde flight from freedom. They would have cordially endorsed that clause in the will of Voltaire's friend which said, " I should like to see, and this will be the last and most ardent of my desires, the last King strangled with the guts of the last priest ". But undoubtedly the great majority of people favoured the return of the old order, seeing in it " that firm foothold of authority in a quaking world which above all else they sought ".[2]

Chateaubriand, the keenest and noblest intellect supporting the Restoration in France, wrote that " Monarchy is an ancient tree on which can be grafted new fruits ".

This observation (though it may have betrayed some ignorance of the practice of the average arboriculturist) was wise and pregnant. It appealed particularly to that confident belief in progress, characteristic of liberalism, which was just beginning to dawn in men's minds. But liberalism and legitimacy were not exactly cosy bedfellows. Nonetheless, under liberalism the kings were struck down but monarchy grew stronger.

The fortunes of the most important dynasties in Europe during the generation following Waterloo show how this

[1] Carlyle, *Life of Sterling*.

[2] *Cambridge Modern History*, vol. x, chap. I.

happened. The old kings "with their high exacting looks, sceptred and globed", as Leigh Hunt once described them, fought tenaciously for the old order. For the most part they lost, retired from the scene and left their heritage to more accommodating branches of their family. In that sense Chateaubriand was proved by history to have been abundantly right.

In France Louis XVIII proved himself a surprisingly competent ruler. Long since impotent and allowing himself no grosser indulgence than an occasional pinch of snuff off the naked back of his mistress, His Most Christian Majesty was in no danger of taking a rash decision. He refused to follow the counsels of the royalist extremists even when, in 1820, his heir-presumptive was murdered and a heartbroken cry rang out from all the faithful that it was *la grande et dernière leçon* of the folly of liberal concessions. Three years later when he died he left the monarchy stronger than when he had begun to reign in 1814. He was succeeded by his brother, Charles X, amusing, intelligent, attractive and cynical, who showed at once that he had learned "*la grande et dernière leçon*". He identified himself closely with the Church, rewarded the *émigrés*, tightened the censorship and quickly alarmed and antagonised liberal opinion. At the General Election in 1830 the Opposition increased their strength by fifty seats and the King immediately dissolved the new Parliament. This provoked a general rising and the King was forced to abdicate in favour of his grandson the Comte de Chambord. It was, however, too late and the new King, who was ten, and his grandfather together left their kingdom. Their departure into exile was leisurely and they made frequent stops at wayside inns, when the Bourbon passion for etiquette was given full rein. At even the smallest pothouse grandfather and grandson had to sit together at the head of the table. Were they not both of equal rank, both *Majestés* of France? So the ancient dynasty retired from the scene. Cultured, agreeable and stately, the Bourbons had brought France prosperity, security and freedom from the armies of her victorious enemies but no real antidote to the toxins of liberal opinions.

They were succeeded by Louis-Philippe — the head of the Orleans branch of the Bourbon family. An astute opportunist, he identified his rule with the prevailing mood of his people, calling himself King of the French, and setting himself up as a liberal King. His rule was not an edifying spectacle, bringing much ridicule on monarchical government, but showing that even the French Bourbons were making great efforts to march with the times.

In Spain, the Bourbons (though more tenacious of power than their cousins in France) did nothing to enhance the reputation of the family. King Ferdinand VII, who had returned from exile at the beginning of 1814, was not stupid but cunning, not courageous but adroit, and he lacked any trace of principle or idealism. Not only was his reign a disaster for Spain while it lasted, but the seeds of faction and intrigue which he had so patiently nurtured were to bear their bitter and poisonous fruit long after his flesh was mouldering in the vasty halls of the Escurial.

The first of the sovereigns of Europe to be restored, Ferdinand, made a public statement to the effect that the Kings of Spain were never despots, "I hate and abhor despotism. The intelligence and culture of Europe no longer suffer it." His actions did not, however, match his brave words and a few weeks after getting back he declared the Constitution null, and ordered the arrest of all liberal deputies. The black dragoons, in the shape of the Jesuits, came rattling back in the wake of royalty and the King imposed that kind of tyranny in which the fat chuckle of the priest drowns the cries and groans of honest men. The King himself used to transact business surrounded by toadies and minions smoking cigars and sucking sweets, every now and again tossing a lollipop to a courtier who pleased him with some outstandingly illiberal remark.

Such rule could not last, and in 1820 risings and disorders were general throughout Spain. King Ferdinand was forced to grant a Constitution and he issued a proclamation ending up, " Let us step out boldly, I at your head along the constitutional path ". All the print shops of Madrid displayed a spirited picture of the King hand in hand with the Constitution — represented by a stout female. The King's idea of stepping out boldly along the constitutional path was to send frantic signals for help to his French cousins. He implored them to rescue him from his difficult and frightening expedition along the constitutional path. Help was quickly forthcoming and 100,000 Frenchmen, calling on God and St. Louis, marched to Spain to save the throne for the descendant of Henry of Navarre. Ferdinand was restored to full absolutism and, in his coarse complacent way, he summed up his relation to his countrymen by saying, " Spain is a bottle of beer. I am the cork. Without me it would all go off in froth."

During King Ferdinand's reign — and this is an astonishing proof of the extent to which the proud people of Spain can support and enjoy the burden of tyranny — a party grew up which demanded an even more effective stopper for the bottle of beer. This party centred round the King's younger brother, Don Carlos, who felt that Ferdinand was bartering the glorious inheritance of the family for the plaudits of liberals and (what he disliked even more) thinkers.

This political tussle between the royal brothers was given a sharper edge by a dynastic squabble. No one could deny that King Ferdinand had made the most valiant efforts to provide his country with an heir. In fairly rapid succession he had buried three childless wives. Still undaunted he married for the fourth time in 1829. On this occasion the lady was his cousin, Princess Maria Christina of Naples. To this princess looked all liberals and progressives, while to Don Carlos rallied all conservatives and clericals. The dynastic battle, especially when the Queen was known to be pregnant, was furious and the King, who was not without a spark of shrewdness, remained most of the time in bed. In 1833 Ferdinand died, having altered the law by which only a male could inherit the throne, and was succeeded by his infant daughter, Queen Isabella II. Naturally enough Don Carlos refused to accept this convenient arrangement and the Battle of the Bourbons was transferred from the King's bedroom to the plains and mountains of Spain, where the bloody Carlist wars were fought out. King Ferdinand's widow acted as Regent for seven years, when she was drummed from the kingdom on the discovery that she had taken a guardsman to her bed — an indiscretion which might have been forgiven if she had not tried to marry the man. Against such a background, surrounded by the intrigues and voluptuous influences of the Court of Madrid, young Queen Isabella began her precocious life of passion. Queen Victoria as a girl of seventeen wrote to her uncle Leopold " and do you know what sort of people are about poor little Queen Isabel, and if she is being *well* or *ill* brought up ?" Modesty must have made King Leopold's task in replying an extremely difficult one. It was truly remarkable that monarchical government in Spain should have survived.

Bad as was Bourbon rule in Spain it was certainly matched by Bourbon rule in Naples and Sicily. It was of this house, the Bourbon-Naples family, that Mr. Gladstone said that their rule was " the negation of God, erected into a system of Government ". The head of this house was Ferdinand I, King of the two Sicilies and of Jerusalem, who reigned, with occasional expulsions, from 1759 to 1825. Promising eternal forgiveness to his faithful Neapolitans he sailed in on the flood tide of reaction and restoration in 1815. He was then sixty-four and his gifts of scholarship had not improved with the years. He could scarcely write or read. To get round his difficulties with a pen he used a special stamp for putting his signature to official documents. This mechanical object he regarded with awe and veneration as the embodiment " of all those solemn and mystical doctrines that made him the autocrat of 5,000,000 men ".[1] King Ferdinand was never happier than when, after a successful fishing expedition, he could sell his fish by public auction in the streets of Naples to a crowd of loafers and *lazzaroni*. On these occasions he showed that he had mastered the Neapolitan dialect and that, if for no other reason than the range of his filthy stories and his command of obscene language, he towered above his subjects.

Determined, like King Charles II of England, never to go on his travels again, but lacking the adroitness of the Stuart King, he found himself obliged, in 1820, to take an oath of loyalty to the Constitution, for the liberal fever in Spain had spread quickly to Naples. Accompanied by the leading members of the constitutional party the King attended divine service, and fixing his wicked old eyes on the cross, he cried out, " Omnipotent God, who with thine infinite powers can read the soul of man and the future, do thou, if I speak falsely or intend to break my oath, in this moment direct the thunders of vengeance on my head." Weeping copiously he turned to his companion and said, " Believe me, General, I have now sworn from the very bottom of my heart." It can have surprised no one — neither King nor General, nor even omnipotent God — that within eighteen months the King, backed by foreign Powers, was once again absolute and was once again assailing liberals with the many-thonged whip and the hangman's rope.

In 1825 this rascally King died and was succeeded by his son, King Francis I, who continued his father's reign of tyranny — at once diabolical in its relentlessness and eastern in its smooth efficiency. King Francis and his wife were in appearance homely and corpulent, and when they went on a state visit to their cousin, King Charles X, in Paris, they looked more like John Gilpin and his wife on their day out than legitimate descendants of le Roi Soleil. Charles X was slightly embarrassed by these seedy relations and was amazed that the Parisians did not laugh

[1] R. N. Johnston, *Napoleonic Empire in Southern Italy*. Macmillan, 1904.

more at them : indeed he seems first to have sensed the imminence of revolution from this visit, because he remarked that the Parisians must have something serious to think of, if they could miss such a splendid opportunity for joking. The excitements of this Parisian trip proved too much for the King and he died shortly afterwards, being succeeded by his son, King Ferdinand II. The tyranny was not abated one jot and the new King's relation, Louis-Philippe, felt constrained to ask him to relax the rigour of his rule. He received the characteristic answer, " My people are not like the French — I do their thinking for them." The reign of King Bomba, as he was familiarly known, had begun.

Chequered and inglorious as was the history of the House of Bourbon in the early years of the nineteenth century it appeared smooth and inspiring compared with that of the Portuguese House of Braganza during the same period. When Napoleon overran Portugal, the Royal Family had to flee from their kingdom in the old world to their empire in the new. In 1807 they embarked at Lisbon and the people of Portugal saw for the first time for years the head of the family, the Empress of Brazil, " Reine de Portugal et des Algarves, en deçà et au delà de la mer en Afrique, Seigneur de la Guinée, par la conquête, la navigation et le commerce d'Éthiopie, d'Arabie, de Perse et de l'Inde, Majesté Très Fidèle ". She had long been hopelessly mad. Fourteen years later, after a not unsuccessful sojourn and not illiberal rule in their Brazilian empire, the Royal Family returned. The Queen was dead, and her son, King John IV, agreed to reign by constitutional methods. Corpulent, melancholy, with large heavy features and a drooping jaw, he liked to show himself to his people in a filthy uniform blazing with stars and orders. He ate his food with his fingers. This liberal-minded monarch was no match for his ambitious wife — a Spanish Bourbon — who was determined that the rule of the House of Braganza should be absolute. In this she was supported by her younger and dashing son, Dom Miguel, but opposed by her elder son, Dom Pedro, who had been left behind in South America as Emperor of Brazil. When King John died he was succeeded in 1826 by Dom Pedro's daughter, Donna Maria da Gloria, who was a few weeks older than Queen Victoria. The child Queen was at once betrothed to her uncle, Dom Miguel, and two years later he landed in Portugal to claim his bride. Greeted everywhere by cries of "Viva Dom Miguel, rei absoluto", he seized the throne, abandoned his matrimonial projects and drove his child bride from her kingdom.

Dom Miguel was not unpopular with governing circles in England, because when staying with King George IV at Windsor he had donned a red coat and gone out stag hunting, taking "his fences like anyone else".[1] However, in spite of this endearing accomplishment, he was not to remain in quiet possession of his hardly-won kingdom, because his elder brother, Dom Pedro, was forced to abdicate from his imperial throne in Brazil and, having nothing much to occupy him, made up his mind to recapture the Portuguese throne for his daughter, Donna Maria. These princes of the House of Braganza were adventurous, romantic and able, but their fraternal squabbles plunged Portugal into a long and bloody civil war. In fact both Spain and Portugal were torn by political battles superimposed on dynastic feuds.

France, Italy and the Peninsula — all had the same tale to tell of sovereigns struggling to keep their power against the deep and swiftly flowing waters of liberal ideas. In Austria, with its scattered empire stretching to Poland and Bohemia in the east and far down the leg of Italy in the south, the House of Habsburg seemed to stand immovable and eternal, set firmly on the rocks of the past, unswayed by the vehement beatings of the waves and winds of reform. Francis I, Emperor of Austria, King of Hungary, Bohemia, Lombardy and Venice, who reigned from 1792 to 1835, was the nephew of Marie-Antoinette, the father-

[1] *Greville Memoirs* (1938), i, 198. It was on this occasion that King George IV — though far too ill and portly to mount a horse — ordered from his tailor a dozen pairs of corduroy riding-breeches.

in-law of Napoleon, and through his four wives — having been thrice a widower — he was connected with all the Roman Catholic ruling houses of Europe and by them was regarded with the respect and veneration reserved for patriarchs. Estimable in character but not enlightened as a sovereign, he was determined that nothing should change. "The Empire was to remain for ever precisely as Francis had found it, its development arrested at 1792."[1] The measure of his political judgment is shown by his belief that wars were inevitable and justified. In explanation of this view he once said, "Mankind requires, from time to time, a copious bleeding, otherwise its condition becomes inflammatory and then the delirium of liberalism breaks out."

He was succeeded by his eldest son, the Emperor Ferdinand, who was feeble in body and mind and turned pale if business was ever mentioned. He lives in our affections to-day for his petulant remark, "I'm the Emperor and I *will* have dumplings." He was quite grateful when the Revolution of 1848 swept him off the throne, and looking back with unwarranted satisfaction to his pitiable efforts at statecraft he could say, "We really did make our people happy, but it was a dog's life after all."[2]

Thus the ebullition of the French Revolution and the long-drawn-out agony of the Napoleonic wars had handed over western and southern Europe to a close corporation of reactionary sovereigns. They were not tyrants, they were not all absolute, they were not even all bad men and women, but their inspiration came from the past and their highest ideal was to reign with that benevolent sternness which had marked the kings and emperors of the eighteenth century. All Roman Catholics and all closely related, they regarded themselves as sent from heaven to drive their peoples into the paths of peace and tranquillity. Each ruler would warmly have echoed the sentiments of the Emperor Francis of Austria, "The people! What of that? I know

[1] A. J. P. Taylor, *The Hapsburg Monarchy, 1815–1918.*

[2] Dr. Doran, *Monarchs Retired from Business.* Bentley, 1857.

nothing of people ; I know only of subjects." However, under the stern impact of liberal opinion, monarchy was, with many protestations, forged into something more appropriate to the age.

In eastern Europe the picture was different. Here the autocrat of all the Russias, his prestige and influence enormously enhanced by the decisive part he had played in the defeat of Napoleon, showed that liberal opinion must not be flouted and repressed if monarchy were to survive. Handsome, agreeable and clever but uncertain, temperamental and haunted by the deadly crime of patricide by which he had stepped to the throne, Emperor Alexander has been well described as "a crowned Hamlet".[1] He was the architect of the Holy Alliance, which was inspired by high ideals and was not designed to be (as it subsequently became) a mere buttress for reaction. Indeed at Vienna, during the negotiations which led up to the signing of the Alliance, he observed, "I count dynasties and so-called hereditary rights as nothing compared with the interests of states." Even more indicative of what his fellow sovereigns regarded as his jacobinical views was his comment on the Bourbons, "They are a bad set of people." When he came on a state visit to England he spent much of his time hobnobbing with Whigs and announced that when he got back to Russia he would start an Opposition. These jaunty remarks thoroughly alarmed his fellow sovereigns, but in practice his political projects all seemed to trail off in religious clouds and mystic vapours. When an English Quaker came to visit the prisons of Russia, he saw the Czar and explained to him how appalled he had been by the conditions in which the prisoners were living. The Czar listened sympathetically, prayed with him, but left the prison system unchanged. By 1825, when he died suddenly at Taganrog, he had had to revoke most of his liberal reforms in Russia. In spite of the failure of the Holy Alliance and in spite of the failure of his

[1] *Cambridge Modern History*, vol. x.

reforms at home, the Emperor Alexander stands out as the one European sovereign with personality and vision who might have been able to graft those new fruits on to the monarchical stock without which it had surely to perish. Perhaps it was not wholly fortuitous that his English goddaughter, Alexandrina Victoria — so named in his honour — was through her long and distinguished reign to bring fresh life and strength to the monarchical ideal, to succeed where her godfather had failed.

For England stood in no less need than did other European countries of an injection of new blood into the royal system. When Napoleon was finally defeated, the English King, George III, was nearly eighty, blind and mad ; his Queen was shrewish and miserly ; his seven sons were all middle-aged and raffish ; his five daughters, of whom only two were married, had no legitimate offspring. In 1815 George III and Queen Charlotte were blessed with twelve adult children and only one legitimate grandchild. Shelley could scarcely be accused of exaggerating when he wrote of this royal family :

> An old, mad, blind, despised and dying King,
> Princes, the dregs of their dull race, who flow
> Through public scorn — mud from a muddy spring —
> Rulers who neither see nor feel nor know,
> But leech-like to their fainting country cling.

In 1820 King George III died and was succeeded by his eldest son, King George IV. Immediately the new King took the remarkable step of arraigning his wife by Act of Parliament for having committed adultery. The public thought, understandably enough, that the King's action was the crowning example of the pot calling the kettle black, and public opinion vociferously espoused the cause of the Queen. The prestige of monarchy in England fell heavily during George IV's reign, and while the personality of his successor, King William IV, did something to revive it, the stability of the throne was assailed by the serious constitutional struggle over the Reform Bill. William IV was not jesting when he said, during the height of the struggle for the Bill, " I feel the crown tottering on my head."

The youth and feminine innocence of Queen Victoria did something to undo the mischief of her uncles, who were not unfairly described by the Duke of Wellington as " the damnedest millstones about the neck of any Government that can be imagined ". Indeed it was a question whether the millstones had not dragged monarchical government in England to depths from which there was no emerging. Our great-grandparents were anxiously wondering whether the romance of youth, which was Queen Victoria's greatest single asset at her accession, would suffice to stabilise the throne. Brave would have been the man or woman who confidently answered that question by " Yes ". Surveying the whole course of monarchical government in Europe since Napoleon they must have argued that only those rulers could survive who were content to reign as the lackeys of liberalism. So the shrewdest observers would have argued in the 1830's or 1840's.

But they would have been wrong. For in the short space of fifty years the scene was to be transformed and, with the exception of France and Switzerland, a constellation of quasi-divine monarchs was to dominate Europe. In characteristically forthright language Mr. H. G. Wells has shown us how mightily monarchy had flourished and how it came to be regarded " with a mystical awe by the ignorant and foolish ". He goes on to say :

> The marriages, the funerals, the coronations, the obstetrics of this amazing breed of idols were matters of almost universal worship . . . their coronations and jubilees interrupted traffic and stimulated trade everywhere. . . . At the dawn of the twentieth century republican freedom seemed a remote dream.[1]

This, Mr. Wells calls the Teutonic dynastic system. He simply remarks upon this system but does not attempt to define it or to explain how the Teutonic system spread with such prodigious

[1] H. G. Wells, *In the Fourth Year.*

force. There was certainly nothing to distinguish the general run of the rulers of Germany, after the fall of Napoleon, from the rest of the sovereigns of Europe. The most important of the German rulers was Frederick William of Prussia, whose mind was given over to religion of a strictly evangelical turn. A certain simplicity mingled with his devout nature, and he was once heard to say, " Godless women I cannot admire, for they are no longer women. What will become of them ? " His nervous hesitancy was well illustrated by his arriving late for the battle of Leipzig because he could not make up his mind whether to appear in Russian or Prussian uniform.

Around Prussia, but not as yet beneath her sway, revolved thirty-eight minor sovereigns — kings, electors, grand dukes, margraves, landgraves, dukes and princes. In almost all their territories was to be seen in miniature the same struggle as in the west of Europe between liberalism and hereditary rights. These petty princelings armed themselves for the fray by assuming fresh titles, by stepping up one rung on the monarchical ladder. The Elector of Hanover became a king, as did the Elector of Bavaria and the Duke of Wurtemberg, while electors, margraves and landgraves comforted themselves and puffed themselves up by taking the title of grand duke. According to Lord Rosebery, they led lives " as dull as those of the aged and torpid carp in their own stew-ponds ". No doubt the recollection of these royal absurdities inspired Swinburne's mordant phrase, " Flights of dim tribes of Kings ".[1]

The might and majesty of " the Teutonic system of monarchy " derived not from the distinctive character of German monarchy but from the statecraft of a single German family — the House of Saxe-Coburg. The gifts and talents of this remarkable family were strengthened and spread by a series of judicious marriages, until its well groomed princes and comely princesses became the most valuable exportable commodity in all Germany.

[1] " Eve of Revolution."

By 1900, descendants of this family occupied the thrones of Great Britain, Belgium, Germany, Portugal, Bulgaria and many of the principalities of Germany. The wife of the Emperor of Russia was of Saxe-Coburg descent, as were the widow of the heir to the Austrian Empire and the wives of the heirs to the thrones of Greece, Rumania and Sweden. More than that, the political talent of the Coburgs had transformed and revivified the whole conception of monarchy : they were the fulfilment of Chateaubriand's ideal — the new fruits grafted on the ancient tree.

CHAPTER II

YOUTH IN COBURG

THE House of Saxe-Coburg was rooted far back in German history and had contributed to mediaeval Germany such eminent figures as John the Constant and Frederick the Bitten, whose mother, in a paroxysm of love, bit his cheek, scarring him for life.

In religion the family had always shown strength and independence and in early days one of the heads of the house was familiarly known throughout Germany as "Praying Ernest". Indeed such was the attachment of these early Coburgs to the reformed religion that it cost them the rich kingdom of Saxony to which, by primogeniture, as heads of the Saxon family, they were entitled. But abandoning the old faith for Protestantism they had to be content with the tiny principality of Coburg, which was very little larger than Rutland. Set among the Thuringian mountains and far removed from the enervating influence of Austria, Coburg formed the very heart of Germany. Thus hedged in from external influences, the inhabitants of the duchy no less than its rulers displayed the characteristic German qualities of rugged determination and unflagging industry coupled with a surprising susceptibility to Romance.

At the close of the eighteenth century the Saxe-Coburg family was represented by a ruling duke — Duke Francis — and his needy but ambitious family of three sons and four daughters. The Duke died in 1806, leaving his family — the youngest of whom was sixteen — to fend for themselves. This youngest son, afterwards King Leopold of the Belgians, once wrote, with that barbed complacency which distinguished him, " Without meaning to say anything unkind of the other branches of the Saxon family, ours was more truly intelligent and more naturally so ".[1] The same sense was put in less flattering terms by Queen Victoria's uncle, the Duke of Cumberland, when he said of the Coburg family, " the spirit of intrigue exists in the whole breed ".[2] Whether the unquestioned gifts of the Coburgs are best described as intelligence or intrigue they were all directed in the early years of the nineteenth century to the achievement of those territorial and commercial prizes — soothing to ambition and comforting in old age — which flow from a prudent marriage. The first of the brothers to show that he had realised the importance of a judicious marriage was Prince Ferdinand — a large, easy-going soldier who married the heiress of the House of Kohary — one of the richest and most powerful families in Hungary. The broad acres and substantial balances of his bride lured Prince Ferdinand from the faith of his fathers into the Roman Church. Their descendants were to sit on the thrones of Portugal and Bulgaria.

A few weeks later Prince Leopold — the youngest of the family — married Princess Charlotte, heiress to the throne of England. Although she unhappily died within eighteen months of the marriage, he was left with a bountiful reminder of her presence in the shape of a pension of £50,000 a year from the groaning taxpayers of England. He became King of the Belgians in 1831 and following the example of his brother he joined the Roman Church. But like Henry of Navarre and other diplomatic converts to that Church he did not allow religion to obtrude unduly on the pleasures of the world. In the following year he married the daughter of King Louis-Philippe. His descendants reigned in Belgium, his daughter married the

[1] General Grey, *Early Years of the Prince Consort.* John Murray. Hereafter referred to as *Early Years.*

[2] *Letters of King of Hanover to Viscount Strangford.* Williams and Norgate, 1925.

Emperor of Mexico, his granddaughter the heir to the Austrian Empire and his great-granddaughter the heir to the throne of Italy.

The marriages of the four sisters — though possibly not so successful as those of the brothers — brought added lustre to the family. The eldest, Sophie, married a French *émigré* called Mensdorf — a character of singular charm,[1] by whom she had a family of able and attractive sons.

The second sister, Antoinette, married a brother of the Empress Marie of Russia. The third sister, Julie, married the Grand Duke Constantine of Russia when she was fifteen and left him when she was twenty-two. The youngest of the sisters, Victoria, married first the Prince of Leiningen and secondly the Duke of Kent, becoming the mother of Queen Victoria.

The last member of the family to marry was the head of it. In 1817 Ernest, the reigning duke, married the daughter and heiress of the Duke of Saxe-Gotha, through whom he acquired Gotha, a small territory roughly the size of Dorset. Of this marriage there were two sons, Prince Ernest, born in 1818, and Prince Albert, the Prince Consort, born on August 26th, 1819.

In later life the Prince frequently told Queen Victoria that his childhood was the happiest period of his whole existence. Such a confession cannot have been particularly flattering to the Queen, who was well aware of the disagreeable elements in the Prince's home life. His father was not a pleasant character, for he was fired with political ambition which he lacked the capacity to realise and in personal habits he was selfish and extravagant. Only a few months after he came to England Prince Albert wrote to his closest friend, "If you could restrain Papa from constantly asking me for money I should be grateful".[2]

The Prince's elder brother was an even more odious character

[1] "A man of noble chivalrous spirit, like uncle Mensdorf, reconciles one to the world which is so full of what is base, foul and corrupt." — The Prince Consort.

[2] Royal Archives.

than his father. In appearance he was as unattractive as Prince Albert was attractive. His complexion was sallow with liver spots, his eyes were bloodshot and his lower teeth, like those of a bulldog, protruded far above his upper ones. In spite of those physical drawbacks he was, in the words of Queen Marie of Rumania, who remembered him well, " a mighty hunter of wine, women and song ".[1] The same impression was made on Queen Victoria's private secretary, who wrote of him :

> Ernest the Great, the Good, the Chaste, the Second, the Father, nay, the Grandfather now of many of his subjects, will appear in state. His Consort and all his other Consorts will be there — all those that have been — that are — and that are going to be — all . . . Send out a Hogarth quick to paint the picture of " La Famille ducale et demi-ducale ".[2]

One who really knew the Coburg family inside out, Baron Stockmar, always thought it astounding that the Prince Consort should have had so fine a character " with such a father and such a brother, both equally unprincipled ".[3]

Nor was this murky picture relieved by the character of the Prince's mother. She was married when she was only sixteen to Duke Ernest, who was seventeen years older than she. Some years after the birth of her sons she fell in love with an officer in the Coburg army. She was divorced by the Duke and died in Paris when she was thirty-one as the Countess von Polzig-Baiersdorf. There seems no other foundation than these facts, which occurred six years after Prince Albert's birth, for the scandalous suggestion, fondly and persistently whispered by all lovers of the unexpected, that the Prince was not the son of Duke Ernest.[4]

[1] Marie, Queen of Roumania, *The Story of My Life*. Cassell.

[2] Lord Ponsonby, *Henry Ponsonby*. Macmillan, 1942.

[3] Royal Archives.

[4] For those who have any sneaking qualms on this subject the true facts are admirably set out by Mr. Hector Bolitho in *Victoria and Albert*. Cobden Sanderson, 1938.

Writers on this topic — and that in part explains why the gossip crept into Lytton Strachey's masterpiece — made the mistake of thinking that Duke Ernest was a serious and high principled ruler (like his brother, King Leopold), who had the misfortune to ally himself, in middle life, with a flighty wife who was steadily unfaithful to him. The facts were otherwise. A charming and vivacious girl, the Duchess was neglected by her husband and disgusted by his unfaithfulness. After enduring this for some years, she chose a life of freedom with a man she truly loved and with whom she eloped. While she was technically the guilty party, no one who really studies the facts can help attributing a large part of the blame to the Duke or agreeing that her character was infinitely finer, more sympathetic and more agreeable than his. The Prince Consort could just remember her and was devoted to her memory. Even Queen Victoria, who was not in the habit of looking favourably on divorced women, wrote in her Journal, " He never saw his poor mother again after. She must have been so clever and fascinating." [1] Did not the Queen set the final seal of approval by perpetuating her mother-in-law's name of Louise in one of her children ?

Fortunately the Prince was not denied feminine influence — at once comfortable and steadying — in his childhood. His father's mother — a Princess of Reuss with a very long nose, which she bequeathed to many of her descendants — lavished affection on him in the critical years following the break up of his parents' marriage. After her death in 1831 her place was filled by his mother's stepmother, a Princess of Hesse-Cassel to whom he was devoted,[2] and by his own stepmother — a Princess of Wurtemberg — whom his father married in 1832.

The Prince was by nature affectionate, intelligent and con-

[1] Queen Victoria's Journal. Hereafter referred to as Journal.

[2] Of her, Stockmar wrote, " She was, as it was fit she should be, a Princess ". Martin, i, 478.

fiding; on these ladies no less than on his father and brother he showered affection as deep as it was unalterable. The follies and faults of his father never shattered his simple little code of loving confidence, first perhaps shown in an infantile letter to his father, written when he was six, "Think of me very often and bring me a doll that nods its head. Your little Albert." [1] Nor did the vices of his brother make any impression on a relationship which was based on youthful association and derived its strength from the soothing haze with which a sentimentalist like the Prince invariably invests the years that are gone.

When the Prince harped on the happiness of his childhood he was thinking not only of the persons who composed his home but of the superb surroundings in which it was set. The most eminent of Victorian novelists has shown us that peaceful and lovely scenery outside the home can do much to compensate for discord and cruelty within. Did not the rural charms of Blunderstone Rookery soften for David Copperfield the horrors of Mr. Murdstone and the atrocities of his sister? Few people can have been brought up amidst more delightful surroundings than was Prince Albert. Coburg, then as now, was far removed from any taint of industrialism. Gotha, not yet marred and seared by the production of the Messerschmitt, could point to its principal product, the *Almanach de Gotha*, which gives the pedigrees of the princely families of Europe, as clear proof that none but the most genteel business was conducted within its boundaries. In both towns there still survived the architecture and manners of the Middle Ages. In the spring and summer the royal family would move out to the Rosenau — a mock mediaeval structure set among the most glorious scenery some four miles out of Coburg. The recollection of this perfect home, whispering the last enchantment of the Middle Ages, coloured the Prince's life and inspired his love for the peace and seclusion of the country and for the fortifying strength of hills. In later life he referred

[1] Grey, *Early Years*.

to it simply but movingly as " the paradise of our childhood ".[1]

As the Prince grew towards manhood he found a most powerful protector against the whims and follies of his father in the friend and confidant of the Coburg family, Baron Stockmar.

Christian Frederick Stockmar was born at Coburg in 1787. He was the son of a lawyer with a passion for book collecting who died from chagrin when his house caught fire and his books were burned. In consequence of this tragedy, which happened when he was still young, Stockmar was brought up by his mother, to whose wit and philosophic turn of mind he paid constant tribute. " Heaven takes good care that the cow's tail shall not grow too long ", was a saying of hers which was handed down by her son to members of the reigning houses of Belgium, Coburg, England and Prussia, and was by them cherished and abundantly quoted. Stockmar was trained as a doctor but after the peace of 1815 he entered the service of King Leopold as a confidential factotum. To him were spoken the last coherent words of Princess Charlotte, " Stocky, they have made me drunk." His advice was eminently shrewd and essentially sound. Above all, he had learned the art (no doubt from his early training as a medical man) of wrapping up his counsel in the most palatable form. To him Coburg princes, and particularly King Leopold and Prince Albert, were the repositories of political power and judgment which, when properly guided, were capable in a fast changing world of restoring the ancient glories of monarchy. To him this ideal was worthy of infinite self-sacrifice and labour. Indeed, for the glory of the cause he left wife, home and children, receiving as his only recompense the gaudy but insubstantial reward of a Saxon barony. Mr. Gladstone, in a burst of spleen not characteristic of his Christian outlook, once called Stockmar " a mischievous old prig ".[2] Against this must be set the verdict

[1] *The Prince Consort and his Brother*, edited by Hector Bolitho. Cobden Sanderson, 1933.

[2] *Life of Lady John Russell*, edited by Desmond MacCarthy and Agatha Russell. Methuen, 1910.

of one of the ablest diplomatists of the nineteenth century, Sir Robert Morier, that his "was the noblest and most beautiful political life which this century has seen".[1] Certain it is that this shrewd, wizened little personage with the piercing eyes and the subfusc suits, listening, writing and whispering, arriving unexpectedly in London from Brussels and then mysteriously popping up in Coburg, did understand politics and played a cardinal part in grafting the new fruits on to the ancient tree of monarchy.

Stockmar placed little confidence in Prince Albert's father, and there can be no doubt that he was responsible, through King Leopold, for the choice of the faithful and devoted tutor, Florschutz, who counteracted the paternal influence and to whose careful grounding the Prince always attributed not only his own orderly habits of mind but his distaste for evil. The Rath, or Councillor, as Florschutz was called, was much more than a mere teacher or tutor; in fact the humdrum tasks of instruction were discharged by lecturers and professors. Florschutz was rather guide, philosopher and friend, embodying those educational benefits which the son of a nineteenth-century country gentleman in England derived from his governess, the village clergyman and the head gardener. But the Prince's upbringing from the age of five to sixteen lacked something of that easiness and elasticity — so essential to frankness and cordiality in manhood — which were enjoyed by his English contemporaries. For the Prince it was a relentless, mechanical time-table, starting with one hour a day when he was six, three hours a day when he was seven, four hours a day when he was nine and rising to a crescendo of five and more hours a day when he was twelve. In this unvarying time-table no break was ever made except by the curious breakfast habits of the Prince's father, who liked to join his sons in a portentous meal in the open air and extended it to hours which should have been sacred to studying the vagaries of gerunds and the tricks of *x*.

[1] *Memoir of Sir R. Morier*, by Mrs. Wemyss. Arnold, 1911.

This formidable curriculum taught the Prince two things — to go to the root of every subject and to deal with everything methodically — lessons for which his temperament, at once thorough and courageously unflagging, provided suitable ground. Throughout life he was to tackle the weighty problems, both political and personal, which faced him, with the weapons of study and system which he had learned in the high, small schoolrooms of Coburg and the Rosenau dominated by the stern, solid form of the Rath, who was ready, as the occasion demanded, to praise or to pinch.

It is a positive relief to learn that the Prince sometimes needed those pinches. For the picture of him in childhood handed down for posterity by previous biographers and by the Queen is of a child never naughty, never ill-tempered, never inconsiderate but always thoughtful, honourable, generous and chivalrous — a sort of Sir Galahad on a hobby-horse. We read of him as a boy storming a ruined tower at the Rosenau with a party of friends, and on being urged to use an easy way in by the back, answering, " Saxon knights should always attack the enemy in front." At the same tender age he gave alms to a beggar, telling his cousin not to mention it because " when you give to the poor, you must see that no one knows of it ". Then there is his tutor's description of him when having a feverish attack.

> His heart seemed then to open to the whole world. He would form the most noble projects for execution after his recovery . . . he displayed a temper and disposition which I may characterize as being, in thought and in deed, perfectly angelic.

In April 1835, when he was nearly sixteen, the close of the Prince's childhood was officially marked by the ceremony of confirmation which took place in the Giants' Hall of the Castle at Coburg. In the presence of their father, their grandmother and a troupe of princely cousins, the Prince and his brother were given an hour's oral examination on the profundities and obscurities of Protestant theology, which they passed through with becoming intelligence and reverence. This theological triumph was celebrated many years later in some spirited lines by the Vicar of Overstrand, near Cromer, written when he was ninety-four :

> Arrived at length to confirmation's age,
> The service was in life a noted page ;
> As valiant soldiers of the Cross to be
> They pledged themselves with marked sincerity.

The sentiment of these lines is far less extravagant than that contained in most of the Prince's biographies, from which the reader is left with the impression that Prince Albert must indeed have been a worthy descendant of Praying Ernest. His brother, with that gentle malice which relieves his very dull book of Memoirs, suggests that this and similar tributes to the Prince's piety were merely sops for the English public and " suited him certainly even less than it did me ".[1] The truth, of course, is that whatever Queen Victoria may have given out for the benefit of the devout, evangelical Englishmen over whom she reigned (and whose partialities she shared) the Prince was not at all religious. By theology and churchmanship he was bored. He preferred to base his life on the widest principles of Christianity prescribed by his wise but worldly uncle Leopold, " the real spirit of Christianity demands that man shall work every moment during life ".[2] This Coburg Christianity would appear to have had behind it little biblical or apostolic authority.

The sure foundations of the Prince's character were not a reliance on Christianity. They were rather a clear, broad and patient mind and a complete absence of selfishness — both plants of slow growth. His childhood and boyhood were not phenomenal ; they were normal, with the gradual deepening and strengthening of character. Once again Stockmar, with that insight into people's character which amounted to genius, traces in

[1] *Memoirs of Ernest II, Duke of Saxe-Coburg-Gotha.* Remington, 1888.
[2] *Memoirs of Ernest II, Duke of Saxe-Coburg-Gotha.*

the Prince not the perfection of a juvenile saint but the qualities and foibles of his erring mother.

He has the same mobility and readiness of mind, and the same intelligence, the same over-ruling desire and talent for appearing kind and amiable to others, the same tendency to *espiéglerie*, to treat things and people in the same amusing fashion, the same habit of not dwelling long on a subject.[1]

As the Prince grew towards manhood, Stockmar surveying the Coburg Court, surrounded by its atmosphere of formality and licence, decided that the Prince must be removed from it as quickly as possible. He and King Leopold, therefore, arranged that after a short visit to England the Prince and his brother should spend ten months studying in Brussels, where they arrived in the summer of 1836. This meant that instead of treading the conventional path of German princes, absorbing the dry conservatism of Berlin or the class prejudices and swashbuckling habits of the older German universities, they were left to the liberal mercies of their uncle and the democratic influences of Brussels. The princely dignitaries of Germany were offended and showed it. The great House of Hesse-Cassel frowned, that potent family the Mecklenburg-Schwerins were shocked and even the Mecklenburg-Strelitzes could not find it in their hearts to approve. Anchored to reaction as were the ruling families of Germany they were horrified by the prospect of members of their caste soaring into the realms of higher mathematics under the tuition of the famous M. Quetelet,[2] and meeting on terms of easy equality the liberals and demagogues who haunted the Court of Brussels. The Princes' other tutors were of almost equal eminence, and for English literature they followed the fashionable Byronic cult, studying under the Reverend Mr. Drury with whom, in spite of

[1] Stockmar's *Memoirs*.

[2] The eminent mathematician. He always remained a friend of the Prince, and made the acute observation that the Prince did not think enough of his own talents, while the King of the Belgians never forgot his.

the barrier of holy orders, Byron had corresponded on such diverse topics as the Turkish for pimp and the charms of three Greek sisters, called Teresa, Mariana and Katinka. The delights and the freedom of life in Brussels played an important part in counteracting the natural bias to conservatism of the Prince's mind.

In the spring of 1837 the brothers moved on from Brussels to Bonn University " in search of more wisdom ",[1] as Prince Albert put it. At Bonn — then a comparatively modern university which had attracted a body of able and enlightened lecturers — the Prince's search was amply rewarded. He and his brother attended lectures on law, the science of government, philosophy, history, literature, history of art and French literature : they filled their notebooks and were consumed by what the elder brother calls " reading rage ".[2] Their eighteen-months study at Bonn bore not the least relation to those gentlemanly dabblings which fell within the curriculum of their English contemporaries at Oxford or Cambridge ; they rather resembled the feverish application of the members of a modern woman's college, and when they left Bonn they could truly say with the sweet girl graduates of Tennyson's fancy, " we issued gorged with knowledge ". But the brothers had not quite the docility of the students imagined by Tennyson, for they would titter in the lecture room if the lecturer showed signs of any narrow ecclesiasticism, and they once absolutely refused to enter in their notebooks the information that the state rested on an original contract between God and man. The antics and oddities of the Professors stirred the Prince's talents for mimicry, and the pitiful struggles of a short-sighted lecturer to recover his spectacles provided him with material not only for the amusement of his contemporaries but, in years to come, for the delight of his children. In its mixture of earnestness and comradeship life at Bonn was typically German, and it undoubtedly had the effect of cramping the Prince's mind within

[1] *Early Years.* [2] *Memoirs.*

strictly German limits from which his more cosmopolitan uncle was entirely free. But on the other hand life at Bonn gave the Prince his fondness for sport, for there he learned to shoot, to skate, to swim and to fence, and when none of these were possible he enjoyed nothing better than a walk by the Rhine to Godesberg. With his masculine character, his fondness for masculine society and his diffidence with women, he loved university life, which in those happy days was as sacred as the pulpit from the chatter of foolish and fashionable women.

This life of studious contemplation against the background of exclusively male society is seldom the keenest spur to matrimony, for a successful undergraduate generally finds in his books, in the study of affairs and in the discipline of argument an ample substitute for the long drudgery of courtship. Foreseeing the danger in this, King Leopold and Stockmar decided that the Prince's coldness towards the opposite sex must be warmed by a visit to Italy. This was, however, to be kept within bounds by the company of Stockmar and a young English soldier, Lieutenant Seymour.[1] The latter was an able and amiable young man who did his utmost to keep all taint of viciousness from entering the Prince's life. Long afterwards Queen Victoria was slightly offended at the thought that anyone should have deemed it necessary to intervene between the Prince and the Devil, for " God knows ", she wrote, " vice itself would ever have recoiled from the look alone of one who wore the lily of a blameless life ".[2] Certainly the tour in Italy left little time for vice. From Florence, which the Prince reached in the early part of 1839, he was writing triumphantly to his old tutor, " Every morning by five o'clock I sit down by my little student's lamp ".[3] Study of French and English occupied the morning, exercises on organ and piano the early afternoon and walks in the country round Florence the later part of the day. Stockmar, who was always crotchety about

[1] Afterwards Sir Francis Seymour, Bart., 1813–90. A distinguished soldier.

[2] *Early Years.*

[3] Letter from the Prince (Mr. Bolitho).

his health, seldom felt strong enough for anything more exciting in the evening than a game of dominoes, but on his good days he and the Prince would enter on those deep and deliberate arguments which are the peculiar attribute of the German political mind. This programme was varied by social calls and parties in which the Prince did not shine, and he wrote sadly to one of his friends, after setting out a catalogue of his formal social life, " I have fairly drained the Carnival cup to the dregs ".[1]

After a few weeks the party moved south to Rome, which the Prince thought no particular improvement on some German towns he knew. He arrived in time to see the Holy Week services, which he thought " absurd ", while to his strictly Protestant eye the Pope looked " like a Pagoda ". The Prince, Stockmar and Seymour were received by the Pope — as resolute a band of Protestants as ever faced the sacred presence. One Roman Catholic accompanied them and turned the whole proceedings into a farce by his valiant efforts to kiss the holy toe. He lay flat down on his stomach and suddenly grasped the Pope by the ankle, throwing the old gentleman off his balance, who in recovering kicked his devout worshipper full in the mouth. Stockmar — grave and imperturbable as ever — led the Prince and Seymour from the room, both shaking with giggles.[2]

In high summer the Prince, not radically changed by his Italian experiences but with his mind broadened and his taste for learning deepened, returned to Germany. His only comment after six months in the sunny land which had driven generations of Englishmen to the wildest excesses was, " My sphere of observation has been doubled." Even his father, that aloof, easy-going personage, was startled by the blend of virtue and scholarship which so surprisingly stamped his son, and ordered him to accompany him to Carlsbad where, in the society of ageing and gout-ridden *beaux*, he was to learn to get more light-hearted and " to take more trouble about women ". " I am not in agreement

[1] Martin, i, 30. [2] Letter from the Prince to Florschutz (Mr. Bolitho).

and Queen were almost lucky, for King George III and Queen Charlotte were merely pen-friends before marriage. As is well known, King George IV nearly collapsed with a mixture of chagrin and brandy when he first saw the wife whom it had been arranged he should marry. At least the Prince and Queen were allowed to meet before betrothal. In 1836 Prince Albert came over, on a brief visit, to stay with his aunt in Kensington Palace, when both he and the Queen were seventeen, and it is obvious that the Queen fell quickly (though not perhaps deeply) in love with him. After the visit was over she wrote to her uncle, King Leopold,

> he possesses every quality that could be desired to render me perfectly happy. He is so sensible, so kind, and so good and so amiable too. He has, besides, the most pleasing and delightful exterior and appearance you can possibly see.[1]

That the Queen, with her particular temperament, should fall in love with the Prince was almost inevitable. Intelligent, deeply affectionate, irrational and impulsive she was all sensibility. Unluckily her upbringing had not matched her gifts or developed them : it had left her clever without being informed, susceptible to prejudice and gossip, anxious to be good but fortified by no real understanding of religion. With the robust and full-blooded habit of her Hanoverian forbears, with a passionate nature and a strong but untrained character, she was ready to be swayed and mastered by the first member of the opposite sex who crossed her path. Her crowning mercy was that in the Prince she found great physical attraction allied to dominating qualities of intellect.

The reactions of the Prince have not survived, but it is clear that both parties regarded the marriage as virtually settled, and thereafter maintained a regular correspondence.

However, this youthful romance was not destined to run

[1] *Letters of Queen Victoria.* Edited by A. C. Benson and Lord Esher. Murray, 1908, i, 49. Hereafter referred to as *Letters*.

smoothly. The reason for this lay in those difficulties by which the Queen was encumbered in her early years. Unlike the Prince, she looked back to the days of her childhood and youth with sorrow and loathing. For these feelings there was good reason. The Queen's half-sister, the Princess Feodore, who was twelve years older than the Queen, made this reference to the time when they had been brought up together by their widowed mother in the Jacobean gloom of Kensington Palace :

When I look back upon those years, which ought to have been the happiest of my life, from fourteen to twenty, I cannot help pitying myself. Not to have enjoyed the pleasures of youth is nothing, but to have been deprived of all intercourse, and not one cheerful thought in that dismal existence of ours, was very hard. . . . I escaped some years of imprisonment, which you, my poor darling sister, had to endure after I was married . . . those years of trial were, I am sure, very useful to us both, though certainly not pleasant. Thank God they are over ! [1]

The Queen herself in a reference to her dismal youth said, " I was extremely crushed and kept under and hardly dared say a word." [2] If the girl did not actually pass behind the purdah, silent and veiled, she was brought up in that kind of tyrannical seclusion which was the unhappy lot of Eastern women. She was not allowed to sleep alone and she was never allowed to see anyone alone ; this supervision, or imprisonment as her sister without exaggeration called it, was maintained rather than relaxed as she grew older. That Queen Victoria endured this treatment without bitterness and without any searing effects on her character is an indication of the nobility of her personality.

To explain why the Queen was subjected to this cruelty is not wholly easy. Some writers even suggest, with a touch of mediaeval imagination, that she was kept under lock and key because her mother feared that her life was threatened by her uncle, the

[1] *Letters*, i, 18. [2] *Letters*, ii, 42.

Duke of Cumberland, who, after her, was next heir to the throne. This fairy story leaves out of account the Princess Feodore, who had nothing to fear from the English Royal Family and was likewise brought up with the savage austerity of a nunnery. The truth seems to be that the Duchess of Kent, who was affectionate but foolish, allowed herself to be swayed by the Comptroller of her household — Sir John Conroy — and that he was really responsible for the severity with which the Queen was brought up. This worthy — an Irish soldier of great ambition but very mean capacity — had been in the confidence of the Duke of Kent and probably shared that Prince's absurdly narrow and tyrannical views. Naturally enough the picture of this swashbuckling Irishman in close domestic confidence with a buxom widow of forty was too much for their scandal-loving contemporaries, who made the obvious conclusion.[1] The Duke of Wellington, who rather enjoyed chattering about matters of this kind, whispered that the Queen had actually seen familiarities between her mother and Conroy. On this delectable topic it can only be said that there is no shred of evidence to prove that Conroy and the Duchess were lovers. As Lady Conroy was one of the Duchess's Women of the Bedchamber, the connexion would seem to have been unlikely, or at any rate rather unusual.

The most probable explanation of the machinations of Conroy and the Duchess — so cruel to the future Queen and not without their repercussions in Coburg — lies in Conroy's passion for power. It was to this passion rather than to anything more romantic that the Duchess tamely surrendered. Slighted and ignored by the English Royal Family and Government, the Duchess contained herself in a kind of self-imposed Coventry, dumbly nursing every grievance and determined that her daughter should be moulded to her imperious will. By 1835 only an ailing septuagenarian — King William IV — stood between the Duchess and the Regency of England. As private secretary to

[1] See references to Conroy in Greville (1938 edition).

the Regent, Conroy would have had boundless chances to gratify his passion for power and cash.

This is the explanation of the remarkable scene at Windsor in August 1836 on the occasion of the King's birthday. At dinner, in the presence of the Court and several guests who included the Duchess of Kent and Princess Victoria, the King burst out in reply to the toast of his health,

> I trust in God that my life may be spared for nine months longer, after which period, in the event of my death, no Regency would take place. I should then have the satisfaction of leaving the royal authority to the personal exercise of that young Lady (pointing to the Princess) the Heiress presumptive of the Crown, and not in the hands of a person now near me, who is surrounded by evil advisers and who is herself incompetent to act with propriety in the station in which she would be placed.[1]

As the weeks rolled by it began to be clear that the King's trust in the Almighty was well founded and that he would survive for those critical nine months. The Duchess then decided to try to force the Princess to agree to a Regency (even though she was technically of age) for a short time, on the grounds of her youth and inexperience. She was also to be made to guarantee that Conroy should be her private secretary. Some rumours of this snug little arrangement seem to have reached King William, who authorised the Princess to urge Stockmar to come over at once to straighten things out.[2] Many years later the Queen was to write of King William:

> He had a truly kind heart . . . and of his kindness to herself and his wish that she should be duly prepared for the duties to which she was so early called, the Queen can only speak in terms of affectionate gratitude.[3]

[1] Greville, iii, 309.

[2] Prussian Archives quoted in *Königin Viktorias Mädchenjahre* (Jagow). Some authorities say that King Leopold sent Stockmar, but the information in the Prussian Archives appears correct.

[3] Martin, ii, 177.

Stockmar arrived in the middle of May 1837, by which time King William was plainly dying. At the same time King Leopold wrote to his niece:

MY DEAREST CHILD

You have had some battles and difficulties of which I am completely in the dark. . . . Stockmar will be able to do much.[1]

Stockmar at once formed the highest opinion of the Princess's abilities,[2] but he was horrified to find that the Princess was to be forced to agree to the scheme for a Regency by a studied system of severity and unkindness.[3] He was hardly less astounded to learn that the Duchess and Conroy were actually in communication with members of the Government representing that it was the Princess's wish that a bill should be brought in to establish a Regency for a short time.[4] Stockmar found it impossible to alter the Duchess of Kent's opinion that the Princess lacked the intellectual ability to reign alone, but he was able to persuade her that the Princess should be further examined on this point by an independent witness agreeable to Conroy and the Duchess. Lord Liverpool, half-brother of a former Prime Minister, was chosen and he interviewed the Princess, who developed her arguments against a Regency " avec une précision et clarté si parfaite " that Lord Liverpool undertook at once to make Conroy and the Duchess see reason.[5] The plot for a Regency was broken, and the circumstances in which this happened help to explain Queen Victoria's peculiarly affectionate feelings for Stockmar.

These intrigues also serve to explain the deep devotion of the Queen to the Baroness Lehzen — often loosely called Queen Victoria's Governess but correctly described as Lady Attendant on Princess Victoria.

1 *Letters*, i, 67, 68.
2 Prussian Archives.
3 Stockmar to Prince Leiningen, quoted by Jagow.
4 Told by Stockmar to Lord Granville (Greville, vii, 67-70).
5 Prussian Archives

Louise Lehzen, though not a wise woman, served the Queen with a matchless devotion, the recollection of which even now must stifle criticism of her faults and follies.[1] The daughter of a Hanoverian clergyman, she was chosen in 1819 by the Duke of Kent to act as governess to his step-daughter — the Princess Feodore. When Queen Victoria was five she was placed in Lehzen's charge. The Baroness was not indulgent but excessively strict and Queen Victoria stood in great awe of her.[2] She was the Princess's best friend in these early days. Indeed it was a curious piece of misfortune for the Duchess of Kent and Conroy that, in walling up the Princess from any outside influence, they had imprisoned with her a dangerous and implacable opponent of their schemes — for the Baroness, from motives which now will probably never be wholly explained, was determined to undermine the authority of the Duchess and Conroy with the Princess. The most charitable explanation is probably right — that, loving the Princess as she did, she felt that the Duchess was treating her daughter with a severity which was wholly unnecessary. She also deeply disapproved of the Duchess's insulting behaviour to the English Royal Family, from whom she herself had received constant kindness, which included a mark of confidence by King George IV when he made her a Baroness of Hanover. Long afterwards, when she was an old woman of over eighty, she wrote to the Queen, showing that her old loyalty to the English family still persisted, "I believe your Majesty has inherited many a beautiful quality of your Royal Father". With engaging complacency the Queen has noted on the letter, "And more from my dear mother".[3]

Whatever the motives which inspired the Baroness to flout

[1] The Austrian Minister in London writing to his Government paid a great tribute to the Baroness's qualities. He observed that in spite of her German origins she had brought up the Queen in English style. "La Reine est éminément Britannique." Jagow, *Königin Viktorias Mädchenjahre.*

[2] Martin, i, 71.

[3] Royal Archives.

the authority of the Duchess, she had her reward, for on that June day in 1837 when Queen Victoria came to the throne she wrote in her Journal, " my *dear* Lehzen will *always* remain with me as my friend ".[1]

All these events may seem far removed from the studious suitor in Coburg, none the less they are strictly relevant to his biography because they not only had momentous effects on the character of the Queen but they postponed his marriage and nearly relegated it to the lugubrious class of those that " will not now take place ". For the Queen has herself explained that when she came to the throne, which was exactly a year after she and the Prince had first met and when each regarded the marriage as virtually settled, " the freedom, the gaiety and the excitements of becoming Queen at eighteen " [2] drove all thoughts of marriage from her mind. It will be noted that she gives pride of place to freedom and naturally enough the transformation from being " the white little slavey in England ",[3] as her uncle called her, to the liberty of being her own mistress, affected her whole outlook. Gloomily the Prince wrote to his old tutor, as he saw visions of his marriage fading :

> Victoria is said to be incredibly stubborn . . . she delights in court ceremonies, etiquette and trivial formalities. These are gloomy prospects. . . . She is said not to take the slightest interest in Nature, to enjoy sitting up at night and sleeping late into the day.[4]

There was, too, an even more serious hitch in that she had fallen completely under the spell of her Prime Minister, Lord Melbourne. Though her feelings may not have amounted to what is vulgarly called " love ", her admiration for Lord Melbourne's worldly wisdom, mordant wit and abounding charm had, for the time being, driven from her mind all thoughts of a more natural, more appropriate passion. Certainly no one could blame the Queen for falling spellbound before the easy accom-

[1] *Letters*, i, 77. [2] *Early Years*. [3] *Letters*, i, 48.
[4] Letter to Florschutz (Mr. Bolitho).

plishments of the finest product of the Whig tradition, but she herself was conscious of her feelings and, in retrospect, disliked them. A few years later she was writing in her Journal:

> Talked afterwards over former days. . . . My unbounded affection and admiration for Lord Melbourne, which I said to Albert I hardly knew from what it arose, excepting the fact that I clung to someone and having very warm feelings. Albert thinks I worked myself up to what really became quite foolish.[1]

The Queen, so often flatteringly compared with Queen Elizabeth, showed some signs of emulating her indecision over marriage. King Leopold and Stockmar, who were really the promoters of the marriage, decided by 1839 that the only way to make the Queen see reason was to let her once again set eyes on those charms, now more fully developed, which had only three years before won her heart. The visit was fixed, and the Prince and his brother arrived at Windsor on the evening of October 10th, 1839. Some weeks before they arrived the Queen wrote very guardedly to her uncle, King Leopold, " one can never answer beforehand for feelings ".[2] Almost as soon as she saw him, " feelings " swept him straight to her heart, where, cherished and adored, he was to remain for evermore. He was at this time in the heyday of his good looks, before they were obscured by his early inclination to baldness and stoutness. He was somewhat heavily built, square-shouldered and tall, though Lockhart thought his shoulders too high and his legs somewhat heavy.[3] Walter Bagehot, afterwards the editor of the *Economist*, was moved to describe the Prince as " very, very handsome ". Similar tributes to his good looks from more conventional sources abound, but his face was lit up and enlivened by something more than the mere manly virility which characterises the average German. He looked what he was — intelligent and

[1] Journal.
[2] *Letters*, i, 177.
[3] *Life of Lockhart*, by Andrew Lang. Nimmo, 1897.

honourable, or, as it was well put by that wise old worthy Sam Rogers, " He is good looking and looks good ".[1]

The effect on the Queen was irresistible and almost instantaneous ; only two days after the Prince's arrival Lord Melbourne wrote to another member of the Government, " A very strong impression is evidently made . . . the mind is, in fact, made up ", and after a tribute to the young Prince's handsomeness and agreeableness the worldly old man went on, " as to character, that we must always take our chance of ".[2] Two days later, on October 15th at the faintly prosaic hour of 12.30 P.M., the Queen with becoming modesty and an emphasis on the drawbacks of the offer she was making, which did her the greatest credit, asked for Prince Albert's hand. He accepted.

On the Queen's side love was complete and abandoned, as countless guileless entries in her Journal and extracts from her letters plainly show. To her on the day of the engagement the Prince wrote, " How is it that I have deserved so much love, so much affection ? " And the letter was signed, " In body and soul ever your slave, your loyal Albert ".[3] More revealing of the Prince's deepest feelings is the letter which he wrote to Stockmar on the day following :

I am writing to you today on one of the happiest days of my life to send you the most joyful possible news. Yesterday in a private audience V. declared her love for me, and offered me her hand, which I seized in both mine and pressed tenderly to my lips. She is so good and kind to me that I can scarcely believe such affection should be mine. I know you take part in all my happiness, and so I can pour out my heart to you. For the present the event is to remain a secret, and is to be announced to the nation before being communicated to anyone else, at the meeting of Parliament. What grieves me is that my aunt (Duchess of Kent) to whom this important step by her daughter touches so nearly is not to know of it. But as everyone

[1] *Mrs. Brookfield and her Circle*, by C. and F. Brookfield. Pitman, 1905.

[2] *Lord Melbourne's Papers*, edited by L. C. Sanders. Longmans, 1889.

[3] Jagow, *Letters of the Prince Consort.*

says she cannot keep her mouth shut and might even make bad use of the secret if it were entrusted to her, I quite see the necessity of it.

V. wishes that the wedding should take place as early as the beginning of February, to which I gladly agreed as the relations between a betrothed pair, when the fact is public property, may often appear indelicate.

I cannot write further or on more serious matters — I am in too great a state of confusion for

Das Auge sieht den Himmel offen,
Es shwimmt das Herz in Seligkeit.[1]

Some writers have suggested, and it has often been whispered, that the Prince was not in love with the Queen, and that he really married her for the gratification of the Coburg passion for political power.[2] Certainly he lacked her passionate nature, but equally certainly he loved her deeply and truly, believing that love would grow and flourish not only on the excitements of passion but through the moulding of character on common sympathy and common experience.

The brothers remained on at Windsor for a month after the engagement and a tactful indulgence in jaundice by Prince Ernest gave the Queen and Prince many hours of their own company in her little blue boudoir. For long no one except Stockmar, King Leopold and Melbourne shared the secret and the Queen wrote guilelessly to one of her intimate friends several days after the engagement, "We have been very gay here, dancing every alternate night and I have become a great galloper".[3] In the weeks of separation which lay ahead, for he went back to Germany while the engagement was still a secret, the Prince would often console himself with thoughts of those

[1] "The eye sees heaven open,
The heart floats on a sea of blessedness." (Royal Archives.)

[2] See particularly Lytton Strachey, who states, "he was not in love with her". *Queen Victoria*, p. 104.

[3] *Memoirs of the Earl of Sandwich*, by Mrs. Erskine. John Murray, 1919.

happy peaceful times in the little blue room or when "I was flying with you through that lovely ballroom".[1] Indeed that halcyon month at Windsor, with the courtship rendered at once more real and more stimulating by the need for secrecy, stirred the Prince's passion. He showed by the letters he wrote to the Queen during their weeks of separation something of the depth of his feelings for her. "Thinking of you makes me so happy"— he wrote —"what a delight it must be to walk through the whole of my life, with its joys and its storms, with you at my side. Love of you fills my whole heart."[2] The Queen had that gift, which even the most highly paid journalist must envy and might study, of revealing herself with every sentence, every word which she wrote. The Prince, on the other hand, has suffered in the eyes of posterity from a stilted and extremely reserved style, which (so far as the English language was concerned) never did justice to his true feelings. This applies both to his conversation and to his letters. No one realised this better than he did, for he wrote to the Queen, "I reproach myself so often, because compared with yours my letters are so cold and stiff, and yet I shrink from boring you with my outpourings".[3]

On November 23rd, 1839, the Queen, "her hands trembling so excessively that I wonder she was able to read the paper she held",[4] announced to the Privy Council her forthcoming marriage. By the eighty assembled privy councillors the news was politely received, but by the country as a whole it was greeted without enthusiasm. The Queen's happiness and the fact that, as King Leopold wrote to her, "You could not exist without having a happy and *agréeable intérieur*",[5] were not considered by the populace: to them the Prince came of an undistinguished and impoverished family, and was quite unworthy

[1] Jagow, *Letters of the Prince Consort* (referred to hereafter as Jagow).
[2] Jagow. [3] Jagow. [4] Greville, iv, 218.
[5] *Letters*, i, 190.

of alliance with the might and majesty of England. As a contemporary satire puts it:

> He comes the bridegroom of Victoria's choice,
> The nominee of Lehzen's vulgar voice;
> He comes to take "for better or for worse"
> England's fat Queen and England's fatter purse. [1]

The purse, however, was not to be so fat as this scribbler imagined. While the Prince was far away in Coburg bracing himself for the farewells to his old life and preparing himself for the new by polishing up his English and ploughing through the tortuous pages of Blackstone's *Commentaries on the Laws of England* which the Queen had given him to read, affairs in England were taking an uncomfortable turn. He had every reason to expect that he would receive £50,000 a year from a grateful and prosperous country. This had always been the allowance for the sovereign's consort — man or woman. If a queen consort with the sober requirements of womanhood was entitled to that sum, then it was obviously only just that it should be given to a prince consort with the open-handed habits of manhood. Nor was the Prince unmindful that the popularity of the Queen Dowager (William IV's widow) largely depended on her magnificent gifts to charity which she was enabled to make by spending on herself only a fraction of her £50,000. Moreover, in the early eighteenth century, when money was worth half as much again as in 1839, Prince George of Denmark, "Queen Anne's very stupid and insignificant husband",[2] as Queen Victoria called him, had been granted £50,000.

The matter was debated in the House of Commons on January 29th, 1840, and the Government, when they brought forward the proposal that the Prince's annuity should be £50,000, found themselves defeated by the huge margin of 104 votes.

[1] *The German Bridegroom; A Satire*, by the Honourable J. W. (Southgate), 1840.

[2] Royal Archives.

The annuity was reduced to £30,000. " Shame, shame ", wrote King Leopold when he heard the news,[1] but oddly enough it was his example which heavily tipped the scales against the Prince. Colonel Sibthorp — an able if eccentric Tory — pointed out that since 1816, when he married Princess Charlotte, King Leopold had drawn over £1,000,000 from England and had flouted the religious opinions of his paymasters by joining the Church of Rome. To the Tories — and to many Englishmen — the lax attachment of the House of Coburg to the Protestant religion was a source of real concern. Queen Victoria dismissed them as " a few stupid people ",[2] but there were many who would anxiously have echoed the question by the anonymous versifier already quoted :

> Or does he worship all the motley crew
> Of Saints and Martyrs as the Romans do ?

They could have pointed not only to the conversion of King Leopold but also to the conversion of the Prince's first cousin, Prince Ferdinand of Coburg, who had recently married the Queen of Portugal. Nor would they have been greatly comforted if they had turned up the Prince's answer to the question whether he intended to remain true to the Evangelical Church put to him at his confirmation. With studied vagueness he replied that he was " determined to remain faithful to the acknowledged truth ".[3]

Naturally these events were extremely mortifying to the Prince and no less so to the Queen. Lord Melbourne had to tell her that " her marriage was liked in the country, but that there was no enthusiasm for it ".[4]

To the Prince the serious aspect of these events was that it was symptomatic of the extent to which the Queen had alienated the Tory Party, who to a man had voted against the £50,000. Her affection for her Whig Prime Minister, and her terror lest

[1] *Letters*, i, 214.
[2] *Letters*, i, 197.
[3] *Memoirs of Duke of Saxe-Coburg*, i, 25.
[4] Journal.

she should lose him, led her to shower favours on members of his Party — male and female — and to exclude from her society anyone with Tory affinities. Almost all the best places at Court were occupied by members of a single Whig family — the Pagets. This family was likened, not unjustly, by the Press, to " a swarm of locusts ".[1] Even so staunch a Whig as Greville was shocked, writing in his diary :

> It is with a mixture of aversion and contempt that people read in the Court Circular of the Ladies Eleanora and Constance Paget tagging after the Queen, on foot, on horseback or in carriage six days out of the seven.[2]

The dominance at Court of the Paget family — haughty, self-seeking and raffish — gave the impression, which was sedulously fostered by the Tories, that morality and respectability counted for nought with the Queen. Whiggery was alone the password to admit the bearer to the charmed presence of the Queen of England. The Tory Party would never have stirred the mud over the Prince's marriage and annuity if the Queen had not shown an utter contempt for their cause and (what is always more painful to bear) a complete indifference to their company.

What worried the Prince most of all was that the Queen soon made it clear that she was determined that he should be no less tightly bound than was she herself to the Whig interest. With scant regard for her bridegroom's feelings she told him that she and Lord Melbourne would choose his household and that he could be quite certain that they would choose people of good character.[3] For the most important post, that of secretary, they chose George Anson — a strong Whig, who had been a parliamentary candidate, and was Lord Melbourne's private secretary. They even proposed that he should act simultaneously as secretary to both the Prince and Melbourne.[4] To this appoint-

[1] *The Age.*
[2] Greville, iv, 225.
[3] *Letters*, i, 204.
[4] *Letters*, i, 200.

ment the Prince strongly objected, saying that he knew nothing of Mr. Anson " except that I have seen him dance a quadrille ".[1] He followed this up by an almost piteous appeal:

> Think of my position, dear Victoria, I am leaving my home with all its old associations, all my bosom friends and going to a country in which everything is new and strange to me. . . . Except yourself I have no one to confide in. And is it not even to be conceded to me that the two or three persons, who are to have the charge of my private affairs, shall be persons who already command my confidence?[2]

Blandly the Queen replied, " Once more I tell you that you can perfectly rely on me."[3] The appointment went through, only one small concession was made to the Prince — Anson did not continue to act as Melbourne's secretary.

The Prince was, however, a good loser and as disappointment crowded fast on disappointment he wrote with simple humility to the Queen, " While I possess your love, they cannot make me unhappy ".[4] At the same time he clearly saw the danger, not only to his relations with the Queen but for the throne itself, if the Whig dominance of the Queen's mind was left unchecked. When the discussion over Anson was at its height Melbourne wrote to the Prince to the effect that he would have to be a Whig and remain one even if the Ministry changed. On this astonishing doctrine the Queen, who saw the letter before it was sent, commented, " It is just what I told you. . . . Follow this advice and you may be sure of success."[5] The entry in her Journal for New Year's Day, 1840, shows how passionately the Queen clung to the Whigs: " I implore Providence to grant that the true and good cause may prosper for this year and many to come under the guidance of my kind Lord Melbourne ".[6] But on personal matters, as distinct from political ones, the Queen showed that

[1] Jagow.
[2] Martin, i, 55.
[3] *Letters*, i, 206.
[4] Martin, i, 55.
[5] *Letters*, i, 208. Royal Archives.
[6] Journal.

she could behave with independence, and she described a few days later as " foolish nonsense " an idea of Melbourne's that it would be improper for the Prince to be under the same roof with her before the wedding. Recording this in her Journal she wrote, " I said laughing that I would show that I could sometimes have my own way, though I was so seldom allowed to have it, which made Lord M. laugh ".[1]

During these weeks of separation the Prince must often have wondered whether the Queen was going to give way to him over anything. He suggested that they should stay at Windsor for some time after the wedding. Back flashed the Queen's reply :

> I am the Sovereign. . . . I am never easy a moment if I am not on the spot . . . and everybody, including all my Aunts (who are very knowing in all these things) say I must come out after the Second day. . . . This is also my own wish in every way.[2]

The Prince could be pardoned for thinking that the lampoonist must have literally peeped behind the scenes when he wrote :

> She's all my Lehzen painted her,
> She's lovely, she is rich,
> But they tell me when I marry her
> That she will wear the *britsch*.

But, as always, difficulties and misunderstandings were almost magically to vanish when the Prince himself appeared on the scene. He had set out from Gotha on January 28th, after an orgy of farewells to the companions and scenes of his childhood, with a caravan of vehicles — the Duke of Coburg's travelling-carriage first, then three travelling-carriages sent by the Queen, then two britzkas and finally a pair of fourgons for the luggage.

[1] Journal.

[2] *Letters*, i, 213. This contrasts oddly with the Queen's views in later life, when she expected ministers to lay aside all public business in order to travel to Osborne or Balmoral.

The Queen had sent out two members of the English aristocracy to invest him with the Order of the Garter, Lord Torrington and Colonel Grey — son of the former Prime Minister. As the Duke of Saxe-Coburg bound the garter round his son's knee, a salvo of 101 guns burst out, and an enthusiastic German commentator wrote that the new Knight of the Garter was certain silently to influence the English aristocracy.[1] He could scarcely have found a better subject to influence than Lord Torrington, who was typical of the kind of courtier by whom the Queen was surrounded. Witty and indiscreet, he gorged himself on royal chat and gossip which he retailed to his fashionable friends in London, and later made a habit of sending regular private letters to the editor of *The Times* about Court events, allocating to himself the title of " Your Windsor Special ". Many years later he was to win the gratitude of generations of greedy ladies by setting up a discarded French mistress as a purveyor of chocolates in Bond Street. Grey, with his patient and masterly grasp of affairs but completely lacking the frothy charms of Torrington, had far more in common with the Prince and the friendship started in those early days paved the way for Grey to become the Englishman most closely in the confidence of the Prince.

The cavalcade halted at Brussels and King Leopold wrote to his niece that the Prince " looks a little interesting ".[2] This was merely a polite way of saying that he looked thoroughly worried, and he himself wrote to the Queen on landing at Dover that his face was more the colour of a wax candle than a human visage after a terrible dusting in the Channel.[3] Then on February 8th, in the afternoon, he arrived at Buckingham Palace and the Queen wrote triumphantly in her Journal, " My dearest precious Albert looking beautiful and so well ", and she added that his being there " put me at ease about everything ".[4] On the following day they read the marriage service together, tried on

[1] Martin, i, 52.
[2] *Letters*, i, 215.
[3] Jagow.
[4] Journal.

the ring [1] and the Prince drove in the London streets with a mob cheering at his heels.[2]

On Monday, February 10th, they were married in the Chapel Royal, St. James's Palace, the bridegroom wearing a British field-marshal's uniform with the Garter. He entered to the tune of "See, the Conquering Hero Comes".[3] As he walked through the splendid throng of the governing classes of England gathered in the Chapel, escorted by his father and brother, he had eyes for one person only — the small, dark, unobtrusive figure of Baron Stockmar standing in one of the pews close to the chancel. The memory of this faithful servant — a sombre patch of black among the blazing jewels and gay uniforms — remained printed on his mind for ever.[4]

The extreme youth of the bridegroom and bride (neither was twenty-one) was emphasised by the antiquity of the English Royal Family — sons, daughters, daughters-in-law and niece of old King George III — who were grouped round the altar rails. The Queen was given away by her aged uncle, the Duke of Sussex, whose superb uniform was rendered slightly bizarre by the addition of a skull-cap. He maintained that without this comforting head-dress he invariably caught cold. A few tears rolled down his kindly face. His brother, the old Duke of Cambridge, was described as "decidedly gay" because of his very audible remarks throughout the more solemn moments of the service. The Queen pronounced the responses in that clear, bell-like voice which was one of her greatest attractions, but the Prince was "a good deal perplexed and agitated in delivering his responses".[5]

The Archbishop of Canterbury, who took the service, enquired beforehand whether the Queen wished to promise to obey her husband.[6] This she wished.

[1] Journal. [2] Greville, iv, 239.

[3] *Personal Life of Queen Victoria*, by Sarah Tooley. Hodder and Stoughton, 1896. [4] Martin, v, 33.

[5] Account by the Duchess of Cleveland, one of the Queen's bridesmaids, quoted in *V.R.I.*, by the Duke of Argyll. [6] Sarah Tooley.

After the service a splendid banquet was held in Buckingham Palace. The wedding cake weighed 300 pounds: this was surmounted by the figure of Britannia blessing the illustrious pair, who were dressed as ancient Romans. Various cupids were scattered round the cake "enjoying themselves as such interesting little individuals generally do".[1]

In the afternoon bride and bridegroom left for Windsor Castle, travelling in what Greville calls a very poor and shabby style because their carriage was not new.[2] The crowd, which was enormous, did not seem to share the aristocratic prejudices of Mr. Greville and cheered so lustily that when the Queen and Prince got to Windsor they were "quite deaf".[3] After the exertions of the day the Queen was worn out, confiding to her Journal, "I had such a sick headache that I could eat nothing at dinner and had to remain on the sofa for the rest of the evening".[4] They were up early the next morning walking in the grounds of the Castle and Greville crustily observed to Lady Palmerston that this "was not the way to provide us with a Prince of Wales".[5]

The wisdom of the Prince's judgment in urging that they should stay for a few weeks quietly at Windsor was endorsed by Greville, who thought the royal honeymoon "more strange than delicate". Two days after the wedding the Queen collected an immense party for a dance, sending up to London for spare members of the Paget family to make up the numbers.[6] But any criticism there may have been did not affect her happiness and she was writing enthusiastically to Stockmar, "There cannot exist a dearer, purer, nobler being in the world than the Prince". The recollection of him at breakfast during those honeymoon days remained with her always — "He wore a black velvet jacket without a cravat, and anything more beautiful — and more youthfully manly and perfect — never was seen".[7]

[1] *A Biography for the People.*
[2] Greville, iv, 240.
[3] Journal.
[4] Journal.
[5] Greville, iv, 241.
[6] Greville, iv, 241.
[7] Royal Archives.

He, for his part, was comforted to find that her nature was cheerful rather than merely pleasure-loving, clinging rather than obstinate. There was yet time to shape her to his pattern and to put into practice what he wrote to her before the wedding, " So should it ever be, dearest Victoria, one heart, one mind ".[1]

[1] Jagow.

CHAPTER IV

PALACE CABALS

THE very warmth of the Queen's feelings made it difficult to attain to that singleness of heart and mind for which the Prince was seeking. She appears to have convinced herself that affairs and political business were deadly to love and passion, and that they would strangle the sickly plant of true love which could only thrive in the bright lights and gentle warmth of leisured grandeur. Love was to be strengthened by long gallops through Windsor Park, by singing and reading in the Blue Boudoir and by dancing in her lover's arms through the brilliantly lit ballroom of the Castle. The Queen's own words, written only a fortnight after her marriage, seem to hammer this home: "I danced several quadrilles and valses and a gallop with dearest Albert, who is a splendid dancer. . . . He (Lord Melbourne) thought it all so bright and gay." [1] Then in a reference to affairs of state she puts the Prince deftly in his place, "Albert helped me with the blotting paper when I signed".[2] And a few weeks later she wrote, "Rested and read Despatches — some of which I read to Albert".[3]

The gilded popinjay of the Palace sternly excluded from the harsh realities of business and affairs was no role for a man of the Prince's capabilities and ordered mind. He quickly chafed and less than three months after his marriage he sadly wrote to his greatest friend, "I am only the husband, and not the master in the house".[4]

Sympathy for the Prince in a position at once equivocal and to some extent humiliating has led writers on these years to treat

[1] Journal. [2] Journal. [3] Journal. [4] Martin, i, 71.

the Queen with great severity. She herself set the pace, for in later years she lashed herself with all the mortifying agony of a Trappist monk battling with his conscience.

A true understanding of the facts shows that the Queen was influenced partly by prudence and partly by circumstances which left her no freedom of action. She would have acted with great recklessness if she had immediately given the Prince a dominating influence in politics and in the Household. However circumspectly and wisely he had acted, he would have made enemies who, by whisper and chatter, would have fanned the terror of foreign influence in high places which lies dormant in every honest British heart. Had the Prince been assailed in 1840 and 1841 (as he was assailed just before the Crimean War) with all the malevolence of the insular mind his position would have been irreparably weakened before he had had time to win the respect and confidence of governing circles.

At any time in English history the influence of a foreign mind behind the political scene is fraught with alarms and danger, but they were magnified by the circumstances in which the Queen was placed. When she came to the throne in 1837 she inherited the tradition — and Melbourne schooled her to maintain it — that the sovereign of England should give unmistakable proof of political partisanship. Only in text-books of a later age, only in the lecture rooms of late Victorian England, was fostered the theory that the sovereign was a gorgeous referee, watching with keen impartiality the manœuvres and struggles of the opposing political teams.

A study of political history in the first half of the nineteenth century shows that the constitutional sovereign never played the game according to those rules. Far from being an impartial referee, he was always calculated to give a series of surreptitious kicks and trips, culminating in a shrill blast on the whistle if his friends were in real danger of defeat. George III, George IV and William IV never pretended to be impartial; they regarded the

Government of the moment as their own and worthy of protection by a full display of royal favours and support. They freely exercised the right to appoint ministers; only ten years before the Queen's accession the sovereign made a personal appointment to the Chancellorship of the Exchequer, forcing through his nominee with the words, "The office requires ability and not aristocracy . . . the King will have those that are proper for their business and if there be room after this — the Cabinet may if they please look out for ornaments".[1] In return for political influence, which was wide, extensive and freely used, the sovereign gave public support to his Government in patronage and by surrounding himself with courtiers who shared the politics of his Government. People of the opposite complexion in politics were excluded from the sovereign's private circle, though they could, naturally, attend the general functions of the Court. Even when the Duke of Wellington, at a time that he was in opposition, called on the King, the latter thought it right to explain to the Prime Minister why he had called and what they had discussed. Traditionally, therefore, the Queen was not constitutionally wrong to give public and constant proof of her complete identification with her Whig Ministers, and to cut herself off entirely from the Tory Party or even from members of the aristocracy who were Tories. Years later the Queen allowed Sir Theodore Martin to say, in the Life of the Prince (and it will be recalled that the book was wholly revised and in part written by her), that Her Majesty's affection for Lord Melbourne caused her

> to drift insensibly into political partisanship and to forget for a time the obvious, but up to that time much neglected, doctrine . . . that it is the paramount duty of a constitutional Monarch to maintain a position of neutrality towards the leaders of party on both sides.[2]

In fact, as the Queen points out, this doctrine was not the constitutional practice of her immediate forbears and it was really

[1] Aspinall, *Letters of George IV*. Cambridge, 1938.

[2] Martin, i, 36, 37.

not so much British constitutionalism as pure Coburgism. Like everything which emerged from the fertile mind of Stockmar it was designed for the greater glory of monarchical power. The Baron's ideal of monarchy was that of a sovereign, wise and laborious, withdrawn from the sordid clash of party and exercising power which was unobtrusive but decisive. The instrument by which he sought both to reform and revivify the British Monarchy was Prince Albert. "Be you therefore the constitutional genius of the Queen", he wrote.[1]

The Queen was perhaps scarcely fair to Lord Melbourne when she suggests that he "allowed her to drift insensibly into political partisanship"; rather he was deliberately guiding her along channels clearly marked by the practice and traditions of her immediate forbears. As events developed she became more and more closely identified with the Whigs, Melbourne acting as her adviser and secretary on all important political matters, and her confidante, Baroness Lehzen, acting as her adviser and secretary on all personal matters. Victoria, Melbourne and Lehzen — the old firm bound together by no articles of partnership except that of perfect understanding — exercised monarchical power with gusto and without disaster. The whole performance was slapdash and informal. Indeed the Queen did most of her work by conversation with Lord Melbourne, and her scrutiny of documents when she had taken his counsel, was generally perfunctory. To admit a fourth member to this cosy triumvirate was not easy. They were enjoying the game; they knew the rules which they kept in their heads and it was a tedious prospect to have to explain everything to a new-comer who was certain to ask questions and to raise objections. Within two months of their marriage the Queen told Lord Melbourne that the Prince was complaining of not being given her confidence in affairs of state, and she added, "It is entirely from indolence. I know it is wrong but when I am with the Prince I prefer talking on other subjects."[2]

[1] Martin, i, 111.

[2] Royal Archives.

In exchange for this exclusive treatment in business and politics, she gave way to him entirely in the domestic sphere. Even so harsh a critic as her brother-in-law wrote to King Leopold in those early months of the Prince's marriage, " She is invariably a loving, attentive and even tender wife to Albert and tries to find out his small preferences ".[1]

With no natural aptitude for either politics or statecraft — in fact Stockmar noted with sorrow that when the Prince was twenty he showed not the slightest interest in politics — he was pitchforked into a position where both had to be practised. A lazy man or a foolish one would have allowed events to take their course, and would have been content to play the humdrum part of a cork in a choppy sea. The Prince, conscious of his limitations, flung himself on the political protection of the Baron and asked him " to sacrifice your time to me for the first year of my life in England ".[2] The Baron was ever at his elbow, goading, prodding, advising. In his niggling handwriting, when business called him back to the Continent, he drenched the Prince with pious bromides. " Be patient, consistent, courageous and worthy." " Human happiness is only to be found on the paths of love and goodness." " By the collision of mind with mind your Royal Highness may often, as by an electric shock, gain impressions and glimpses of intelligence which expand the limits of your being." " Not outward show — but Truth and Reality be the aim." " Never fail in princely worth and nobleness." [3]

How were " nobleness " and " princely worth " to be indulged if the Prince was kept, as the triumvirate clearly intended he should be kept, as the plaything of the blue boudoir ? [4]

To appreciate the full difficulties of the Prince's position it is necessary to go back to those battles of the Queen's early years, the smoke of which still hung heavily over Castle and Palace. One of the strongest qualities of Queen Victoria — and one which

[1] *Duke of Saxe-Coburg Gotha*, i, 93. [2] Jagow.

[3] Martin, *passim*. [4] The Queen's private room at Windsor.

greatly contributed to her nobility of character — was her passionate loyalty to her friends and dependents. In her early years this quality was concentrated with all the force of her determined nature on the Baroness Lehzen, who had been her only friend in those wild days at Kensington Palace before she ascended the throne.

This narrow-minded, jealous, devoted spinster became a figure of the greatest influence and the first importance so soon as the Queen ascended the throne. Queen Victoria had wanted to appoint Stockmar as her private secretary, but he wisely declined on the ground that he was a foreigner.[1] After some discussion with the Government, who were jealous of anyone coming between them and the sovereign, it was arranged that no secretary should be appointed but that Lord Melbourne should combine the offices of Prime Minister and Private Secretary to the Queen. Naturally enough Lord Melbourne, who was not remarkable for industry, could not be bothered with many of the trivialities and formalities falling to the lot of a private secretary. He could hardly be expected to adjust himself, fresh from the splendours of Downing Street, to the behaviour of a bell-boy. In consequence, the Baroness became the Queen's personal private secretary with particular authority in all Household affairs.

Devotion to the Queen, amiability and an anxiety to please (the cardinal qualities of Lehzen) were no substitute for capacity. Each night, in the small hours, the faithful Baroness, in slippered feet, padded through Windsor Castle or Buckingham Palace to make certain that all was quiet and that no fire was raging. She was never once known to have a day off, but it is impossible not to blame her directly and Lord Melbourne indirectly for the grave disorders by which the Queen was encompassed.

The Baroness's choice of persons to fill the chief places at Court — and Melbourne must of course share with her some of the responsibility — was disastrous. She allowed Lord Conyng-

[1] Martin, ii, 554.

ham, whose wife was a Paget, to remain Lord Chamberlain after he had installed his mistress as housekeeper in Buckingham Palace. They were, on one occasion, observed rushing into each others arms.[1] The Vice-Chamberlain was Lord Charles FitzRoy and in old age the Queen said that she remembered him because of the vigour of his language.[2] The Lord Steward was Lord Uxbridge — the head of the Paget faction — and he followed the example of the Lord Chamberlain by providing for his mistress in the domestic staff of the Palace. He became Lord Chamberlain in 1839. These matters were not, of course, known to the general public but they were whispered by busybodies outside, and the scurrilous newspapers used to refer to Windsor Castle as the Paget Club House. The loose habits of these eminent courtiers did not encourage a high tone of morality among the Queen's guests, and on one occasion Lord Palmerston, who was staying at the Castle when he was Secretary of State for Foreign Affairs, burst into the bedroom of Mrs. Brand, one of the Queen's Ladies of the Bedchamber and subsequently Lady Dacre. Her protests roused the Castle (though happily not the Queen) and Palmerston, caught red-handed, passed it off with a nonchalant air.[3]

These sins and follies, any one of which might have blown up into a scandal beside which the phantom pregnancy of Lady Flora Hastings would have read like a Sunday School tract, were the penalty which the Queen had to pay for her dependence on Melbourne.

Greville, who enjoyed retailing scandals but always accompanied them with shrewd and penetrating observations, remarked

[1] Royal Archives.

[2] *Memoirs of Sir Almeric FitzRoy*. Hutchinson.

[3] Greville (vi, 441) is wrong in saying that this came to the Queen's ears at the time. She only knew of it much later and pardonably thought it the grossest insult to herself, for which she never forgave Palmerston. The episode had serious political consequences because it provided the foundations for the Queen's violent hostility to Palmerston. According to Anson, Palmerston had been accustomed to sleeping with another lady in that bedroom and " probably from force of habit floundered in ". (Royal Archives.)

of the *tracasserie* at Court about Lady Flora, "It is inconceivable how Melbourne can have permitted this disgraceful and mischievous scandal".[1] This and the other scandals of the Palace and Castle were the rotten fruits of Whiggery which lay behind the bland gossip and fat chuckle of "dear Lord M.". The Queen, who during all these events was an innocent girl, was ignorant of what was going on, except when, as in the case of Lady Flora, the scandal came to the surface.

It was Lehzen's self-appointed task, in addition to her many other duties, to hide all these yawning chasms from the Queen, to keep up the fiction that life was gaiety and amusement, all tittle-tattle and all pretty nonsense like her note-paper, which was adorned with a railway engine in gold, and the inscription, "I am coming".[2]

From the moment of his marriage the Prince was determined that the Baroness's motto must be changed as quickly as possible to "I am going". No one, not even Melbourne, challenged the wisdom of this decision. That being so, most people would have expected the Prince to go frankly to the Queen and ask her to dismiss the Baroness or at least to subordinate her to his authority. There was, however, in the Prince's character a certain hesitancy and tortuousness spotted by Greville at first sight, who speaks of "rather a slouching air".[3] This streak of indirectness and hesitancy in the Prince was frequently touched on by Stockmar in those long, spun-out letters from Germany by which he fancied he was making the marionettes of Windsor dance to his manipulations. "Your character has to gain force, endurance and the necessary hardness", he wrote in the summer of 1840.[4] Anson referred to it as "constitutional timidity".[5] Nonetheless, it was not easy to talk openly and frankly with the Queen on this topic. The reason for this was that the whole Whig structure of her household was based on the Baroness.

[1] Greville, iv, 133. [2] Royal Archives.
[3] Greville, iv, 260. [4] Martin, i, 91. [5] Royal Archives.

All details of the courtiers' duties, including their spells in waiting, were arranged by Lehzen and she could be relied on to keep the wheels of court life revolving smoothly, deriving their force from the sacred principles of Whiggery. The Prince, on the other hand — as was shown by his struggles to introduce men of all parties into his own household — would have introduced a jarring note destructive of the apparent harmony of the Court.

This policy of keeping the Prince in a water-tight compartment was, of course, strongly encouraged by the Baroness since her power rested on his exclusion ; when he was out or busy the Baroness would come sidling in, sit down with the Queen and they would enjoy a feminine chit-chat about the world of rank and fashion — that world which bored and irritated the Prince. The letters of Lehzen which survive at Windsor show her to have been strong-minded and forceful but delighting in malicious gossip. She was extremely worldly and, even for a clergyman's daughter, she was astonishingly ignorant of religion and she once wrote to Stockmar to know whether immortal souls would be allowed to meet in a future world. The Baron, for all his lore and learning, must have been hard put to it to find an answer. She dreaded anything which would estrange the Queen's mind from worldly things, and she strongly disapproved of the Prince reading religious books to the Queen on Sundays.[1]

Unluckily a public event in the summer of 1840 somewhat strengthened the Baroness's hand. Owing to the Queen's pregnancy it was necessary to appoint a regent in case she should die leaving an infant sovereign. The Prince was appointed by Parliament sole regent in such an eventuality, but not without opposition from the Royal Family, who thought there should have been a Council of Regency. This opposition was led by the Queen's uncle, the Duke of Sussex, who, after alluding to the Prince having passions like other men, ended a remarkable oration by suddenly ejaculating, " God's will be done ! "[2]

[1] Royal Archives. [2] Hansard, July 21st, 1840.

Emboldened by this lead from the Royal Family and taking full advantage of it, Lehzen and some of the courtiers suddenly announced that the Prince had no right to drive in the state coach with the Queen when she went to prorogue Parliament, and they also raised the question where he should sit at the prorogation ceremony in the House of Lords. This was evidently not frankly discussed between the Queen and Prince, though the Queen talked it over with Lord Melbourne, who characteristically told her, "We must see what happened to that infernal George of Denmark to whom we are always referring."[1]

Then one day when the Queen and Prince were at luncheon she received a box from Lord Melbourne. Opening it she turned very red and said to the Prince, "I asked Lord Melbourne about the House of Lords, for I was very much concerned about it, and I see George of Denmark went with the Queen. . . . I thought it had not been so, but I am very pleased. . . . You will lead me in and sit there." Wearily the Prince replied "I don't much mind about going there."[2]

A few weeks later, in August 1840, an official box came in from one of the government departments labelled "Sign Immediately". The Prince thought it most unbecoming that the Queen should be thus ordered to discharge her functions (as though she were an overworked Civil Servant) and he urged her to hold up her signature for a day or two. The Queen was extremely annoyed at his interference, said she knew he was opposed to everything and signed at once.[3]

The Prince was, therefore, cut off from a full share in the Queen's life except for the private and social side, where his influence and authority were fully recognised. Melbourne and Lehzen stood on guard to warn him off ground where they felt he did not belong. During this time he had to be content with such despatches and papers as the Queen tossed across for him to

[1] Journal. [2] The Prince to Stockmar. Royal Archives.
[3] Royal Archives.

see. Gratefully accepting these scraps he commentated on them in the best Stockmar tradition and forwarded his memorandum to Melbourne. He had sadly to confess that he seldom had any reply.[1]

However, in spite of these ups and downs the Queen showed him much more confidence after his position at the prorogation of Parliament was publicly recognised. In September he was able to write to Stockmar, "I am constantly provided with interesting papers. . . . I have come to be extremely pleased with Victoria during the past few months. She has only twice had the sulks. . . . Altogether she puts more confidence in me daily."[2]

He made his first public speech in June 1840 at a public meeting on behalf of the abolition of slavery. The speech, unexceptionable in sentiment, consisted of less than two hundred words and began, somewhat ungraciously, "I have been induced to preside at the meeting of this Society . . ." He was excessively nervous and had repeated it by heart to the Queen just before starting. The speech was excellently received. To occupy his time he began with characteristic thoroughness to study the British Constitution, reading Hallam aloud with the Queen, and taking lessons from a distinguished Chancery lawyer — Mr. William Selwyn, the Treasurer of Lincoln's Inn. He was described by the Prince as "old, bald-headed, lame, with staring eyes, skin like parchment and a voice like a lion".[3] This rough diamond, hardened in the rugged confines of Lincoln's Inn, somewhat shocked the Prince by "sitting down without much ceremony" and by "his lack of method". For the rest, he passed his time in laying out the pleasure grounds round Windsor Castle and he was successful in saving the remains of George IV's Cottage (the Royal Lodge) and the fishing temple on Virginia Water from being pulled down.

[1] Martin, i, 95. [2] Royal Archives.

[3] To Stockmar. Royal Archives.

In May 1840 he was put in full possession of all the facts about the Duchess of Kent and he was able to do much to straighten out her affairs, both financial and personal, and to restore normal relations between mother and daughter. For her part, the Duchess was devoted to him and he always treated her with a species of good-natured banter exactly suited to her warm heart and simple nature. Each Christmas with monotonous regularity she presented him with a gay and gaudy waistcoat. He always maintained that the troubles between mother and daughter need never have arisen if King Leopold had taken the trouble to advise the Duchess.

But increasingly he saw that he must win the full trust and confidence of the Queen in all her duties if his marriage was to be completely happy and if he was to render her the maximum service. His desire to help in politics sprang from his love for the Queen, not, as his aunt the Duchess of Cambridge (who never cared for him) put it, from his " very stirring and ambitious views ".[1] Stockmar shrewdly cautioned him against the danger of wishing for political power " all at once ".[2]

With the birth of the Princess Royal in November 1840 things began to go better, showing that this cautious policy was bearing fruit. In the first letter which the Queen wrote to Lord Melbourne, after recovering from the birth of the Princess Royal, she said that she wished

> Lord Melbourne would order her likewise a key for the Secret Boxes (Chubbs) as she wishes to give it to the Prince to whom it would be a great convenience to have — the Queen thinks as well as Sir H. Taylor [3] had the use of these keys, the Prince may, as his discretion may be relied on, and the Despatches interest him to read.[4]

This letter marks what Anson called " an important advance " in the Prince's political position and from the beginning of 1841 he was, in all but name, the Queen's private secretary. Dark

[1] *Sir Robert Peel*, by C. S. Parker. [2] *Letters*, i, 224.
[3] Private Secretary to King William IV. [4] Royal Archives.

political storms were gathering, and it was providential that the Queen should have had the Prince's help in the nick of time.

For months Melbourne's Government had been tottery. As far back as the summer of 1839 their majority had fallen to five and they had resigned. They were, however, given a reprieve because the Queen refused to admit a Tory Government on terms which would have meant a change of courtiers — the so-called Bed Chamber question. It was, however, only a reprieve and by 1841 Melbourne's Government clearly could not last. In the first few weeks of the year they lost four by-elections and they were day after day held up to scorn and obloquy in the matchless prose of Delane and Barnes in *The Times* newspaper.

Things looked so threatening that at the end of April the Prince took the unusual course of asking Lord Melbourne to come and see him after he had had an audience with the Queen. He urged Melbourne to tell the Queen quite frankly that she must send for Peel (if the Whigs resigned) "through me". He also asked Lord Melbourne to make it clear that from the moment the Whigs resigned "I must be alone her adviser". Lord Melbourne did nothing. "The old man has probably fallen into his old lazy ways", wrote the Prince angrily,[1] but it is more likely that he took no action not because of laziness or disrespect to the Prince but because he was shrewdly biding his time. Meanwhile the Queen's wrath was mounting as the prospect of losing "Lord M." came alarmingly near. "Nothing will induce me to send for that bad man Peel who behaved so wickedly," she cried with something of the spirit of Queen Elizabeth.[2]

At this juncture the Prince took the remarkable step of sending Anson to discuss with Peel the position of the courtiers if Peel were summoned to form a Government. This was done without the knowledge of the Queen.[3] With much emphasis on his feelings as a gentleman, Peel readily agreed to a compromise about the ladies and it seemed in those bright days of May that the change of

[1] Royal Archives. [2] Royal Archives. [3] Royal Archives.

Government was virtually accomplished. However, colossal exertions were made by the Whigs to rally every conceivable supporter to the division lobbies in Westminster ; they fought tenaciously, even whipping up the sick and dying to vote. Perhaps their greatest triumph lay in wheeling William Beckford's brother-in-law, Lord Douglas Hallyburton, through the lobby in a bath-chair. He had long been hopelessly mad.[1]

At the same time a powerful section of the Cabinet urged during May that the Government, instead of resigning, should ask the Queen to dissolve Parliament, which still had three years to run, having been elected at the Queen's Accession, and the Septennial Act being still in force. In the middle of May, Lord Melbourne came to discuss this point which touched on the very nerve-centre of the sovereign's constitutional powers — the right to grant or withhold a dissolution. The Queen noted in her Journal, " Albert was present and joined in ". This appears to have been the first occasion on which the Prince was present at an official audience between the Queen and her Prime Minister.

Lord Melbourne, who had a very nice sense of the constitutional power of the sovereign, was lukewarm about a dissolution because in his heart of hearts he felt that the Whigs would be smashed if they went to the country. He felt it was constitutionally wrong to ask the Crown to intervene on behalf of a Ministry which was doomed. He pointed out to the Queen that since the days of the Stuarts the Crown, when it had intervened to dissolve Parliament, had always had a majority returned in its favour. " I am afraid ", he added, " that for the first time the Crown would have an Opposition returned smack against it ; and that would be an affront to which I am very unwilling to expose the Crown." [2]

In a letter of great force and power Lord Brougham, himself a Whig and an erstwhile Lord Chancellor, wrote to the Queen counselling her not to grant a dissolution, thereby " perverting to

[1] Greville, iv, 383. [2] *Letters*, i, 276.

BARONESS LEHZEN
From the miniature by C. F. Koepke

the mere purposes of party by far the most eminent of the Royal prerogatives ".[1] There can be no doubt that, looking to the by-elections, the general feeling in the country expressed by the newspapers and to the half-hearted request for a dissolution by the Prime Minister, the Queen would have been amply justified in withholding her consent. Young and inexperienced as both she and the Prince were, they received no clear and sound advice from any quarter. Even the faithful Stockmar was far from the point. Scratch, scratch went the baronial quill in Coburg to the Prince.

> Let us cleave devoutly but unceasingly to high thoughts and noble purposes. . . . [Do not] rest satisfied with mere *talk*, where *action* is alone appropriate. . . . Turn the events of the hour to account as an instructive practical lesson. . . . All men, still more all women, yield to the omnipotence of events. . . . A man can always accomplish what is right, if he set himself resolutely to do so.[2]

They needed advice, not pulpit oratory; they had no lack of high thoughts and noble purposes, but even on that lofty plane the question still had to be answered, " Should they agree to dissolve ? "

Evidently the Prince saw the dangers of agreeing to a dissolution and Anson had expressed the opinion to Melbourne that he should not ask the Queen to dissolve unless he thought there was some chance of increasing his strength.[3] The Queen, perhaps naturally, welcomed a dissolution because it provided a possible means of keeping the Whigs and " Lord M." When the Government was beaten on June 4th by one vote on a motion of No Confidence she agreed to dissolve Parliament. Plainly somewhat nervous of what she had done, she wrote to her uncle, " it is the fairest and most constitutional mode of proceeding ".[4]

[1] *Letters*, i, 293. [2] Martin, chap. vii. [3] *Letters*, i, 268.

[4] *Letters*, i, 291. Subsequently the Queen felt strongly that she made a mistake in agreeing to a dissolution. She defined the power to dissolve Parliament as " a most valuable and powerful instrument in the hands of the Crown, but which ought not to be used except in extreme cases and with a certainty of success ".

In a valiant effort on behalf of her political allies Baroness Lehzen spent £15,000 of the Queen's money on behalf of the Whig Party.[1] When the Prince heard what she was doing he was alarmed and horrified and strongly remonstrated with Melbourne at this royal interference in elections. The loyal old Whig pooh-poohed it all, characteristically adding that £15,000 was nothing compared with what George III used to spend at elections.[2] This lavish expenditure of cash may explain why the Queen and Prince were much gratified, on attending the Ascot races, to be met with loud cheers and cries of, " Melbourne for ever ; no Peel." But the views of the touts and tipsters of Ascot were not those of the electors of England, who butchered the Government and sent them back to Westminster in a minority of at least seventy.

Even the passage of a hundred years cannot wholly stifle the observer's feelings of sympathy for the Queen as the prospect of losing Lord Melbourne was translated into a certainty. Her health was not robust as she was expecting a second child within a few weeks. In this condition she was called upon to exchange those political friends with whose leader she was on terms of affectionate intimacy for a party of complete strangers led by Peel whom she herself described two years before as " such a cold, odd man ".[3] Her uncle, the Duke of Cumberland, had summed him up, with reference to his cotton-spinning father, no less picturesquely, " You will always see the jenny ; the manufacturer's blood will show." When the dreaded moment of parting came and she had to face the ordeal of the ceremony of handing over the seals of office, she was very flushed but comported herself with such distinction and courage that even Greville was swayed by emotions of pity and admiration.[4] Only to Lord Melbourne she betrayed her true feelings, and writing to him on the day of the formation of the new Government she said " she was dreadfully affected for some time after, but is

[1] Royal Archives. [2] Journal.
[3] *Letters*, i, 159. [4] Greville, iv, 408.

calm now. It is very, very sad", and then throwing aside the cold formality of the third person, she burst out, "We do, and shall, miss you so dreadfully".[1]

As the well-loved figure of Lord Melbourne, at once intellectual and gentlemanly, shrewd, kind, amusing and paternal, backed for the last time as Minister from the presence of the Queen he bequeathed to her his greatest gift — the advice to trust her husband and lover. On the last evening at Windsor, with tears in his eyes, he began, "I have seen you daily and I liked it better every day." He went on to explain that it was easier to leave her then than it would have been in 1839 because she had the Prince, and, simply and without affected exaggeration, he numbered and praised the Prince's gifts. "I am so glad to hear Lord M. say this. Perhaps this may be a good lesson for me."[2]

The improvement in the political influence of the Prince was not matched by his influence in the Household. Here, where Lehzen was still supreme, affairs went worse rather than better. Unknown to the Prince and to the Queen an officer, Captain Childe, attached to the Court, fancied himself madly in love with the Queen and drew some attention to himself. Anson got wind of this and asked the Baroness why on earth she had not told the Prince. She said that she had done all that was necessary in putting the matter in the hands of Lord Uxbridge. (Even the grave Anson must have smiled at the picture of Uxbridge as the custodian of morality.) When Anson said that she ought at once to have told the Prince she broke out into a tirade against him, saying that he had slighted her, and that his conduct to her made it impossible for her to consult him. She added that the Prince had once told her to leave the Palace, but "I replied that he had not the power to turn me out of the Queen's house."[3] It was scarcely surprising that after this the Prince referred to her, in writing to Stockmar, as "the House Dragon spitting fire" or as "the yellow lady". The explanation of this last description lay in the frequent attacks

[1] *Letters*, i, 311. [2] Journal. [3] Royal Archives.

of jaundice with which the poor Baroness was smitten. On one occasion she was delirious for two days. The Queen's doctor, whose diagnoses were a constant menace to the lives of the Royal Family, opined that it was a proof of the weakness of Lehzen's intellect that she became so easily delirious.[1] However (yellow or not), the Baroness was not without allies — notably Lord Uxbridge — and these two formed a strong cabal against the Prince's influence. On one occasion the Queen was much annoyed when two of the Ladies Paget, during a Drawing Room, remained close by her, chattering and giggling and making a great disturbance. The Queen told Lehzen to rebuke Lord Uxbridge but she refused to carry out this command because of Lord Uxbridge's notoriously fiery temper.

He had always treated the Prince with studied insolence ever since the Prince in the first summer of his marriage removed him from his private rooms in the Palace.

> I summoned Uxbridge about the room. He did not come till after a few lines from me, he could not do anything else. I told him he must give up his rooms. He could not get over his anger. He said he must first put it before Lord Melbourne.[2]

With however ill a grace, Lord Uxbridge had eventually to go, and the Prince wrote gleefully to his brother, "I can boast of the master stroke of having driven the Lord Chamberlain and Saunders [3] out of their rooms".[4]

Such episodes as these more than justified the Queen's comment some years later, "Poor Lehzen, how ill everything went while she was there." [5] Stockmar told Lehzen to her face that she had been justified by events in coming between mother and daughter but that the country would never forgive her if she came between husband and wife.[6] Certainly it strikes the reader

[1] Royal Archives.
[2] Royal Archives.
[3] A clerk in the Household.
[4] *The Prince Consort and his Brother*. Bolitho.
[5] Journal.
[6] Royal Archives.

of a later age as most odd that no one — not Stockmar, Melbourne or the Prince — had the courage to tackle this thorny problem boldly with the Queen. The Queen's letters give a clear example of the roundabout methods which were employed to try to influence her. In May 1840, when Palace difficulties were proving particularly wearisome to the Prince, King Leopold (plainly put up by Stockmar) wrote to the Queen about his own experiences with Princess Charlotte — the moral of which was obvious. "I know that you have been told that she ordered everything in the house, and liked to show that she was mistress. It was not so. On the contrary, her pride was to make me appear to the best advantage. . . ." [1]

But this tortuous policy had some justification in results, and by 1841 things began to improve. At the beginning of that year the nursery was put under the control of a Superintendent who was independent of the Baroness. The latter made a desperate effort to keep control by charging the nursery establishment to the Wardrobe Accounts which were her province. This was contested by the Prince, who had to enlist the support of the Queen. He wrote to Stockmar, "Victoria is annoyed that I should disturb her with such quarrels. She takes everything about the Baroness so much to heart and feels she ought to be her champion." [2]

That summer of 1841 the Queen and Prince went on a round of country-house visits and, as the Prince put it, the public could see that at last "the moon was on the wane" [3] from the fact that Lehzen was not of the party. It was the first time that the Queen had ever been separated from her since she was a child of five, and she confessed to "feeling a little low". [4]

After the General Election of 1841 Lord Uxbridge was replaced by a Tory Lord Chamberlain and the walls of Whiggery, so faithfully built round the Queen by Lehzen and Melbourne,

[1] *Letters*, i, 222.
[2] Royal Archives.
[3] Royal Archives.
[4] Journal.

finally collapsed. From that time onwards the Baroness, " narrow jealous, provincial ",[1] sucking her caraway seeds to the last, fades from the scene, till in September 1842 she left England for ever, retiring to Hanover, where she died in 1870 surrounded by pictures of the Queen whom she faithfully loved and whose character she had sternly moulded.

Over and over again Anson refers to the blessed consequences of Lehzen's departure.[2] So long as she haunted Castle and Palace, her spirit — not deliberately malignant but nonetheless mortal to happiness and comfort — was destructive of full confidence between husband and wife. The Baroness was, to use the slang of the modern world, a spinster gremlin. Not till she was gone did " my lord and master ", words which the Queen had once used of the Prince, half in jest at her own passionate love of power and independence, become an established reality. After she had gone, the Prince, for the first time, put the Queen wise about Lehzen and she was horrified as several entries in her Journal show. " I blame myself for my blindness. . . . I shudder to think what my beloved Albert had to go through . . . it makes my blood boil to think of it."[3] In writing to Stockmar the Prince says that he often had to fight " to prevent her from regarding herself as too guilty ". The old firm of Victoria, Melbourne and Lehzen was now finally dissolved : from henceforth it was to be Victoria and Albert.

[1] Lytton Strachey. [2] Royal Archives.

[3] Journal. This explains why the Queen only saw Lehzen once again. This was when the Prince and Queen visited Germany in 1845, when the Queen thought her " much quieter ". In 1858, when they were also on a visit to Germany, Lehzen stood on Buckeburg station waving her handkerchief. The royal train did not stop.

CHAPTER V

HOME LIFE

PLAINLY the Prince Consort's life would have been intolerable without plenty to do. The hapless plight of the drone after it has performed its vital duties with the queen bee provided a lesson which he could not ignore. The experience of previous consorts of English Queens drove home the truth. The consort of Queen Mary I, having regard to the jealousy of the English and the plainness of his wife, wisely decided to spend only the minimum of time in England. The consort of Queen Mary II shrewdly seized the political power which belonged to his wife. Only poor Prince George of Denmark, who was described as " very fat, loving news, his bottle and the Queen ", had no occupation on which to sharpen his meagre wits, and shuffling through one of the most glorious eras in English history invites our sympathy and laughter.

From the first, Prince Albert was determined to lead a life full, active and conformable with the dignity of manhood. In these early years before his political powers were fully stretched, the management and expansion of the Queen's property and the organisation of the Household gave him plenty to do. Here in particular " the blessed retirement of Lehzen " made itself felt and gave the Prince his chance to take over the reform of the Household, though the work was not wholly congenial, because it entailed " an infinitude of small trivialities ".[1] The chaos and confusion in the Royal Household arose because of the lack of any central controlling authority : every person working in the

[1] Martin, i, 155.

Queen's establishments was subject to one of three great officers of state — the Lord Chamberlain, the Lord Steward or the Master of the Horse. The fabric of the buildings and all outside work were under the Office of Woods and Forests. Between all these august personages there was no " liaison " and since the Lord Chamberlain and the Master of the Horse had no one in authority living in the Palace two-thirds of the servants had virtually no supervision. In short, the arrangements combined to make a paradise for officials and bumbles in which, unhurried and undisturbed, they could twang their harps regardless of harmony and the mournful screeches of their neighbours. They could echo the hymn-writer's conception of this paradise as " bliss beyond compare ". For the performers it was indubitably bliss, but for those who depended on their ministrations it was chaotic rather than blissful.

The prevailing disorder in the Queen's houses was brought home to the public when it was learned that a boy had broken into Buckingham Palace and had been found close to the room where the Queen was sleeping. To the Queen this lack of organisation was brought home more forcibly when the Foreign Secretary of France, who was staying as her guest in Buckingham Palace, by mistake blundered into her dressing-room when she was dressing for dinner. Reform was not, however, easy. All members of the Household — from the great officers of state down to the meanest tweeny and the dirtiest scullery-boy — had a personal interest in maintaining the existing system which abounded in light work and vast perquisites. Not till 1844 was the Prince finally able to make a complete reorganisation, putting everything within doors under the single authority of the Master of the Household.[1]

Scarcely less formidable than the question of internal economy was the housing problem. Superficially the housing accommodation for the Royal Family appeared ample — even extravagant.

[1] Martin, i, 153-61.

Buckingham Palace, Windsor Castle, Claremont (lent to them by King Leopold) and the Pavilion at Brighton seemed more than adequate for their needs and tastes, but in fact none was wholly satisfactory for the youthful parents and their expanding family.

The Pavilion at Brighton with exotic birds, mandarins, serpents and Chinese dragons springing from every wall and ceiling, each room haunted by the rich laugh of the Regent, was no home for children. On first seeing it the Prince was struck dumb by the strangeness of it all.[1] Greater familiarity with the building did not endear it to him and he was quick to discover that, as was the case with most Regency houses, the bedrooms were sacrificed to the living-rooms. In fact it would have been as difficult as a jig-saw puzzle to find sleeping accommodation in the Pavilion for the Royal Family and their attendants. The growth of Brighton had destroyed the privacy of the property and after two or three visits in their early married life they used it as a convalescent home where their children could throw off the infectious disorders of infancy. They were never there again after 1845, when they were much troubled by mobbing, and the building was finally sold to the Brighton Corporation in 1850.

Even at Buckingham Palace things were little better. In the Prince's words, his children were worse off than those in any private house since they had to occupy servants' attics and as they grew up " there was literally not a hole to put them into ".[2] For entertaining, the Queen needed a room which would hold 5000, whereas no room held more than 200. But the Government discouraged the Prince's ambitious schemes for rebuilding the Palace and he notes that whenever he brought up the subject " Peel puts on his wooden face ".[3] Though the Prince was not allowed to rebuild the Palace, it was improved and enlarged by him in the years following 1846.

At Windsor they were far better housed, but here the drawback was the lack of any private garden near the Castle and any

[1] Journal. [2] Royal Archives. [3] Royal Archives.

considerable acreage where the Prince could express his tastes for gardening, planting and country life. He had, it is true, enjoyed laying out the drives and paths in the Home Park. Lord Melbourne, surveying his work, observed that it was "quite the making of the place"[1] — an observation well suited to a pretty lawn round a suburban villa but somewhat singular when applied to the mediaeval glories of Windsor Castle. Over all the park and farm land at Windsor loomed the Office of Woods and Forests which had to be consulted at every turn. The Prince pined for something of his own where his personal tastes and fondness for experiment could be freely indulged. They both longed for something secluded, for as the Queen expressed it, "Windsor is beautiful and comfortable but it is a *palace*".[2]

At Claremont they were certainly private and peaceable but standing in the parish of Esher it was close to London in a district where the population was rapidly spreading. Claremont had been the English home of King Leopold since 1816 and to him it still legally belonged. A revolution in Belgium or the upheaval of a general European war might send him scurrying back to his English home, so that here they were, at best, tenants-at-will of their uncle.

Walking together round the gardens of Buckingham Palace in the autumn of 1843 they first discussed the feasibility of buying something of their own. The Prince broached the project to Sir Robert Peel and through him they heard of two properties for sale in the Isle of Wight. Enquiries were made through Mr. Sewell — a member of a distinguished family and a prominent solicitor in the island — who recommended Osborne as the more suitable of the two properties. He explained that the house was fitted for the residence of a gentleman, that there was a park of 200 acres, that a farm and a wood went with it. The owner, Lady Isabella Blachford,[3] was asking £30,000 for the estate —

[1] Journal. [2] *Letters*, ii, 5.

[3] She was the daughter of the 3rd Duke of Grafton, Prime Minister in 1769.

an exorbitant price based on the fact that the estate was "ripe for building development". The farm was on copyhold tenure — the freehold belonging to Winchester College and, with that remarkable capacity of scholars and gentlemen to drive a hard bargain, they were asking £20,000 for the purchase of the freehold. Both Peel and Anson considered the outlay excessive and they urged the Prince to abandon the project and to be content with taking over and developing the Royal Lodge [1] in Windsor Park. The Prince was, however, adamant and after lengthy negotiations it was agreed that the Queen should take Osborne for one year at a rent of £1000 to see how it suited. They went down in the autumn of 1844, and after a few weeks the Prince was writing enthusiastically to Peel:

> Now I come to an advantage which this place offers which no other spot in England could give us so well, which is the facility for maritime excursions of every kind. Yachting, rowing, etc. etc. We have been out at sea daily in various ways and have notwithstanding very boisterous weather found great enjoyment. . . . This will be very well received in the Navy with whom it brings us in constant contact, teaches us and will teach the Prince of Wales, the nature of this glorious profession.[2]

In the result they were able to buy the whole estate for £26,000, the Prince pointing out that the Queen had been able to save £70,000 since she came to the throne and that they proposed to make a substantial economy by selling the Pavilion at Brighton.

The house itself at Osborne was too small for their needs and three months after buying the property the Queen and Prince, with their characteristic fondness for a little ceremony, laid the foundation stone of the new building planned by the Prince and designed in detail by Cubitt. This house was habitable in 1846 but it was not finally finished till 1851. The Queen and Prince moved in on September 16th, 1846, and one of the ladies-in-

[1] Built by Nash for King George IV; since 1931 the home of King George the Sixth.

[2] Royal Archives.

waiting, who was a Scotswoman, insisted on hurling an old shoe after the Queen as she crossed the threshold of the new home. These crude antics of the barbarous northerner were followed by a solemn drinking of the health of Queen and Prince, to which the Prince, deeply moved, replied in a German paraphrase of the 121st Psalm.

Unsern Ausgang segne Gott,
Unsern Eingang gleicher-massen.

Here among the lush greenery and sparkling atmosphere of the island the Prince was blissfully, idyllically happy. "Our island home", as he invariably called it, so completely his own conception and creation, gladdened his heart. Writing to his Coburg relations in 1850 he says, "In our island home we are wholly given up to the enjoyment of the warm summer weather. The children catch butterflies, Victoria sits under the trees, I drink the Kissingen water, Ragotzky." [1] At Osborne the Prince can be pictured, as the Queen described him, strolling through the woods, rich and various with trees and shrubs of his own planting, whistling to the nightingales "in their own long peculiar note" or standing on the balcony at night to listen to their song. The inhabitants of the island were familiar with glimpses of him and the Queen, each in a wideawake hat, cantering on horseback with merely a lad following them to open the gates.

At Osborne life was simple, free and informal, and London with its social gaieties and political squabbles seemed a world apart, only occasionally sending down emissaries, in the shape of distinguished politicians, to bridge the gulf between the mustiness of city and the brilliance of country. Very grumpy they seemed, these stiff, black and white creatures redolent of the smoke and feuds of Westminster and Whitehall. Very odd and startled they looked in the sea-washed garden, sparkling with sun and bright with blossom ; they were like the villains marauding through

[1] Martin, ii, 287.

the homes of innocence in the gay coloured symphonies of the cinema. Once, soon after the Royal Family had acquired Osborne, Greville as clerk to the Council came down with Ministers. Waiting for the Council to start, the party stumped round the grounds, Greville thinking the place " miserable ", the house " vile " and the new one which was building " very ugly ". In conversation with Sir James Graham — a pompous and haughty renegade from the Liberal cause—Greville grumbled away about the monstrous expense of the place, and this pair of crows chortled with delight over the recollection of the reduction in the Prince's allowance and they agreed (without the slightest justification) that the Queen was secretly delighted that it had been cut because it gave her more power over the Prince. After this truly Christian chat, they no doubt adjusted their faces with appropriate fawns and cringes to pass into the presence of their host and hostess.[1]

With Buckingham Palace enlarged, with Osborne rebuilt and with Windsor Castle the Queen may be felt to have been housed with a style and comfort commensurate with her rank. The addition of Balmoral to the list was made partly to gratify the people of Scotland and partly to give the Prince that mountain scenery which he deeply loved.

Before settling at Balmoral in 1848 they went three times to Scotland and on each occasion the Prince was in rhapsodies over the honesty and simplicity of the Scottish people, over the mountain air recalling his beloved Rosenau and over the chance of " field sports ". After these visits they decided to rent Balmoral, with a view to purchase, on the advice of their doctor, Sir James Clark, who considered the air there was primarily what was wanted " for the peculiar constitution of the Queen and Prince ". For one with the high nervous sensibility of the Prince, the air of Balmoral — clear, cold and bracing — acted, as he said himself, " like a tonic to the nerves ".[2]

[1] Greville, v, 229. [2] Martin, i, 234.

Oddly enough, one of the first official visitors to Balmoral was the ubiquitous Greville. In spite of being too gouty to grace the royal dinner table he considered the Queen and Prince in their Highland retreat were to be seen at their best. "They live with the greatest simplicity and ease . . . she is running in and out of the house all day long, and often goes about alone, walks into the cottages and chats with the old women." To the Prince he pays this tribute — impressive from one who was notoriously sparing in praise: "I was greatly struck with him. I saw at once (what I had always heard) that he is very intelligent and highly cultivated."[1]

To fit naturally into a Highland background was not perhaps easy. While it is known that Queen Victoria was indomitably proud of her Scottish blood which flowed so sturdily in the veins of her great-great-great-great-great-great-grand father (King James I) it has to be admitted that it was somewhat diluted by the time it reached her. A free flaunting of the Royal Stuart tartan, in which in later life Prince Albert looked somewhat bizarre, and a careful draping of the Castle in the Balmoral tartan, could not disguise the fact that the master and mistress were not wholly Scottish. Nonetheless, the Prince and Queen appeared to great advantage in their Highland home. Not only did they enjoy themselves in Scotland but they made their enjoyment obvious. They did not make the mistake of trying to play the part of a Scottish laird *manqué*, though they did not stand aloof from the traditional enjoyment of the Scots.

> Seven whole days in castle and forest — gay in the mazy
> Moving, imbibing the rosy, and pointing a gun at the horny.[2]

They went to Balmoral primarily for health. To them it was the nineteenth-century equivalent of hydro, clinic, sea voyage and watering-place rolled into one.

Such was the setting. Buckingham Palace, Windsor Castle,

[1] Greville, vi, 185-7.

[2] Clough, *Bothie of Tober-na-Vuolich.*

Osborne House and Balmoral Castle — arranged, cherished and enriched by the care and taste of the Prince for the long-drawn-out pageant of royalty. Each house had to be at once a home and a place for official entertaining — the comforts and privacy of domestic life had, at a moment's notice, to be capable of transformation into state entertainment. The home had to embrace the Assembly Rooms.

In 1842 the Queen and Prince had their first experience of state entertaining when the King of Prussia came to England for the christening of the Prince of Wales. The splendour of the banquets in the Waterloo Chamber at Windsor, with the gold plate flashing with myriads of lights, was a scene of fairyland magnificence which would have warmed the heart of King George IV. Nor was the ball which followed less splendid, though the King, who had the mind and appearance of a plump archdeacon, scarcely adorned the scene. Bald and stout, with Protestant theology whizzing through his brain, and having long given up dancing, he bumped his way through the quadrille with the Queen. As always, her deportment, "perfect in Grace and Dignity", redeemed a situation which might have degenerated into the ridiculous.[1]

The full glories of the exchange of visits between heads of states and their full political significance were perhaps first shown in the following year when the Queen and Prince went to France. The project was the Prince's and was arranged by him with the Prime Minister before the Queen knew of it.[2] After a cruise off the coast of Devonshire in the royal yacht, where Queen and Prince delighted in what the Queen calls "this semi-sailor gipsy life",[3] they landed in state at Tréport. For a few days they stayed with the King of the French and his large family at the Château d'Eu, originally built by Louis XIV's mistress, Madame de Montpensier. The weather was radiant, the Prince bathed and

[1] *Memoirs of Baron Bunsen.* Longmans, 1868.
[2] Journal. [3] Journal.

both royal families went out each day for picnics in the forest. "It was so pretty, so merry, so *champêtre*", writes the Queen.[1] She was greatly amused by the oddities of the old King of the French, and it was noticed that she was always roaring with laughter and showing, as a French journalist remarked, "une superbe rangée des dents".[2]

The visit was not, however, all social gaities, luncheon baskets, *chars-à-banc*, gifts of Gobelins tapestry and Sèvres china, with the King mouthing avuncular civilities. Stockmar feared that this had been so, and he wrote to the Prince imploring heaven to "give you *great fertile thoughts and a pure heart* valiantly to withstand the seduction of the world's vanities".[3]

In fact politics were discussed and it was at this meeting between the two families that the King gave the important undertaking that no son of his, and he had five, should aspire to the hand of young Queen Isabella of Spain. So soon as Stockmar heard the full details of the expedition, and in particular of this undertaking of the King, he was delighted and in his turgid analytical way wrote to the Prince,

> Let us pause to ask why it was a success? Because it was thought well over beforehand, because it was undertaken upon a definite plan, because the plan *was adhered to to the letter*. Let us make a vow *to carry on like things in the like way*.[4]

The visit was in fact an important and unconventional diplomatic stroke. The royal families of Europe had completely cold-shouldered Louis Philippe, regarding him as a traitor to his family and traditions. His wife and daughters complained to Queen Victoria at Eu that they had been treated as if they were lepers by all Europe ever since the King had seized power. Consequently the visit of the Queen of England was of vital importance to them, comparable to a visit from Lady Lufton to a slightly suspect family in Framley. With spirit the Queen

[1] Martin, i, 179.
[2] *The Times*, September 4th, 1843.
[3] Martin, i, 184.
[4] Martin, i, 191 and 192.

THE ENGLISH ROYAL FAMILY GREETING THE KING OF THE FRENCH
IN WINDSOR CASTLE

Reproduced from the painting by Winterhalter, 1844, by gracious permission of His Majesty the King

wrote of the visit, "The Emperor of Russia will be very much annoyed, but that is neither here nor there".[1]

In fact it turned out to be very much here, because in the following May the Queen and Prince suddenly learned that the Emperor was on his way to England to visit them. At the time they were quietly entertaining their relative the King of Saxony — a model guest because, as the Queen puts it, "He is out sight-seeing all day, and enchanted with everything".[2] The visit of the Emperor could scarcely have been more inopportune, because they only had forty-eight hours in which to prepare and the Queen was seven months gone with child. Prince, statesmen, courtiers and servants rushed to get everything ready and so effective were their labours that when the Emperor arrived he said, "the English Court is conducted on the noblest scale of any Court I have ever seen. Everything appears to be done without effort."[3]

The Emperor, whose death was to be so loudly acclaimed in England during the Crimean War, was a curious blend of the formal and informal. His first action on getting to Windsor was to send to the stables for a bundle of straw on which to sleep. At the same time he complained bitterly to the Queen of the custom of the English Court in not wearing uniform, adding that when wearing a frock-coat he felt as if he had lost a skin. He was, however, very gracious and easy, entering quite naturally into the simple life of the Queen and Prince, going out for drives with the Queen and amusing her by his habit of ogling the pretty ladies.

As became a Russian autocrat there were about the Czar few manners and no diplomatic niceties. Though he did not talk politics to the Queen he bellowed them to the Prince and Prime Minister, and on one occasion they had to move him from an open window at Buckingham Palace for fear that people in the street would overhear what he was saying. He ranged over Europe — pronounced Turkey on the verge of disintegration and

[1] Martin, i, 182. [2] *Letters*, ii, 14. [3] Martin, i, 214.

emphasised his loathing of France. "As to what the French say of me, I care not. I spit upon it." Quietly, with courage and ability, the Prince countered these outbursts with the English point of view — their desire to maintain the *status quo* in Turkey — and stressed the pivot of British policy, the maintenance of good relations with France.

Not unnaturally the King of the French looked somewhat askance at the Emperor's visit to the Queen and came over to England as quickly as he could to repair any possible damage. In September he came to Windsor. As Queen Victoria observed, the last occasion on which a King of France had visited England was in 1356 after the Battle of Poitiers, when the French King was brought to Windsor as a prisoner of war. Louis Philippe was old, and slightly shaky but full of chat and cordiality, repeating over and over again to the Queen how happy he was to be in England. Like the King of Saxony he was all bustle and curiosity, full of ecstatic praise, poking his nose everywhere. Though easy and amiable he was more of an anxiety than the Emperor because his family, who did not accompany him, had sent special instructions to the Queen to see that he did not overeat.[1] He came to the White Drawing-Room at the Castle and sat talking politics with the Queen and Prince in the place where the Emperor had sat three months before. The Queen took him driving to Twickenham and she noticed that he did not betray the roving eye for female beauty which the Emperor and even King Leopold made no effort to control although driving with her. Instead, the King showed business-like attention to the matter in hand, revelling in the cheers and bowing low over his hat, observing to the Queen that he had never had such a reception. He was given the Garter; this the Prince placed in position and the Queen gave it its final adjustment. As the visit closed he burst out in his voluble way in paeans of praise of the Prince. "Merveille . . . si sage . . . il vous donnera toujours

[1] *Letters*, ii, 23.

de bons conseils . . . il sera comme son oncle aussi sage et aussi bon." [1]

Perhaps more gratifying to the Prince was the statement by the Prime Minister in Parliament that the Queen had given a reception to two of the most powerful sovereigns in the habitable globe, which struck everyone by its magnificence, without adding one tithe to the burden of the country. The Prince's reforms of the Household had borne fruit.[2]

These entertainments of visiting royalties were, of course, additional to the normal entertaining of the Court by balls, concerts and afternoon parties at Buckingham Palace, carried out with impeccable taste and with great profusion during the early years of the Queen's reign. Perhaps the most spectacular was the *Bal Costumé* of 1842 which was given to promote English trade. The Prince appeared as Edward III and the Queen as Queen Philippa. A vast procession of 120 people headed by the Duchess of Cambridge, representing the contemporary French, Spaniards and Italians, paid deference to the mighty Plantagenet sovereigns. This gave great offence in France, where it was felt that the English Court was needlessly disinterring the ancient humiliations of the French.

Any visitor to Buckingham Palace in the early years of the Queen's reign was impressed by the splendour and effortless machinery of the entertaining. As King Leopold expressed it: "There is hardly a country where such magnificence exists: Austria has some of the means but the Court is not elegant from its nature." [3] This was a polite allusion by King Leopold to the imbecile or (to use the language of Greville) to the "wretched crétin" who was at this time Emperor of Austria.[4]

Improvements in the internal economy of English Royalty did not satisfy the Prince: he felt the need of order and beauty in the grounds and land which surrounded the homes of the

[1] Martin, i, 235-42.
[2] Martin, i, 235-42.
[3] *Letters*, i, 396.
[4] Greville, vi, 42.

sovereign. King George IV, who had done much to introduce dignity and taste into the houses of the monarch, had been essentially an indoor personality. A view through a window of a well-heated room was his idea of landscape. The suggestion that he should have gone out to plant, cut, level and drain would have seemed outrageous. Prince Albert was, on the other hand, a countryman by nature. Though not a conventional sportsman he had the country interests of an English gentleman and he was, in this respect, the natural heir of King George III.

Always a warm supporter of the Royal Agricultural Society, he roused great enthusiasm at their annual meeting in 1848 by alluding to the company as "We Agriculturalists of England assembled together" and by referring to himself as "having experienced the pleasures and the little pangs attending these noble pursuits". His claim was more than justified as he had taken the closest personal interest in improving the farmland at Windsor. In 1844 he won his first prize at Smithfield for pigs and after that year the Windsor farm stock never lacked a prize or medal during his life-time.

At Windsor he farmed almost two thousand acres divided into three farms — Home, Norfolk and Flemish. He kept a herd of Herefords on the Flemish farm and a herd of Devons on the Norfolk farm. With the rough wit of a farmer he allowed all the bulls to be named after members of the Royal Family and, lest the bastards should feel slighted, a very fine bull was called FitzClarence after William IV's illegitimate offspring. The most famous of the royal bulls was Prince Alfred, named after the Queen's second son, which was lent for a time to Napoleon III.

At the end of the forties the Prince began to bring the Windsor farms up to date. He extended the Home farm by taking in Shaw farm, rebuilt most of the farm buildings and introduced the very latest agricultural machinery. The farm-houses themselves were rebuilt and he also built a school in the Great Park which was to be attended by agricultural labourers in the evening: each scholar was given a Bible by the Prince. The drawback to Windsor farming was that all had to be done with the cumbersome approval of the Department of Woods and Forests — once described by the Queen as "the plague of one's life".[1] This department was not outstandingly efficient as it was regarded as an appropriate grazing ground for Whig politicians retired from the hurly-burly of party politics. Not until 1851, when Mr. Charles Gore — formerly Lord John Russell's private secretary who had been given a job at £1200 per annum in this department when he was twenty-eight — became sole commissioner, could the Prince work whole-heartedly on agricultural reforms at Windsor. Gore was efficient and co-operative and the Prince was able to show that a royal personage and a government department could jog along together as that beloved figure of the Victorian countryside — the improving landlord.

Naturally enough the Prince found farming at Osborne, where he was free from the watchful eye of the Civil Service, far more congenial. Here, as a result of additional purchases, the Queen had 600 acres of parkland, 400 acres of woodland and 700 acres of arable. To the west of Osborne House, where the public roads were nearest to it, he planted himself a mass of shrubs and soft-wood trees, including Araucaria — the famous monkey-puzzle tree for the popularity of which in England generations of landlords have not thanked him.

At Osborne he worked really hard and he himself described his life there as "partly forester, partly builder, partly farmer and partly gardener".[2] As the Queen was quick to notice, "the planting and transplanting of trees is such an amusement to him".[3]

In a letter to his eldest daughter he described the deep satisfaction afforded to him by gardening. After referring to the extraordinary attractions which this art had had for him since

[1] *Letters*, ii, 35. [2] Martin, i, 322. [3] Journal.

childhood, he writes, " the artist who lays out the work, and devises a garment for a piece of ground, has the delight of seeing his work live and grow hour by hour ; and, while it is growing, he is able to polish, to cut and carve, to fill up here and there, to hope and to love ".[1]

He did not make the mistake — common to many agriculturalists — of being too busy with improvements and alterations to enjoy the pursuits of open-air life. These he loved and nowhere was his influence over the Queen more marked than in breaking down her partiality for town life and late hours in favour of the fresh simplicity of country life.

His favourite pastime was shooting and the first record of his going out in England was in the early autumn after his marriage, when he shot at Richmond.

As the following letter shows, he went to great trouble to improve the shooting at Windsor. Writing to the Queen's aunt, the Duchess of Gloucester, who lived at Bagshot, he says :

My dear Aunt

You have once been so kind as to tell me that when the Rapley Estate was bought by the Crown you would then allow me to have the shooting at Bagshot. I feel extreme delicacy in bringing this matter before you, but I have a double reason for not postponing it as I have lately made an acquisition of a hundred and fifty hares which I am going to turn out in that country and who might find their way into your park. I will be bold and come out at once with a proposition. It is that I will engage to supply you with any quantity of game you may require and that I will take upon myself the expence (*sic*) of the preservation of the game in Bagshot Park — and beg from you the exclusive right of shooting, as the person who has the shooting at Bagshot has entire command over the result of my exertions and expense in getting up a good stock of game at Rapley and Swinley. I have lately got from the University of Cambridge a large tract of heath adjoining Bagshot and hire some other tracts of land thereabouts.

[1] Martin, i, 324.

I hope you will excuse the boldness with which I bring this request before you — and should you not like it I beg you will not hesitate a moment in saying no.

Ever yours,

ALBERT.

WINDSOR CASTLE
February 2nd, 1843.[1]

At this period of English history shooting was still a modest and gentlemanly pursuit: two or three guns, a loader and beater and a couple of setters could spend an agreeable day of exertion and slaughter. The huge shooting-party with hordes of minions, the "slap-up" luncheon and the minimum of exercise, beloved by the best county families of Surrey, had not as yet made its expensive appearance. Regretfully it must be recorded that Prince Albert played his part in that development, thereby making himself unpopular with the older generation of sportsmen.

He thoroughly enjoyed a *battue*. The Queen records his delight when he himself shot 100 pheasants between breakfast and luncheon.[2] In very early days when visiting Scotland he allowed Lord Breadalbane himself, with 300 Highlanders, to tramp and puff "o'er moor and fen, o'er crag and torrent" to beat up the roe-deer for the royal gun.

Another factor destructive of simplicity in the Prince's shooting was his dislike for cold food. Writing to the Queen of the prospect of cold food he says, "Heaven defend my stomach".[3] In country-houses at this time luncheons were always cold, with hot food for the children. The Prince introduced the habit of hot luncheons and he insisted on interrupting the sport to eat them. As an English peer indignantly expressed it, "He stops shooting to devour his German mittagessen".[4]

His partiality for a *battue*, his passion for hot food and his inability to hide his chagrin if he shot badly, combined to give the impression that he was not a sportsman in the English sense

[1] Royal Archives. [2] Journal. [3] Martin, ii, 88.
[4] *Sixty-Three Years*, by Lord Onslow. Hutchinson, 1944.

of the word. It was even said that when out shooting with his secretary, he would blaze away himself, miss and then turn round to Anson and call out, " Anson, di gonn," and seize Anson's gun before the unlucky secretary had time to fire a shot.[1]

In fact, the Prince was a fine shot and he quickly learned to hide his impatience. General Grey, his assistant private secretary, writing to his wife, says, " I do not think I ever shot with a pleasanter and more cheery person than the Prince and how all these stories they still tell of him and the shooting have come to be invented I cannot conceive ".[2]

Lord Ellesmere — a peer of great standing and influence, said of the Prince, " He is the best shot I ever saw though I think if I had three guns and men to load I could run him hard myself." [3]

Out shooting, the Prince used to wear a black velvet jacket and long boots of scarlet leather. Accompanied by two *jägers* in appropriate costume he looked, according to the Queen, " very picturesque ",[4] but to the more conventional eye of an English gentleman he must have looked very garish. Nonetheless, in spite of aristocratic sneers, it was left to an English peer, Lord Canning, when shooting at Windsor with the Prince, to pepper General Grey in the face and narrowly to miss the infant Prince of Wales who had been brought out by the Queen to watch the sport. (When Lord Canning saw what he had done, he fainted.) Nor did the Prince rival the prowess of his uncle, the large easy-going Prince Ferdinand, who discharged his barrel at the Prince's favourite dog. In her Journal the Queen noted, " Uncle Ferdinand shot good Eos in the lung ", while King Leopold was so indignant that he thought Prince Ferdinand had much better have shot his own son.[5]

[1] *Memoirs of A. M. W. Pickering*. Hodder & Stoughton, 1903.

[2] From a letter in the possession of Louisa Lady Antrim.

[3] *Correspondence of Charles Arbuthnot*, edited by A. Aspinall. Camden Society, 1941.

[4] Journal.

[5] *Letters*, i, 379. The son in question was Prince Augustus, father of the Tsar Ferdinand of Bulgaria.

The Prince thoroughly enjoyed the easy relationship which was possible between himself and the keepers. His head keeper had a selection of ugly words which he used to let fly when things went wrong. On one occasion the Prince felt he must remonstrate and he could not hide his amusement when the keeper replied, "I beg your Royal Highness's pardon but they did not mind swearing in my last place." (He had been in the employ of Melbourne's friend, Lord Lichfield.) It was this keeper who said to Sidney Herbert after a day's shooting, "We should have done better if it had not been for the damned farmer." As they drove off, the Prince explained that he was the damned farmer.[1]

From infancy the Queen had hated shooting because her uncle Leopold had always disorganised the Household on the days he was out shooting. She was not reconciled to the pursuit when she married because it meant that the Prince was out and she could not go too. Above all she was, perhaps understandably, scared of firearms, though the Prince tried to persuade her to fire a little gun of his which she wished greatly to be brave enough to use.[2]

In addition to being a fine shot the Prince skated magnificently, and whenever the frost held he organised games of ice hockey with members of the Household. He played with great animation and vigour till well on in the 1850's when his sons were old enough to join in. He was, in addition, a keen rider to hounds, going out at Windsor constantly, either with his private pack of harriers or with the Buckhounds.

When there was snow he used to enjoy driving the Queen in a sledge, and the citizens of London must have been rather startled to see the Prince driving the Queen and their two eldest children in a smart little sledge down the Fulham Road.[3] When the weather was hopelessly bad he used to take his exercise on a velocipede.

In summer his chief exercise was swimming and he used to

[1] *Life of Lord Granville*, by FitzMaurice. Longmans, 1905.
[2] Royal Archives. [3] Journal.

bathe at Osborne regularly all his life. In early days he swam in the Thames at Windsor. He also played tennis at Hampton Court, and in London in the summer he was fond of a game of skittles in the gardens of Buckingham Palace, invariably taking Stockmar out for a game when he was staying there. The observer can almost hear the voice of the Baron across the years, as he stoops to bowl his skittle, " Frivolity, my dear Prince, undermines all morality, and suffers no deep thought, and no pure and deep feeling to germinate."[1]

Beyond the walls of Windsor Castle or the gates of Buckingham Palace the outdoor occupations and accomplishments of the Prince were unknown. Sporting men of rank and fashion regarded him as a namby-pamby of the drawing-room, a kind of pretty curate dancing attendance on the Queen. Consequently the news that he could ride to hounds descended on his critics like a thunderclap. In 1843, when staying with the Duke of Rutland, he took the opportunity of hunting with the Belvoir. He thoroughly enjoyed it, keeping well up with the hounds, skimming over the countryside, "like a swallow on a summer evening". His attendants could not stand the pace and dropped like ninepins — Anson, a great rider to hounds, had a fall on his left, and Colonel Bouverie, his equerry, dropped on his right. In many a dreary country-house in Leicestershire tough and bony sportsmen talked with amazement of the Prince's prowess. Paragraphs in the papers were given over to his horsemanship and it provided the principal topic of chat in the London clubs. Both Queen and Prince thought the fuss very silly but Stockmar more shrewdly thought that the Prince's popularity with fox-hunters was "not without practical value".[2]

Just as the fox-hunters, through ignorance, misjudged the Prince, so generations of Englishmen have, through the same cause, misjudged him in relation to his children. To them he is supposed to have shown the indifference of a Dombey coupled

[1] Martin, i, 472. [2] Martin, i, 199.

with the stern deportment of a Murdstone. With his children he was, as Lady Lyttelton, their governess, makes abundantly clear, a delightful companion. As she watched him helping a struggling infant into some garment she could not avoid exclaiming, " It is not every papa who would have the patience and kindness." She records him at Osborne " noisily and eagerly managing a new kite with his two elder sons ". The Queen describes him playing " hide and seek with Vicky and Bertie " with the dash and gusto of a boy. She tells of the same trio, armed with nets, in pursuit of butterflies at Osborne, and the Prince turning somersaults on a hay stack " to show Bertie how to do it ".[1] In 1848 when the Queen was going round the Palace garden in her pony chair she saw the Prince playing with the children and wrote : " He is so kind to them and romps with them so delightfully, and manages them so beautifully and firmly". In his relations with his children the Prince was serious but companionable, always ready, in the sound tradition of Victorian fatherhood, to point the moral and adorn the tale, but likewise ready to join in any game or recreation. He treated them as intelligent human beings, with the dignity to which they were entitled, avoiding that boisterous chaff — crushing to youthful spirits — with which King Edward was to treat his own offspring and on which so shrewd an observer as Mr. Asquith commented, " It is not my idea of family fun." [2] Essentially Prince Albert was a family man, revealing to his wife and children alone the finer shades of his character and personality. Outside that tiny circle with Stockmar, King Leopold and one or two members of the Royal Household on its fringes, the Prince was friendless and unknown.

Normally a Prince Consort would be expected to have personal friends among the English aristocracy. Indeed, there is no easier way for a member of the Royal Family to become popular. An analysis of the popularity of King George IV as Prince of

[1] Journal. [2] *More Memories*, by Margot Oxford. Cassell, 1933.

Wales or of King Edward VII shows that it was based on the easy friendship of those sovereigns with individual members of the aristocracy. Their views and opinions on the King — like the views on morality of Miss Beal and Miss Buss — permeated the community which they adorned, spreading quickly and universally from the top. Little anecdotes about the graciousness and bonhomie of the royal personage darted swiftly among the well-to-do, penetrated to all classes, and reached newspaper men ; instances of affability and openhandedness were noticed and retailed by servants, buoying up the illustrious Prince with an easy reputation for amiability and humanity. Every schoolboy knows that George IV had fascination in his very bow, but the bow was kept for the club-house, the dance floor and the drawing-room. It was a private and social bow, not a public one : the man in the street knew of the bow only by hearsay, he never saw that splendid pointing of the toe, that display of shapely calf, that flourish of the gorgeous hand, that dazzling smile and that calculated adjustment of awkward protuberances.

Prince Albert's position would have been immensely strengthened, and popularity could have been easily acquired, if only he had troubled to make a handful of English friends. By joining White's, which in those days was truly a club of fashion, by occasionally staying in country-houses for shooting-parties, by sometimes giving a dinner-party for members of his own sex, he could have won the loud-voiced loyalty of those on whom the personal popularity of the Crown ultimately depended. In London clubs, to the stimulating accompaniment of negus and toddy, and in country-houses, as the cross-stitch needle flashed and the gaily coloured bead was strung, chatter and gossip turned on the Prince, so manly, so comely but so unaccountably distant. With the Queen it was different. She had several personal friends among the aristocracy — notably the Duchess of Sutherland — and her character and vivacity were freely canvassed and discussed. But the Prince stood aloof, friendless and unknown.

One reason why the Prince kept himself to himself was that he had absorbed — and allowed himself to betray — the disapproval of the British aristocracy which at that time was current on the Continent, especially in Germany. There was much to justify this disapproval. The glimpses which the public, at home or abroad, obtained of English high life through a number of *causes célèbres* were sufficient to make them (according to taste) start back in horror or pine for more.

The Prime Minister, Lord Melbourne, was twice cited as a co-respondent, and although both cases collapsed, the public generally would have endorsed his brother's observation, "no man's luck can go further". When Lord Hertford's will was disputed he was revealed not only as a father of a host of bastards but as the lord of a troupe of prostitutes who were the solace of his closing hours in this transitory world. In the same year Lord Chesterfield was sued because, as a trustee, he had agreed to pay £300 a year to an immoral woman who had been the paramour of the beneficiary of the trust. Before this there had been the long-drawn-out action arising from the question of Lord de Ros cheating at cards, and shortly afterwards Lord Frankfort de Montmorency was sent to prison for twelve months for an indecent libel. He sent out a number of printed letters offering to keep husbands "insensibly asleep" while wives and their lovers were "amorously engaged in the drawing-room". He elected to send one of these attractive prospectuses to the vicar of St. Martin-in-the-Fields.

A friend of Greville's, returning from Germany in the '40, told him that the Germans believed "the state of society in England and the character of its aristocracy was to the last degree profligate and unprincipled".[1] In the light of all these scandalous cases, Greville thought such a view understandable.

The Prince shared to the full the German prejudice against English aristocratic life, and being himself repelled and bored by the peccadilloes of others he deliberately shunned the company of

[1] Greville, v, 41.

the nobility. In the domestic circle at Windsor he once observed that he never feared temptation with regard to women because he had no inclinations in that respect and that that species of vice disgusted him.[1] No doubt there were many members of the English aristocracy who shared his simple, virtuous code in these matters and who, like him, had no wish to sample Lord Frankfort de Montmorency's system of dalliance in the drawing-room with other men's wives. But he made the mistake of thinking that well-born Englishmen were all raffish and dissolute, and he made no effort to cultivate the society of those who, by identity of taste, would have been congenial to him.

There were, however, more personal reasons than disapproval of the well-to-do classes in England which accounted for the Prince's failure to make friends. His was a curiously ungracious personality. His handshake was peculiarly stiff and formidable as he always kept his elbow tucked firmly into his side. A newspaper noticed that "like King Leopold, that sneaking, plotting and most jesuitical monarch, he never looks anyone full in the face".[2] Nor was his habit of speaking German with the Queen endearing to the Court, and Anson summoned up the courage to reprove him on the ground that his English did not improve.[3]

He was far too open in his criticism of the English. His remark that "no tailor in England can make a coat"[4] was given wide circulation and caused general offence. Nor was it prudent to say to a distinguished clergyman that in England "there is nothing to do but to turn rogue or marry".[5]

His unpopularity was first brought home to him when he designed a new headdress for the Infantry. This was a kind of hessian cap, common in the German armies, but described by *Punch* as "a cross between a muff, a coal scuttle and a slop pail". "These unhappy military caps", as he called them, were freely

[1] Memorandum by Anson, Royal Archives.
[2] *The Age.* [3] Royal Archives.
[4] *Sir Robert Peel*, by C. S. Parker. John Murray, 1899.
[5] *Life of Samuel Wilberforce*, by A. R. Ashwell. John Murray, 1880.

ridiculed in the Army and in clubs. "I have seen in this" — he wrote — "how very petty and prejudicial (*sic*) the public can be in this country. Anson and I snuffed round and conclude that many people dislike me either from dislike or picque."[1]

The Prince's brother in a passage in his memoirs, which deserves to rank with that species of princely chit-chat commemorated in masterly fashion by the skill of Mr. Cecil Beaton in *My Royal Past*, dilates on his brother's character. After groping and fumbling through a mass of words, and after some fairly obvious digs at Queen Victoria, he suddenly lets fly an illuminating observation "of mankind in general he was contemptuous".[2]

Many writers have argued that the Prince was unpopular in England because he was a foreigner: for this there is no evidence. His unpopularity largely sprang from a curious streak of arrogance which he indulged and never controlled. Only in the presence of the Queen and of his family did he raise the protective visor of his superiority and reveal the nobility, the pathos and the gaiety of which he was so curiously compounded.

Yet what oppressed him always in England and what he was ever seeking to escape was the sense of being perpetually on show. Most people who met him immediately noted how reserved and cautious he was in conversation, and this undoubtedly sprang from the fear that his words, either through mistake or malice, would be twisted or distorted. The German philosopher von Humboldt, for example, published a private observation of the Prince to the effect that "the Poles were as little deserving of sympathy as the Irish".[3] This naturally caused an outburst against him in the Polish and Irish newspapers. He felt that every movement of his, every manifestation of his personality, was the subject of comment and scrutiny.

The strain on the sovereign and his or her family of ever appearing in public agreeable, smiling, fit and fashionable is considerable and has been frequently remarked. An even greater

[1] Royal Archives. [2] *Memoirs of Duke of Saxe-Coburg-Gotha.* [3] Jagow.

strain — though less frequently observed — is the lack of complete privacy at home. There were very few occasions in each day when the Queen and Prince could really escape from servants, secretaries or courtiers. However amiable and discreet these persons may have been, they were not unlike warders and wardresses, attentive but all-seeing, gazing on the inmates of the cell.

At that time of day when the average Victorian husband and wife sent away their prodigious nursery parties and were settling down to enjoy each other's company, the Queen and her husband were still on show — the centre of a circle of at least a dozen courtiers. Even when they were not entertaining they usually dined with the ladies- and gentlemen-in-waiting, who remained with them till they retired for the night.

The Prince always went down to dinner before the Queen, looking in at her dressing-room on the way through. He would admire her toilette (in fact she never bought a dress or bonnet without consulting him) and then, like many a husband before, and since, he would gently chaff her for being late.[1] On getting downstairs he entertained the assembled guests, keeping half an eye on the door through which the Queen must come. After some minutes of suspense two gentlemen of the Household would enter and, turning, make a series of profound obeisances when the small figure, gay and sparkling, in bright clothes and jewels would glide in with just the suggestion of an amused smile towards the Prince, which he would return. On one of the rare occasions when they dined alone with some of their Coburg relations the Queen at once noted "how delightful these dinners *intimes* are without any *gêne* and Albert always so merry".[2]

When dinner was over, the Prince, in early years, generally played a game of chess — a gentle game with Queen Adelaide, a losing one with Colonel Murray, who combined somewhat uneasily the position of Master of the Household with a Fellow-

[1] Royal Archives. [2] Journal.

ship of All Souls, or a fierce tussle with Archdeacon Wilberforce. One Sunday evening the Archdeacon was made somewhat uncomfortable by the Prince challenging him to a game, for he rightly thought that a clergyman should devote that day to more celestial objects than bishops, castles and knights. However, he wisely decided that the rank of his opponent justified a breach of Sabbath etiquette.

The Queen disliked the Prince playing chess because it inevitably meant that she was left to make conversation with the guests and courtiers by herself and she was always apprehensive lest cônversation should take a scholarly turn revealing the gaps in her education. In deference to the wishes of the Queen, the Prince abandoned chess and the whole party generally played a round game of cards — a game called "The Yellow Dwarf", which was introduced by the Prince, being the favourite. Naturally enough some visitors seemed to find these evenings rather tame and the Prince's brother tried to liven things up by teaching the party Macao — a variant of *Vingt-et-un*. "Too gambling a game for my taste," observed the Queen disapprovingly.[1] Some visitors found the evening's entertainment intolerably slow and when the Italian Prince of Lucca — who was quickly dubbed "Filthy Lucre" by the ribald English — was on a visit to Windsor, he tried to entice gentlemen of the Household to join him in a cigar in the billiard-room.

Both the Queen and the Prince disapproved of the English custom by which gentlemen enjoyed manly wine and manly chat after the ladies had left the dinner-table. Consequently, the time for after-dinner port was very severely cut. The Prince invariably left the dining-room a quarter of an hour before the rest of the men, and he and the Queen sang duets before the ladies — the Queen not caring to sing in front of gentlemen, who, in the absence of their host and hostess, were regaling themselves with coffee.

[1] Journal.

At Osborne etiquette was cut to the minimum and if the weather were fine the Queen and Prince would often indulge themselves to the extent of being half an hour late for dinner. The Prince, the ladies and gentlemen of the Household and any visitors assembled in the drawing-room. A servant would then announce that the Queen was coming. The ladies and gentlemen of the Household moved to the door and, bowing low, escorted her into the room. She immediately took the Prince's arm and they went in to dinner. During dinner conversation was general and informal and after dinner the Queen had individual talks with her guests. These were always rather a strain because of her shyness and it was noticed that she blushed deeply on starting to talk. The Prince designed the drawing-room at Osborne with a large recess where was a billiard-table and easy-chairs. There the gentlemen, hidden from view, could sit down although they were technically in the same room with the Queen. The Prince loved a game of billiards and when playing was noticed to be " not only cheerful but mirthful and joyous ".[1]

Yet however much etiquette and formality were reduced their lives lacked privacy and only the merciful shadow of death broke the unrelenting glare of publicity. The decease of a Coburg duke or an English aunt gave them an excuse for a dinner *intime*. Both were tender-hearted, and even in that sentimental age their sentimentality was remarkable. When his father died the Prince wrote, " Here we sit together, poor Mama,[2] Victoria and myself and weep, with a great cold public around us, insensible as a stone ".[3] When Queen Adelaide died in 1849 the Queen writes, " We dined alone and after dinner talked of the funeral and of building a Mausoleum for ourselves ".[4] But that, of course, was to be many, many years ahead as the Queen observed, " May our present happiness continue until in our old age we close our eyes to be reunited in a better world." [5] More ominously the Prince

[1] *Adam Sedgwick's Life and Letters*, by Clark and Hughes, 1890.
[2] Duchess of Kent. [3] Martin, i, 202. [4] Journal. [5] Journal.

once said to Lord Hardwicke when he found a piece of four-leaved clover, "I have no wish for myself and but one wish for the future, and that is, for the long life of the Queen."[1] That wish was abundantly granted, but in the circumstances which were to prevail it was not a wish which the Queen would have echoed. She was to be the wife for twenty years and the relict for forty.

The very publicity which encompassed them made their companionship together doubly precious and sharpened the solace and recreation which each felt in the society of the other. After breakfasting together they always went out for a short walk before settling down to the papers and despatches which had to be read. They did not as a rule work in the same room, but the Prince would come into the Queen's room at the end of the morning's work — his face lighting up at sight of her with that tender look in the clear blue eyes which "went straight to my soul".[2] In their times of leisure together they played duets, sketched and painted. The Prince taught the Queen to paint in oils and her first venture was a kneeling nun. They were fond of reading out loud to each other and in those early years their books were Hallam's *Constitutional History*, recommended by Lord Melbourne, *Marmion*, *Lay of the Last Minstrel*, *St. Simon's Memoirs* and Dr. Arnold's *Sermons*. The Queen's sense of humour was keen and the Prince's, though not so light as her's, was far more developed than is commonly supposed. The Queen was thrown into ecstasies when he successfully made her an April fool.[3] With her confiding nature she was perhaps an easy target.

Those who seek a picture, clear and complete, of what Prince Albert was like will not find his character and quality revealed by politics, by his speeches and appearances in public or by the observation of those who saw him as one of the centres of the Court. Like a swan whose beauty and dignity is only revealed

[1] *Twenty Years at Court*, by Mrs. Erskine. Nisbet & Co., 1916.
[2] Journal.
[3] Journal.

on the water, the Prince is only seen in the full grace and nobility of his character in relation to the Queen.

"Love of you fills my whole heart", he wrote in a passage already quoted. Whether that love sprang originally from grand passion or a joy in domestic life is immaterial. He was perfectly content so long as he made her happy: he grudged no amount of work or trouble so long as his labours eased her path. "He is so good and kind and loves me for myself", wrote the Queen to Sir Robert Peel.[1] The very strength of his devotion to the Queen and his complete satisfaction in her company deflected him from friendship. Like a domestic animal barred from the wide world he yet led his life — full, happy and complete in a narrow compass, revealing himself only to those who shared his restrictions. George Anson, an Englishman through and through, with the cynical twist of the true Whig, and a member of the intimate domestic circle of the Court, paid this tribute to the Prince who at the time was a young man of twenty-four: "Mr. Anson has seen much of the world, but in no Person in any Profession has he ever seen so spotless and so pure a character as the Prince's."[2]

On another occasion he notes that "the Prince has no serious faults". His two outstanding weaknesses were childish irritability over trifles and nervous hesitation in making up his mind — an unfortunate trait reacting unfavourably on the nervous excitability of the Queen.[3] But these were merely blemishes, and with a character noble and manly, and a mind clear and earnest, he set himself the task of moulding the Queen to his fashion. Over and over again Anson refers to the baneful influence of Lehzen over the Queen's mind, going so far as to say that her presence was an insuperable obstacle to any moral improvement in the Queen's character. As soon as Lehzen was gone Anson shows that the Prince systematically went over the Queen's education, "reforming her mind and drawing out her powers".[4]

[1] Royal Archives.
[2] Royal Archives.
[3] Royal Archives.
[4] Royal Archives.

Of this the Queen was fully conscious. She records in her Journal how she told the Prince, " it is you who have entirely formed me ".[1] People outside were quick to notice the change and Brougham referred to her with scorn as " Queen Albertine ". However much elderly Whigs might curl their lips at the change in their sovereign there is no doubt that as her intellectual powers were developed they combined with her zest for life, her sense of fun and her depth of feeling to make her, in the Prince's own words, " the most delightful companion a man can wish for ".[2]

[1] Journal. [2] Royal Archives.

CHAPTER VI

PRINCE AND PALMERSTON

"HE shows not the slightest interest in politics . . . while declaring that the Augsburg *Allgemeine Zeitung* is the only paper one wants, or that is worth reading, he does not even read it." This was Stockmar's considered verdict on the Prince only a few months before his marriage.[1] Prince Albert's tastes were scholarly and artistic, not political. The explanation of the large political part he was to play in England does not lie in the gratification of any private or dynastic ambitions but only in a desire that the Queen should be well served and safeguarded from mistakes in judgment. Indeed his political exertions, which did not come naturally to him, were perhaps his crowning unselfishness towards the Queen.

He was broken in to English politics by the rough and ready hand of Melbourne. The laziness, redeemed by judgment and enlivened by wit, with which this statesman ruled was puzzling and antipathetic to the Prince. His supreme good fortune was to find in Melbourne's successor, Peel, a careful and sympathetic friend — a kindred spirit. Without exaggeration Prince Albert can be called the political pupil and heir of Sir Robert Peel.

Peel was thoughtful, high-minded and laborious — qualities which the Prince understood because they were his own. He derived from Peel just the degree of confidence which he needed and which he could never have gained from reams of the Baron's moralising essays. Peel's habit of mind — he was a party man but not a partisan — made a strong appeal to the Prince who, like

[1] Martin, i, 34.

every royal politician, was apprehensive of any violent displays of party passion. Again his programme of rebuilding Toryism on the foundation of hard work and efficient government was easily understood by the Prince.

Moreover the two men were curiously alike in character and tastes. Each was reserved, nervous of giving himself away in public and only completely natural and at ease in the company of one person — his wife. Both Prince and Prime Minister had a fine natural appreciation of the arts and a broad understanding of the fate and aspirations of the ordinary man.

The Queen, on the other hand, regarded Peel with antipathy of long standing. Memories of the Bedchamber crisis still rankled and she felt uneasy in his company because he was no gentleman and because he had the appearance and deportment of a dancing-master. The Prince was unaffected by these parlour deficiencies. Like all members of continental royal families he was conscious that he belonged to a caste and that anyone outside the caste was "much of a muchness". None was royal, therefore all were equal. Uninhibited in his relations with Peel by any feelings that he was dealing with someone less socially desirable than Lord Melbourne or by any spectres of spinning jennies and commercial ancestry, the Prince trusted, respected and loved him. After Peel's untimely death he took the unusual course of paying public tribute to him in a speech in which he spoke of "my admiration for his talents and character, and gratitude for his devotion to the Queen, and private friendship towards myself".[1]

The Prince was likewise fortunate in Peel's choice of foreign secretary — Lord Aberdeen. Though not a showy man — Mr. Gladstone once expressed this by saying that Lord Aberdeen could not have been an actor — he brought to the Foreign Office a penetrating mind of outstanding fairness and one singularly free from insular partialities. Though a Tory, when Toryism was

[1] *Speeches of the Prince Consort*. Murray, 1862 (hereafter referred to as *Speeches*), pp. 121 and 122.

out of fashion, he was among the greatest of nineteenth-century statesmen, but he has been somewhat shouldered from the stage by politicians with attainments more meretricious and personalities more flashy than his. A deeper study of nineteenth-century history will show that Aberdeen, with the Prince, can lay claim to the compliment, coveted by many English statesmen though achieved by few, of being called a good European.

It would be difficult to give the three men a political label except the generic one of Peelite, which embraced the particular brand of progressive conservatism stamping the mind of the Prime Minister. All three were out of sympathy with reactionary Toryism which at this date had attached itself to the broad acres of the landed interest and to the deep pockets of the Church. Nor had the three men any sympathy with the narrow reforming policy, which straight-jacketed the Whig Party. Firm believers in established authority, they held — and here they parted company with the great majority of their contemporaries — that more could be done through politics to relieve the misfortunes and assuage the injustices of the ordinary working man. Their foreign policy was conservative : their home policy was radical. As Mr. Gladstone — himself a Peelite — expressed it, " Their minds were eminently just and liberal, but they clung — especially in foreign politics — to traditions which were outmoded ".[1]

When Melbourne's Government fell in 1841, the immediate task which confronted the Prince — and it was a formidable one — was to break down the Queen's hostility to the new Government of Peel. This she made no attempt to hide and in writing to her uncle she said, " I own I am much happier when I need not see the Ministers ".[2] She continued to correspond freely with

[1] *Church Quarterly Review*, January 1878. The influence of the Peelites, with only a small following, rested on the character and ability of their leaders.

[2] *Letters*, i, 322. The same sentiment was once expressed more vigorously by King William IV who said, " I would rather see the Devil than anyone of them in my house ".

Lord Melbourne. So long as this correspondence was confined to social chit-chat there was no harm in it, although both the Prince and Stockmar disapproved of it because these letters undoubtedly fanned the Queen's partiality for Melbourne. From the constitutional angle it was plainly wrong that a political enemy of the Queen's Ministers should have been in confidential political correspondence with her. Lord Melbourne was not always judicious in what he wrote, even passing on to the Queen frank comments on personalities in the new Government. He told her, for example, that it was Lord Palmerston's opinion that "Lord Aberdeen was likely to let down the character and influence of the country".[1] But by degrees the Queen's hostility to her Prime Minister lessened and within eighteen months she was writing that Peel was "undoubtedly a great statesman, a man who thinks but little of party and never of himself".[2]

When the Queen was lying-in for the birth of the Prince of Wales in November 1841, it was to the Prince that Peel sent nightly reports of the debates in the House of Commons and a summary of what was discussed in Cabinet. (The year before, when the Queen was similarly incapacitated, the Prince was not even in possession of a key for the secret cabinet boxes.) The following letter, written in February 1842, shows the degree of confidence established between the Prince and Peel:

> Sir, when I had the honour of last seeing your Royal Highness at Windsor Castle, I stated to your Royal Highness that it would give me great satisfaction to have the opportunity from time to time of apprizing your Royal Highness of the legislative measures in contemplation of Her Majesty's servants, and of explaining in detail any matters in which your Royal Highness might wish for information.[3]

Two years later he sent for the Prince's perusal all the papers relating to education in Ireland "printed privately for the sole use of members of the Cabinet".[4] (This was a highly controversial

[1] *Letters*, i, 375.
[2] Martin, i, 163.
[3] *Letters*, i. 382.
[4] Royal Archives.

question, loosely known as The Maynooth Grant, on which Gladstone resigned from the Government.) Naturally enough the Prince commented with gusto on all the topics submitted to him and expected Ministers to allay any royal anxieties and heart searchings. Although he and the Queen were consulted at every turn, they did not, at this period, directly interfere with Ministers except on certain questions of foreign policy.

During the years of Peel's Government, which lasted from 1841 to 1846, the Prince's chief political preoccupation was centred in the Peninsula. Although the Queen of Spain was only eleven when Peel's Government was formed, she was precocious and the choice of a husband for her stimulated the zeal of the match-makers of Europe. The Austrians wanted a Spanish Bourbon, the French wanted a son of Louis Philippe and the Prince wanted a Coburg — his first cousin Prince Leopold of Saxe-Coburg-Kohary. In a memorandum to Lord Aberdeen, as early as December 1841, he laid down the principles which should govern this choice — namely that it should be left to the Spanish people and to the predilections of the Queen. He ended up by saying, "I have no wish to press my cousin, if he should not be asked for by Spain herself, or to sacrifice him, should he have no inclination to undertake so troublesome a task".[1]

When King Louis Philippe and Queen Victoria met for the second time at Eu, which was in 1845, the King modified the pledge which he gave to the Queen at the previous Eu meeting in 1843. He undertook that he would not work for an Orleanist prince as husband to the Queen of Spain, but he stipulated that one of his sons should marry the Queen of Spain's younger sister after the Queen had had children. In return the English Court and Foreign Office undertook not to push the Coburg candidate. Just before the Eu meeting the Prince wrote as follows to Lord Aberdeen and the letter is revealing because it shows the degree to which he was directing policy :

[1] Jagow, pp. 75, 76.

MY DEAR LORD ABERDEEN

. . . the Queen thinks it right that you should inform Lord Howard [1] that the possibility of a marriage between Prince Leopold and the Queen of Spain had been for some time a favourite thought of hers and mine, and that you thought that this combination had some advantages which hardly any other could offer. But that the matter had been and was treated here as one purely and solely Spanish. . . . That you wished him to take the same view, but not to lose sight of it, and to report to you whatever he might hear bearing upon the subject.

Believe me, etc.

ALBERT [2]

The flaw in the Prince's reasoning was that the English had everything to gain from a free choice by the Queen of Spain. Their candidate had all the virile and manly charms of the Coburgs whereas his rivals, particularly the most obvious of them, Don Francis of Spain, betrayed unmistakable signs of effeminacy and impotence. It was against nature to expect the passionate Spaniard to pass over the Coburg prince in favour of a Spanish bridegroom who sought to hide his impotence by bribing immoral ladies to live beneath his roof.[3] Those things are not so easily hidden.

During this period, Portugal, where the Coburg candidate's brother was married to the Queen, became a sounding board for all the intrigues in Spain. Consequently the Prince took a lively interest in affairs in Portugal, and in the summer of 1843 he wrote to Peel, on information he had received from Portuguese sources, asking him to intervene with the President of the Board of Trade (Mr. Gladstone) to smooth out certain difficulties which had arisen in the commercial negotiations between the two countries.[4]

In 1844 the Queen, Prince and Peel discussed the British Ambassador in Lisbon, Lord Howard de Walden. The Prime

[1] Lord Howard de Walden, British Ambassador in Lisbon.

[2] *Letters*, i, 485, 486. [3] Greville, vii, 307. [4] Royal Archives.

Minister was urged to remove him from Lisbon because, as the Queen expressed it, " he was very injudicious, dissatisfied and ill-tempered, and his wife not kind in what she says and thinks of the Court ".[1]

Nor was royal interference confined to foreign and diplomatic matters. In 1844 the Queen, helped by the Prince, wrote a vigorous protest against the recall of the Governor-General of India who had just annexed Scinde and Gwalior. The royal views did not prevail either in the case of the British Ambassador or of the Governor-General, but throughout Peel's administration it was made clear that the ready acquiescence of the sovereign in all measures and appointments, which had been a marked feature in Lord Melbourne's day, was a thing of the past. On his side, Peel always managed to give the Queen and Prince the impression that even if he had to disagree with them, their arguments and point of view had been fully pondered. This perfectly satisfied them, as they did not seek to overbear ministers; they were only anxious that their independent point of view should be fully weighed.

For his part the Prince was determined that the Queen should be provided with as good sources of information as were possessed by the Foreign Office, with papers as well arranged and with business as promptly discharged as in any department of the public service. Thus his first and perhaps his most lasting contribution to monarchical government was that business should be orderly and no longer haphazard.

With the departure of Melbourne and Lehzen he became in fact the Queen's private secretary. With the help of his own secretarial staff[2] he prepared the papers which the Queen was to see, commented on them when necessary and kept a careful record of everything passing through his hands. He drafted almost all the Queen's important letters to Ministers. His slightly stilted style — though the Queen was always careful to correct

[1] Journal. [2] Mr. Anson, General Grey and Sir Charles Phipps.

his idiom — stamps all her official communications after 1844. Sometimes she would produce the first draft, dashed off in her flowing handwriting with its characteristic abbreviations, and the Prince would pencil in alterations and amendments to the sense though not to the style.

He kept the most careful record of every conversation which he or the Queen had with Ministers, heading it in red ink, and writing it in his almost copperplate handwriting, every word of which is crystal clear. He himself made copies of all important letters, compiled memoranda on all the topics of the day, filed and marked newspaper cuttings. "They are gospel now," sobbed the heart-broken Queen, after the Prince's death, gazing on the hundreds of beautifully bound volumes ranging over every aspect of home and foreign policy. Alas! like many another gospel, events moving (as Lord Palmerston once expressed it) "at a hand gallop" were to make their message uncertain and slightly musty. The Prince himself had sometimes hoped that they might become a vast storehouse of lore and learning for the Prince of Wales where he might seek guidance and counsel.[1] That was not to be, but the volumes survive to-day to impress the reader with the scrupulous integrity of the Prince's mind and the infinite labour with which he toiled for the Queen, to guide her through problems of great complexity and difficulty. In a very frank exposition to the Duke of Wellington of his duties as consort of the sovereign, a position which he described as "most peculiar and delicate", he emphasised that he "must continually and anxiously watch every part of the public business, in order to be able to advise and assist her at any moment in any of the multifarious and difficult questions or duties brought before her".[2]

[1] To the King of Prussia the Prince once wrote, "We are gradually amassing a treasure of political knowledge which grows daily more valuable to us and which we hope one day to hand down to the Prince of Wales, your dear godson, as the best endowment for his future kingly office". Jagow, *Letters*, p. 108.

[2] Martin, ii, 260.

In pursuit of this objective he elevated the business side of the monarchy to the dignity of a government department. He would have been a rash Prime Minister who failed to give the Palace the same freedom to comment on and object to legislation as belonged to his Cabinet colleagues.

More than that, the curious eye of the Prince ranged over government departments, and he asked questions and urged action in a manner more reminiscent of a modern Prime Minister than of the Sovereign. His questions to the War Office and Admiralty on the danger of invasion arising from the development of steam were incessant. He wished to be informed of the number of troops which the railways could carry. No detail escaped him and he fancied that the trucks on the Eastern Counties Railway were unsuitable for the transport of horses. He demanded to know the best type of ball for muskets, feeling himself a preference for the all lead ball. To a Prime Minister notoriously weak on economic questions [1] he used to send the *Economist*, marking articles which he felt were worthy of careful study.

If he asked for information he gave back generously in return, showing that he had mastered one cardinal lesson of the Civil Service that information must be shared and that secrets must not be coddled. His confidential political correspondence with his foreign connexions gave the court news from abroad which was frequently quicker in arriving and more accurate than that possessed by the Foreign Office. He was in regular correspondence with his uncle in Brussels, his brother at Coburg, his cousin in Lisbon, the Queen's half-brother in Leiningen, the King of Prussia, Prince William of Prussia, the King of Saxony and the Archduke John of Austria. Lord Palmerston once observed that "it was unheard of that a foreign sovereign should write to the Sovereign of England *on politics*",[2] and he used to slit open these letters in the Foreign Office until he was stopped by a protest from

[1] Lord John Russell. [2] Bunsen, ii, 150.

the Palace.[1] As a general rule the Prince did not withhold the contents of these letters from the Government and he would himself translate the letters, or part of them, and circulate them to the Prime Minister with the request that he would show them to one or two influential members of the Cabinet. On very confidential matters, which he did not care to entrust to the diplomatic bag, the Prince used a private courier in the person of his librarian, Dr. Praetor.[2]

For example, his correspondence with the King of Prussia was of a particularly confidential character and was not shown to Ministers. The Prince made it a condition of this correspondence that it should be treated with the greatest secrecy and "withheld from everyone including our Governments". This was understandable when the Prince could write of the British Minister at Athens who had caused offence to the Prussians, "Your Majesty may rely on us watching Sir E. Lyons with anxious attention and seizing upon any action of his not in conformity with his duties to demand his immediate recall".[3]

Above all else he was anxious to break down the insular ignorance of the English on foreign countries. On occasions he would put down on paper his views on an issue of foreign politics for the benefit of the Cabinet. For example, in 1849 he wrote to the Prime Minister:

I have put down my views on the different questions now at issue in Germany and send them to you. The subject being of the highest importance I would beg you to let my Memorandum circulate amongst your colleagues of the Cabinet, many of whom may not have the time to follow this complicated matter into all its details.[4]

When Cracow — the last remnant of independent Poland — was absorbed by Austria in 1846, the Prince was most anxious that opinion in England should be fully informed of the arguments on both sides. Writing to the Prime Minister he deprecated

[1] Royal Archives.
[2] Royal Archives.
[3] Jagow, p. 111.
[4] Royal Archives.

the partisan articles on Cracow " written in an off-hand style " in the Press, and he went on to say that he was arranging for a well-informed statement of all the facts to be published. This was done by one of the foreign leader-writers on the staff of *The Times* [1] and was published, after it had been corrected by the Prince, in the *Edinburgh Review*.[2]

Inevitably perhaps, he was betrayed into expressions of opinion on political topics which were not always judicious when addressed to people outside the Government circle. For example, he wrote to Lord Ashley when he introduced his Mines and Collieries Bill, which increased the age at which children could be employed in the pits, " I know you do not wish for praise, and I therefore withhold it, but God's best blessing will rest with you and support you in your arduous task ".[3] Elementarily humane as Lord Ashley's measure may appear to the modern mind, it was a political measure arousing fierce opposition in the House of Lords, on which the Crown should not have taken sides. Likewise he made a mistake in going down to the House of Commons when Peel introduced that glorious measure which made England a Free Trade country. He laid himself open to a grandiloquent rebuke from Lord George Bentinck.

> If so humble an individual as myself might be permitted to whisper a word in the ear of that illustrious and Royal personage . . . I would take leave to say that I can not but think he listened to ill advice when on the first night of this great discussion he allowed himself to be seduced by the first Minister of the Crown to come down to this House to usher in, to give *éclat* . . . to a measure, which, be it for good or for evil, a great majority at least of the landed aristocracy of England, of Scotland and of Ireland imagine fraught with deep injury if not ruin to them.[4]

Nor was it wise for the Prince to air his views on socialism to a notorious chatterbox like Lord Brougham who had asked him

[1] Henry Reeve. [2] Royal Archives.

[3] *Life of Lord Shaftesbury*, by Edwin Hodder. Cassell, 1886.

[4] Martin, i, 321.

BARON STOCKMAR

Reproduced from the painting by John Partridge, by gracious permission of His Majesty the King

to present a memorial from the veteran socialist, Robert Owen, to the Queen requesting the appointment of a Royal Commission to investigate socialism. In reply the Prince said:

MY DEAR LORD BROUGHAM

I think I can take it upon myself to present Mr. Owen's memorial to the Queen because in so doing I do not commit either Her Majesty or myself to any opinion upon its subject matter.

I think you might, as from yourself, tell your old friend that the appointment of a commission to report upon the Theory of Socialism would not be likely to be attended with any satisfactory result. Its principles could only be tested by their practical adaptation. Unfortunately such practical experiments have always been found to be *exceedingly expensive* to the Nations in which they have been tried. One, however, upon a large scale is now being carried on in France which I think might be fairly considered to be a "Monster Commission" for the instruction of the rest of Europe.

Ever etc.

ALBERT.

BUCKINGHAM PALACE, *June 15, 1848.*[1]

Yet for so young a man — still in his twenties and unaccustomed in youth to the scrupulosities of English politics — he made astonishingly few mistakes and gave to his critics astonishingly few openings.

While it is true that he enjoyed affairs and the bustle of political business, he contrived never to obtrude himself but always to bring forward the Queen. She was even mildly embarrassed to receive congratulations from the Prime Minister for proposals which were entirely his. She records in her Journal, "He always lets me get the credit for his excellent ideas, which pains me". Greville, as early as 1845, woke up to the true facts and with a kind of frightened squawk put in his diary, "He is King to all intents and purposes".[2] This was no exaggeration, for in fact the Prince enjoyed more political power and influence than any English sovereign since King Charles II.

[1] Royal Archives. [2] Greville, v, 257.

The occasion of Greville's outburst was the political crisis of December 1845 arising out of the disruption of Peel's Government on his proposal to repeal the Corn Laws. Peel went down to Osborne and resigned, and the Queen sent for Lord John Russell. (Lord Melbourne had by this time had a seizure and confessed that he was no more capable of making the sea voyage to the Isle of Wight than of crossing the Atlantic, but the Queen sent him a touching letter expressing unabated confidence in him but feeling that he was physically unfit for the task of forming a government.) Lord John behaved with great feebleness. Agreeing to form a government after keeping the Queen waiting for several days, he suddenly threw up the sponge because of personal difficulties which he seemed incompetent to resolve.[1] Peel, therefore, agreed to re-form his Government and to carry a measure of Free Trade. Lord John and the other Whig leaders who went to Osborne were astounded at the change from the old days of Melbourne's Government. They were no longer received by the Queen alone, but the Prince was present at all interviews and the Sovereigns, as Greville calls them, referred throughout to "*We* think this," or "How should *we* act now?"

In fact the position of the Prince was even more powerful than Greville and the Whigs supposed. When Peel came down to resign he was received by the Prince alone as the Queen's Journal shows:

> Albert saw Sir Robert Peel first, and it was an hour before he came back, and I felt very anxious and fidgety. Alas! my anxiety was justified when Albert told me that the dissolution of the Government and the resignation of Sir Robert Peel were inevitable.[2]

The royal pair conducted themselves with judgment and spirit in a situation of great perplexity and some danger. According to a very bitter radical writer, who was no friend of royalty,

[1] Lord Grey, son of Grey of the Reform Bill, an advanced Liberal, objected to the inclusion of Lord Palmerston at the Foreign Office.

[2] Journal.

they played their part " faultlessly ". This writer, Mr. Albany Fonblanque, went on:

> In the pages of history, the directness, the sincerity, the scrupulous observance of constitutional rules, which have marked Her Majesty's conduct in circumstances the most trying, will have their place of honour.

To Stockmar the Prince wrote with unconscious humour (because was he not really praising himself?), " The advance Victoria has made is very striking when I compare her conduct in this crisis with that of 1841 ".[1]

Peel's new Government was from the first in an impossible position with the most stolid of his supporters growling at his heels, whipped on by the embittered Jew, Disraeli, and by Lord George Bentinck. Amid the jeers and jibes of " this choice pair ", as Greville called them, Peel made his last speech as Prime Minister in July 1846, saying, " It may be that I shall leave a name sometimes remembered with expressions of goodwill in the abodes of those whose lot it is to labour, and to earn their bread by the sweat of their brow."[2] Certainly in one house where labour was the order of the day, Peel's name was ever remembered with respect and devotion. The Queen admitted to being " much overset "[3] at having to say goodbye to him and the Prince took the remarkable course of asking him to continue in confidential correspondence with them.[4]

For almost five years the Queen and Prince had had the gratifying experience of ruling with the tide gently and smoothly carrying them along. Between the Court, Peel and Aberdeen there was no conflict of aim, no clash of personality. " We felt so safe with them ", wrote the Queen.[5]

With the new Government which was Whig, with Lord John Russell as Prime Minister and Lord Palmerston as Foreign Secretary, they first experienced the strains and stresses of cross-

[1] Royal Archives. [2] Greville, v, 329.
[3] *Letters*, ii, 87. [4] Royal Archives. [5] *Letters*, ii, 87.

currents and divided aims. Rightly the Queen had little confidence in the strength of character of Lord John. The well-known drawing in *Punch* of the Queen saying to Lord John in the guise of a button-boy, " I'm afraid you are not strong enough for the place, John ", precisely summed up their relationship. His flabby conduct of the crisis in December 1845 was destructive of the Queen's confidence. He has been well described by a distinguished Oxford historian as " the arch Whig of the nineteenth century ",[1] and he was far more concerned with cherishing the fast putrefying principles of Whiggery than with practical politics. High-minded but obstinate, impetuous but with no width of interest, awkward and crusty in dealings with his colleagues, he provided an almost impossible foundation on which to build a powerful government. Superimposed on this shaky structure was an administration nicely divided between old-fashioned Whigs and up-to-date Liberals with the volatile personality of Palmerston radiating activity at the Foreign Office.

Surveying the Government the Queen and Prince saw that it was not good and they made themselves ready for battle. Ringing in their ears was the advice of Lord Aberdeen, that " delightful companion " as the Queen called him[2] who had said to the Queen of Lord Palmerston, " You must try to keep him straight." [3] The political history of England during the next five years was the battle of the Court *versus* Palmerston.

The first serious clash between Palmerston and the Sovereign developed over Portugal in 1847. By the close of 1846 Portugal was on the verge of civil war. The constitutional party, known as the Junta, was under arms preparing to strike at the Queen and her followers. The Queen, Donna Maria, was, as Queen Victoria well puts it, " as foolish as ever ".[4] Obstinate and reactionary, she was determined to make no concessions to the Junta. Prince Albert saw very clearly that she must negotiate

[1] Mr. Woodward, *The Age of Reform*. Oxford Press, 1938.
[2] *Letters*, ii, 87. [3] Journal. [4] Journal.

with the rebels, and with an effort to bring this about, he sent a personal adviser to Lisbon in the shape of Colonel Wylde—one of his equerries. (Wylde's mission was also sponsored by the Government.) The English Court felt that while these private and delicate negotiations were going on, nothing should be done to exacerbate the rebel Junta by the Foreign Office in London. Needless to say Lord Palmerston was constantly poking up the official English diplomatic representatives in Lisbon to show sympathy with the Junta, and the Queen of Portugal's letters to the English Court were filled with lamentation at the conduct of English diplomacy. The following letter shows the extent to which the Prince and the English Foreign Secretary were at cross purposes, and it will not be overlooked that the writer was a youth of twenty-six, while the recipient had been prominent in English politics for forty years.

January 28, 1847

MY DEAR LORD PALMERSTON

I return the copy of your letter to Colonel Wylde which you have sent me. We could not help *being very much* disappointed with it.[1] The Queen (of Portugal) had told Wylde that the belief that England wished well to the cause of the rebels was one of the chief causes of their strength and she begged that the English Government would state that this was not so. We thought you would be entirely justified as Minister of England to comply with that request and you would be anxious to seize the opportunity to prove that you do not sympathise with the insurgents as is believed. . . . Our only hope is that Wylde will not show your letter at Lisbon where it could do no good.

Ever etc.

ALBERT.[2]

The degree of mistrust between the English Foreign Office and the Prince is shown by the following letter to the Prince

[1] In his letter Lord Palmerston had told Colonel Wylde to make the Queen of Portugal promise constitutional government and undertake to call a Cortes in return for submission by the Junta.

[2] Royal Archives.

written by Wylde after a vitally important interview with Donna Maria.

I have therefore ventured to take the liberty of enclosing my letter to Lord Palmerston to your Royal Highness trusting that your Royal Highness will be pleased to consider it as addressed to yourself and not forward it, if you think I have taken a mistaken view of the matter in communicating its contents to his Lordship [1]

This is a remarkable letter from one who was conducting a mission on behalf of the British Government.

It is scarcely surprising that, with England speaking with two voices, the Wylde mission proved a complete failure. Following this Queen Victoria, in March 1847, sent a strong protest to the Prime Minister against British policy in Portugal. She pointed out that the English Ambassador confirmed that England was believed to be favourable to the rebels and that this was justified by the peremptory notes over trifles sent to the Court threatening them " with our men of war ". The letter ended :

Once more the Queen earnestly warns Lord John of the imminent danger of England losing *all* legitimate influence in Portugal, which ought now, more than ever, to be of the greatest *importance* to us.

The Queen has in all this spoken solely of English influence, but this influence becomes of still greater importance to her when the Sovereigns of that country are her near and dear relations.[2]

Palmerston's reply to the Prime Minister, which was to be shown to the Queen, was not exactly calculated to turn away wrath and he belaboured the Portuguese Court with all the gusto of a Punch and Judy show. He wrote :

The Court is guided, I might almost say governed, by a pedantic and bigotted tutor, by a furious political Portuguese Fanatic (Fronteira), by a newspaper Editor, a vulgar man suddenly raised to power and full of low resentments (Castillo) and by a gambling, drinking, unscrupulous Priest (Padre Marcus).[3]

[1] Royal Archives. [2] *Letters*, ii, 120. [3] Royal Archives.

For the Prince and Queen this was not a very comforting picture of the home life of their near and dear relations.

However, the gloves were off and two months later the Prince took the astonishing step of writing to the British Ambassador in Lisbon, whom he knew (from reading his despatches) to be critical of Foreign Office policy. He wrote :

> I must write a line to you in order to express to you how much the Queen and myself are pleased with the mode in which you discharge your very difficult duties, how much moderation, good sense and firmness you display. You are a valuable friend to the Queen and King of Portugal, and I am sure they recognise you as such.[1]

Happily, Portuguese affairs were settled without any considerable bloodshed by a conference in London of the interested Powers, but not before there had been a debate in Parliament in which Mr. Bernal Osborne — a fine type of independent member and at that time a close associate of Lord Palmerston — had referred to " whispers of mysterious influence " and to " backstairs intrigue " and then more openly to Colonel Wylde — " a mere partisan " and to " meddling with the petty politics of the Court ".[2]

From Portugal the struggle of Court and Foreign Office was transferred to Spain and France. Shortly after Palmerston became Foreign Secretary the French, scrapping the agreement reached at Eu between Louis Philippe and the Queen, simultaneously announced the marriage of the Queen of Spain to her cousin Don Francis, and of her sister to Louis Philippe's son, the Duc de Montpensier. (It will be remembered that the previous year Louis Philippe had promised Queen Victoria to delay Montpensier's marriage until the Queen of Spain was married and had children.) With some cunning and a fine display of Gallic subtlety they had chosen for the Queen, in Don Francis, a man believed to be impotent. Indeed historians have sometimes fancied, having regard to the character of the Queen of Spain,

[1] Royal Archives. [2] Hansard, vol. xciii.

that the children which she subsequently bore were not really proof of her husband's manhood. Be that as it may, the *coup* of the Spanish marriages was a triumph for France and a sharp rebuff to the progressive party in Spain which was fostered by England. The Queen and Prince betrayed great indignation against the King of the French and had none to spare for Palmerston, who was perhaps innocent except so far as his very presence at the Foreign Office had provoked the French into this violent and faithless action.

So soon as Louis Philippe was drummed out of France by the Revolution of 1848, Palmerston elected to write to the British Ambassador in Madrid telling him to advise the Spanish Ministry to profit by recent events in Paris and to broaden the basis of the government by including in it representatives of Liberal opinion. Our Ambassador was Sir Henry Bulwer, brother of Bulwer Lytton, the novelist, and distinguished by the wit, lively intelligence and irresponsibility which marked that family. A particular crony of Lord Palmerston — he subsequently wrote his biography — he had long been stirring up opposition to the Spanish Government in Spain. That Government, incensed by Lord Palmerston's dictatorial note, took this golden opportunity to order Bulwer out of the country at forty-eight hours' notice. Greville, who saw Bulwer shortly after he got back, said, "The thing that struck me was the knowledge which he betrayed of the plots or intrigues that were going on against the (Spanish) Government."[1] The Queen wrote firmly to Palmerston saying that she was not surprised at what had happened since Sir Henry Bulwer had always been "sporting with political intrigues". She showed how angry she was by referring to Bulwer's "extreme vanity" and "the not very creditable company which he is said to keep". She demanded to know what steps were to be taken to keep her diplomatists in order for the future and she asked that the letter should be shown

[1] Greville, vi, 66.

to the Prime Minister. This was a shrewd cut since she well knew that Lord Palmerston's orders to Bulwer were sent in flat defiance of the Prime Minister's instructions that they should be altered.[1]

Not the least remarkable of Lord Palmerston's gifts was his capacity for jauntily disregarding what was difficult and disagreeable. As Greville said of him on this occasion, "I expect that Palmerston's audacity and good fortune, his rare dexterity, and total absence of sensitiveness will carry him through".[2] They did.

However, by the summer of 1848 the Crown and Palmerston were again at cross purposes — this time over Italy. Starting in Milan, a general revolt had spread rapidly throughout north Italy against Austrian rule of the North Italian provinces. Charles Albert, King of Sardinia, put himself at the head of the rebels, who began to assume the air of an Army of Liberation. They met with great initial successes but they finally endured the humiliation of being routed by an Austrian general of eighty-two. The Austrians, however, hesitated to exploit their victory for fear of drawing down a French army in support of Charles Albert. At this point it was proposed that England should mediate.

The Austrian victory, unexpected because the Austrians were always fighting battles and never winning them, was most unwelcome to the English Foreign Secretary, who was determined that they should be totally expelled from Italy. Palmerston was of course anxious to mediate so long as the revolutionaries were winning, but as soon as the tables were turned, there was silence from Whitehall. The Queen and Prince were anxious that Charles Albert should be firmly told that England could not support the creation of an independent North Italian state under his rule. In a letter to the Prime Minister she wrote on July 25th, 1848, "Why this has not been done long ago, or should not be done now, the Queen cannot comprehend".[3]

[1] *Letters*, ii, 175, and Greville, vi, *passim*.

[2] Greville, vi, 56.

[3] *Letters*, ii, 187.

This was followed up by a letter from the Prince to the Prime Minister.

> You cannot be more uneasy *now* about these Italian affairs than the Queen and myself have been all along . . . we have been repeatedly put in possession of the views of the Austrian Cabinet but have never made any fresh proposals, confining our diplomatic correspondence to that species of angry, irritating, *Bullying* which has long characterised our relations with Spain, Portugal, etc.[1]

Baulked of his objective — the expulsion of Austria from Italy — Palmerston showed unmistakable signs that he was flirting with the French Government to exert pressure on the Austrians, who had not unnaturally, after their victory in the field, snapped their fingers at Palmerston, saying that they no longer desired English mediation.

The use of the French Government for this purpose filled the Queen and the Prince with consternation, and to understand the full force of their alarm it is necessary to recall what had happened in France. When Louis Philippe and his family were expelled from France in the early spring of 1848, Palmerston, in his knockabout style, wrote to the Queen that their adventures were " like one of Walter Scott's best tales ".[2] The Queen, when she first saw the French Royal Family, recalling the King's duplicity over the Spanish marriages, could not help a small expression of triumph ; " humbled, poor people they looked ",[3] she wrote. But very soon the tone changed to one of horror at the new French Government and to a feeling that " the poor old King is sufficiently punished for his faults ".[4]

The *sans-culotte* style of the new French Government — so repellent to the Queen and the Prince — was, needless to say, attractive to Palmerston and he began to agitate, at the time of the failure of the English mediation in the Austro-Italian quarrel, for the re-establishment of diplomatic relations with France.

[1] Royal Archives.
[2] *Letters*, ii, 163.
[3] *Letters*, ii, 163.
[4] *Letters*, ii, 165.

This is clear from a letter which the Queen wrote to Lord John a few months after the expulsion of Louis Philippe :

Lord Palmerston, the Queen is afraid, would be glad of it [an Entente Cordiale between France and England against Austria] merely to gratify a personal feeling against the King, Louis Philippe, M. Guizot and Lord Aberdeen. For vindictiveness is one of the main features in Lord Palmerston's character. . . . The Queen must say, she is afraid that she will have no peace of mind and there will be no end of troubles as long as Lord Palmerston remains at the head of the Foreign Office.[1]

Then, in the peace and quiet of Balmoral that September, the Queen told her Prime Minister that she really felt she could hardly go on with Lord Palmerston. . . .

I had no confidence in him. . . . I felt very uneasy from one day to another as to what might happen. . . . I was afraid that some day I should have to tell Lord John that I could not put up with Lord Palmerston which might be very disagreeable and awkward.[2]

With relations thus strained to breaking-point, Lord Palmerston could write to the Queen from the deathbed of Lord Melbourne with a dignity of language and an oblivion of personal differences which were characteristic.

Viscount Palmerston is here engaged in the melancholy occupation of watching the gradual extinction of the lamp of life of one who was not more distinguished by his brilliant talents, his warm affections, and his first-rate understanding, than by those sentiments of attachment to your Majesty which rendered him the most devoted subject who ever had the honour to serve a sovereign.

The devoted service to the sovereign on which Lord Palmerston thus expatiated provided an example on which he could comment but one by which he seemed totally unable to profit. After referring, in a letter to her uncle, to the grief of Lady Palmerston

[1] Royal Archives. All these important political letters were drafted by the Prince, though signed by the Queen.

[2] *Letters*, ii, 195.

— Lord Melbourne's sister — the Queen tartly expressed the wish that it might soften her " caro sposo ".[1]

For the next eighteen months matters jolted along with frequent groans and grumbles from the Court but without any spectacular explosion. However, during 1849 the Foreign Secretary began to cast his roving eye on the affairs of Russia and the Porte. Having inflamed Russian opinion by his support of Turkey, he suddenly alarmed both Russia and France by an unwarranted display of British arms in Greece. The ostensible causes for this were that an English subject, Mr. Finlay, had been deprived of a small piece of land, which he owned, to make a pleasure garden for the King of Greece, and that a Portuguese Jew, variously described as Mr. or Don Pacifico, who had had the good luck to be born in a British colony and was, therefore, a British subject, had had his house in Athens pillaged. The first diplomatic consequence of Lord Palmerston's bombardment of Greece was that the French recalled their Ambassador in London.

By February 1850 things had reached the usual pass of Court and Prime Minister modifying drafts only to find that the Foreign Secretary had sent them off unchanged. On February 17th, 1850, the Queen wrote to Palmerston that she must

> plainly tell Lord Palmerston that this must not happen again . . . she cannot allow a servant of the Crown and her Minister to act contrary to her orders, and this without her knowledge.[2]

The force of this could scarcely be overlooked and a fortnight later Lord John Russell saw the Queen and Prince with a concrete proposal for moving Palmerston from the Foreign Office. He proposed that he himself should go to the Lords, Lord Palmerston should have the Home Office, with the lead in the Commons, and Lord Minto should have the Foreign Office. This proposal had been discussed by one or two leading members of the Government, including Lord Palmerston, and was agreeable to them.

[1] *Letters*, ii, 204. [2] *Letters*, ii, 234.

Lord Palmerston had mentioned to the Prime Minister that he knew he had lost the Queen's confidence but that he did not think that this was on personal grounds. Lord John mentioned this observation to the Queen, who immediately chipped in with the remark that she did distrust him on personal grounds, but the Prince covered this up without going into it further. Incapable of hiding her feelings, the Queen started with surprise at the suggestion of Lord Minto's appointment to the Foreign Office. He was Lord John's father-in-law, a booby who had clowned his way through minor office and regarded politics as a superior type of bran-pie where all the best dips were reserved for his large retinue of needy and seedy relations.[1] The Prince gravely said that he thought Lord Palmerston ought to be succeeded by a statesman of approximately equal ability. They objected even more strongly to the proposal that Palmerston should lead the Commons. Lord John said that he was too old to do much in the future, but the Prince thought " he might so easily force himself back into office ".[2]

Plainly the Prince's mind was at this stage moving towards the possibility that the Queen should dismiss Palmerston. Stockmar, who was called in to advise, thought that when a Minister was guilty of an act of dishonesty towards the Crown — such as altering something to which the Queen had given her approval — the Crown has " an undoubted constitutional right " to dismiss that Minister.[3] Fortunately, however, no arbitrary decision was taken and on April 2nd the Prince wrote as follows to the Prime Minister :

Private and Confidential

MY DEAR LORD JOHN

In the quiet of the country and the leisure of the Easter Holidays, I have found time more thoroughly to consider the proposition which you made to the Queen some time ago with reference to Lord Palmerston. The result of my reflection has entirely confirmed the

[1] See Greville, *passim*, vol. iv. [2] *Letters*, ii, 237. [3] *Letters*, ii. 238.

first impression which your proposal made upon me and which I believe to have communicated to you then, viz. that it would be a most dangerous experiment to give Lord Palmerston the lead in the House of Commons as a compensation for his loss of the Foreign Office.

Lord Palmerston is an able politician with large views and an energetic mind, an indefatigable man of business, a good speaker; but a man of expediency, of easy temper, no very high standard of honour and not a grain of moral feeling.

Yours etc.

ALBERT.[1]

Three weeks later Palmerston administered a quick snub to the Queen, who had objected to a proposed diplomatic appointment in Spain and had asked the Foreign Secretary to show her objection to the Prime Minister. Lord Palmerston coolly and swiftly made the appointment without communicating with Lord John. The Queen wrote to Lord John that Palmerston's conduct " is really too bad . . . she can really hardly communicate with him any more; indeed it would be better she should not ".[2] More ominously the Prince at the same time wrote to Lord John, " the Queen may feel that her duty demands her not to be content with mere warning without any effect ".[3]

Then in the bright spring days of 1850 it suddenly seemed as if liberation was at hand. As the full implications of the bullying of Greece on behalf of Messrs. Finlay and Pacifico dawned on the public the hue and cry against the Foreign Secretary became loud and general. At the end of May, on every morning, *The Times* published articles shredding the Foreign Secretary who, not without exaggeration, was said to have " roused the indignation of the civilised world ".[4] Thus led, the politicians followed and in June the House of Lords carried a vote of censure on Palmerston by a majority of thirty-seven. In Buckingham Palace the Queen and Prince could scarcely contain their glee. But the hunters had

[1] Royal Archives.
[2] *Letters*, ii, 241.
[3] *Letters*, ii, 243.
[4] *History of " The Times "*, p. 241.

reckoned without their prey. Brought to bay in the House of Commons, he turned on his critics and, in the words of Mr. Gladstone, " from the dusk of one day to the dawn of the next " he defended himself in a speech of titanic force and overwhelming verve, closing with the ringing challenge,

as the Roman in days of old held himself free from indignity, when he could say *Civis Romanus sum*, so also a British subject, in whatever land he may be, shall feel confident that the watchful eye and the strong arm of England will protect him against injustice and wrong.

The House of Commons gave him a comfortable majority. *The Times* (ever sensitive to the prevailing wind) held out an olive branch ; only in Buckingham Palace did the enemy dare to raise its head. There the most constant of Palmerston's enemies remained angry, unrelenting and resourceful. To his brother the Prince wrote :

You and all Europe certainly feel with us in the unhappy combinations of circumstances that granted our *immoral one for foreign affairs* such a triumph in the Commons. We are still more weakened by it, we and all those who advise Christian straightforwardness, peace and love.[1]

Within a fortnight of Palmerston's triumph the Prince wrote to Lord John urging that the Foreign Secretary be moved. He argued that no single man of weight or of respectability supported the Foreign Secretary and that the verdict of his opponents in the debate — Peel, Gladstone, Lord John Manners and Mr. Cobden — " may be taken as the verdict of the public opinion of England ".[2]

In reply to this letter Lord John came to see the Queen and Prince in Buckingham Palace on July 11th and once more they traversed the familiar ground. At the end of this conference the Prince followed Lord John out of the room and they had a long conversation. The Prince began by saying that the full extent of

[1] Hector Bolitho, *The Prince Consort and his Brother*. Cobden Sanderson.

[2] Royal Archives.

the Queen's objections to Palmerston were connected with "her knowledge of Lord Palmerston's worthless private character", and that he wished to explain what the Queen had meant by saying to Lord John, at their previous interview, that she did distrust him on personal grounds.

How could the Queen consent to take a man as her chief adviser and confidential counsellor in all matters of state, religion, society, etc. etc. who as her Secretary of State and while a guest under her roof at Windsor Castle had committed a brutal attack on one of her ladies?

Warming to his task the Prince went on to say

how he had at night by stealth (*sic*) introduced himself to her apartment, barricaded afterwards the door and would have consummated his fiendish scheme by violence had not the miraculous efforts of his victim and assistance — attracted by her screams — saved her.

From the memorandum of this conversation, which the Prince wrote, the reader seems to sense the prim, respectable nineteenth century protesting with squeamish horror at the last lingering indulgences of the eighteenth century. Ever calm and unruffled Lord John observed in his tight-lipped fashion, "This is very bad." He did, however, agree that the Queen had to be protected against having Lord Palmerston thrust upon her as Prime Minister.[1]

Reprehensible and scandalous as Lord Palmerston's conduct had been in indulging the habits of fashionable Whig society in Windsor Castle, he had in the interval grown ten years older and had married a wife to whom he was devotedly attached. In those altered circumstances to attempt to exclude him from the premiership for a gross but ancient insult to the Queen was unfair and, had it been generally known, would have seemed ridiculous to the public. Lord John was, as always, weak in leading the Prince to believe that the Queen could — or even had any right to —

[1] Royal Archives.

UNFINISHED DRAWING OF THE PRINCE CONSORT
By Carl Haag

expect protection against Palmerston becoming her Prime Minister.

Even more serious was the general constitutional argument which the Prince deduced from this episode. He stated correctly that, as he understood the English Constitution, the sovereign could not interfere with the Government or the management of Parliament, but he added, "I differ completely from that doctrine. I hold that the sovereign has an immense moral responsibility upon his shoulders with regard to his Government and the duty to whatch (*sic*) and control it." He went on to say that while it was true that by the Constitution the sovereign had a free choice of any Member of Parliament to be his Prime Minister, "in fact that amounted to no choice at all", because, as the Prince expressed it, "the circumstances of the time always indicated who was to succeed". Therefore, he argued that a sagacious sovereign should take his share in "the preparatory arrangement of party organisation", so that he should only have those presented to him whom "he had before recognised as eligible".[1]

The doctrine is certainly an astonishing one, but even more astonishing is the fact that Lord John accepted it without demur.

The Prince had, however, sufficient experience of Lord John to know that action was unlikely to follow from his undertaking that the Queen must be protected from the possibility of Palmerston's premiership. The Queen and Prince accordingly asked Lord John's elder brother, the Duke of Bedford, a personal friend of theirs with great influence and authority in Whig circles, to come down to Osborne. Seeing how strongly the Queen and Prince felt, and realising that Lord John had given a kind of undertaking to move Palmerston, the Duke came back to London and told his brother that he really must take action. Feebly and reluctantly Lord John approached his Foreign Secretary. Palmerston was very friendly and easy but he said that he really could

[1] Royal Archives.

not be expected to step down from the Foreign Office after a personal triumph in the House of Commons and when his bitterest enemy, *The Times* newspaper, was prepared to make lasting peace with him.[1]

However, the expression of the Queen's disapproval, as passed on by Lord John, was so strong and unmistakable that he asked for an interview with the Prince. In recording this interview the Prince wrote, "I saw Lord Palmerston. . . . He was very much agitated, shook and had tears in his eyes so as quite to move me, who never under any circumstances had known him otherwise than with a bland smile on his face." Palmerston explained that the imputation that he had been wanting in respect to the Queen affected "his honour as a gentleman" and if justified meant that he was "no longer fit to be tolerated in society". He went on to explain that the pressure of business in his department, coupled with his House of Commons duties, made it difficult for him to keep the Palace as fully informed as he would wish. They then branched off into a discussion on the question of Schleswig-Holstein, and they parted with the Prince seeing Palmerston "so low and agitated" as almost to pity him. Lord John, to whom the interview was reported, thought that it had done a great deal of good.[2]

The Queen, however, set down on paper the gist of the advice which Stockmar had given her earlier in the year — namely, that a Minister who altered what she had approved laid himself open to the exercise by the Crown of the constitutional right of dismissal.[3] She sent this to the Prime Minister and asked him to show it to Lord Palmerston.

For a short time things were better, and in September 1850 the Prince wrote to Lord John, "Ld. Palmerston is exceedingly attentive and active, writing and explaining to the Queen all that is going on".[4]

[1] *Letters*, ii, 261. [2] Martin, ii, 307.
[3] *Letters*, ii, 264. [4] Royal Archives.

However, within a few weeks their relations were again as bad as ever — this time over General Haynau, an Austrian with a record of sadistic atrocities — who was paying a private visit to England. While going round Barclay's Brewery he was set on by the draymen, who with lusty cries of " General Hyaena " dragged him through the gutter by the moustache, of which he possessed an inordinately fine specimen. In apologising for this affray to the Austrian Government, Palmerston could not help rubbing in some allusions to the illiberal nature of the Austrian régime. The Queen was highly indignant at this, but in reply Palmerston branched off into a series of flippancies about the folly of the General in flaunting such long moustachios and a comparison between him and Mrs. Manning — an English lady's-maid who had been recently hanged for murder.

Not, however, until a year later, in 1851, did the quarrel burst into its final combustion. In October and November of that year Palmerston tried the patience of Court and Cabinet by a vigorous flirtation with Kossuth — the Hungarian patriot, who was on a visit to England. A few weeks later Louis Napoleon ruffled the smooth waters of European politics by carrying out a successful *coup d'état* against the Second Republic. In private conversation with the French Ambassador in London, without a word to his colleagues, Palmerston gave his " entire approbation " to Napoleon's assumption of power. In correspondence with her brother-in-law, who was one of the Prince's private secretaries, Lady Normanby (the wife of the British Ambassador in Paris) poured out vituperative complaints against the Foreign Secretary and it was from one of these effusions that the Prince learned that Palmerston had given the *coup d'état* his approval. The information was immediately forwarded to Lord John, who, with the unanimous approval of the Cabinet, demanded Palmerston's resignation. This he gave on December 20th, 1851.[1]

Long and loud were the trumpetings of joy at Windsor. To

[1] *Letters*, ii, 336-45.

her uncle the Queen wrote with the customary vigorous underlinings, "I have the greatest pleasure in announcing to you a piece of news. . . . *Lord Palmerston* is *no longer Foreign Secretary*."[1] The Prince notes that his secretaries, Phipps and Grey, were absolutely delighted at the great news, and the sole surviving child of George III — the last link with the days of the open political power of the Crown — wrote "to wish us joy of Lord Palmerston's dismissal".[2]

The significance of the long-drawn-out tussle between the Crown and Palmerston lies in the degree of political power which, through it, the Prince won for the Queen. In the first place, he established the right of the Crown to dismiss an individual Minister. Though they never exercised this right its existence was accepted by the Prime Minister, by Palmerston and by the Cabinet as a correct statement of the constitutional position. There can be no doubt that it was the knowledge that the Queen and Prince intended to use this power which made the Prime Minister himself dismiss Palmerston in December 1851, to avoid the direct intervention of the Crown which must otherwise have followed. He would never have done it if left to himself, and he admitted in his old age that "he had been too hasty and precipitate".[3] Even more revealing was his statement to Lord Clarendon, "I have had for five years a most harassing warfare, not in the Cabinet, but as umpire between Windsor and Broadlands."[4] (Broadlands was Lord Palmerston's house in the country.) Perhaps even more important than the establishment of the right to dismiss a Minister and the virtual display of that right was the personal appointment by the Prince and Queen of his successor.

The obvious person to succeed Palmerston was Lord Clarendon — at that time Viceroy of Ireland and formerly trained in

[1] *Letters*, ii, 344. [2] Royal Archives.

[3] Quoted by Professor Woodward, *Age of Reform*.

[4] *A Vanished Victorian*, by George Villiers. Eyre and Spottiswoode, 1938.

the diplomatic service. He was known to be in the confidence of the Queen and Prince, who often had poured out to his receptive ear their grievances against Palmerston and Lord John. Palmerston was known to be jealous of him and on one occasion Clarendon told the Prince that he cared nothing for Lord Palmerston's jealousies — "they are the jealousies of a footman".[1] Yet there was in Clarendon a curious strain of weakness which, coupled with a propensity to intrigue, set the Court against him as Palmerston's successor. Both the Prime Minister and the Cabinet wanted Clarendon, but the Queen strongly objected and was backed up by the Prince, as the following memorandum, describing an interview of Lord John with the Queen and Prince, shows :

> I assisted the Queen by giving it as my opinion that we would have Lord Palmerston over again in Lord Clarendon, as, with the difference of a milder temper and more gentlemanly feeling he possessed the same love for intrigue and the same lax morality [2] which formed the chief dangers in the character of a Foreign Secretary. Everything depended (I said) on inspiring confidence in the honesty and straightforwardness of the British Government. Lord Clarendon would fail in inspiring that confidence.[3]

In the result Lord Granville, who was still in the middle thirties and had worked in close harmony with the Prince over the Great Exhibition, was chosen by the Court, and Lord John agreed to his appointment. Clarendon was, perhaps understandably, annoyed, and he attributed his snub to having told the Prince

> *the truth* about their wish to send troops to defend the imbecile Queen of Portugal . . . the Queen and Prince are wrong in wishing that courtiers rather than Ministers should conduct the affairs of the country. They labour under the curious mistake that the Foreign Office is their peculiar department and that they have a right to control, if not to direct, the Foreign Policy of England.[4]

[1] Royal Archives. [2] The Prince means by this, lax political morality.
[3] Royal Archives. [4] *A Vanished Victorian.*

This indignant explosion from a disappointed politician need not be taken too literally. The Prince would have never claimed the right to direct or control foreign policy: all he asked was that his point of view should be weighed and considered before policy was settled.

His opposition to Palmerston derived much more from Palmerston's methods than from specific questions of policy. As the following letter to Stockmar, written in 1847, shows, he was broadly in agreement with the policy which England ought to follow as the Liberal sympathies of European peoples began to make themselves felt.

> I am very anxious that England should declare in time that she will not allow independent states to be prevented by force from introducing such internal reforms as may seem to them good. This appears to me to be the right standpoint *vis-à-vis* Germany, Switzerland and Italy. We are often inclined to plunge states which have no wish for them into constitutional reforms — this I regard as quite wrong (*vide* Spain, Portugal, Greece) although it is Lord Palmerston's hobby-horse. I, on the other hand, regard England's true position to be that of a protecting power for those states whose independent development may be hindered from without.[1]

Had Lord Palmerston seen that letter he could scarcely have disagreed with it.

There was no element of Germanic or Coburg sympathies in the quarrel between Prince and Foreign Minister. With his natural fairness and integrity of mind, the Prince, though a great believer in German unity, looked at these problems through the eyes of an Englishman. With unusual asperity he noted after Palmerston's dismissal in 1851:

> There was no interest of the House of Coburg involved in any of the questions upon which we quarrelled with Lord P. . . . Why are princes alone to be denied the credit of having political opinions based upon an anxiety for the national interests and honour of their country and the welfare of mankind? [2]

[1] Royal Archives. [2] Royal Archives.

The disagreements of the Prince and Palmerston covered the whole map of Europe — Greece, Italy, Schleswig-Holstein, Hungary, Austria, Portugal, Spain and France but they rested on something higher than the twists and turns of politics, on the day-to-day manifestations of Liberal feeling — they stood on principle. The Prince freely admitted that there was nothing in the laws of nations to prevent one country from intermeddling (short of military force) in the affairs of another but he argued that such conduct was precluded by "the laws of Morality", and he firmly held that "these form a code under which a statesman ought to act".[1] On that code, as he understood it, he took his stand and for it he was prepared to fight with all the strength and ability with which he had been endowed by his Maker.

Whether Lord Palmerston's foreign policy was right, successful or justified by events is a question which will be debated till the last history book on nineteenth-century politics is written. Ignorant personages, and some who should know better, often sigh and chatter for a Palmerstonian foreign policy, forgetting that if that policy entailed great successes, it likewise entailed great humiliations. "He had to eat dirt", as Greville puts it, "that no man of any delicacy would have consented to do."[2] He had to make grovelling apologies to France, to Austria and to the wretched King Bomba of Naples — a humiliation which the Queen felt deeply, "to have to make an apology to the Government of Naples, which stands so very low".[3] The Prince told the Emperor Napoleon that the attacks on Palmerston by foreign countries gave him a large personal following in England. This he used to coerce the Sovereign and his Cabinet colleagues into acquiescing in his policy.[4]

Of all the politicians who have adorned the public life of England Palmerston is, perhaps, the most remarkable, probably the least intellectual and certainly the most English. As the

[1] Royal Archives. [2] Greville, vi, 149.
[3] *Letters*, ii, 211. [4] Martin, iii, 112.

Prince with dogged persistence was ever emphasising, he had no guiding principle and no sense of morality ; his bustling policy as Foreign Secretary was solely inspired by a sense of the majesty and glory of the nation for whom he was spokesman. He enriched the stilted language of diplomacy with the free and easy chat of a smoking-room in a London club and, on occasions, with the more downright language of the best parlour of a pot-house. His words struck terror into foreign ears because they were backed by the solid ring of English guineas, for it was his good fortune to rise to power while the commercial prosperity of England was flowing to its flood.

His conception of guiding English foreign policy was to lay on the whip, driving ahead with infinite spirit and gusto, tossing out light-hearted apologies and regrets to all whom he ran down in the process. The dash and gaiety of his conduct of affairs made a great impression on Englishmen, perhaps best expressed by a versatile Jewish Member of Parliament.[1]

> Reverse the foreign policy of this country and your commerce is crippled. There is not a petty despot who will not peep from his hole and rejoice, not in the humiliation of the noble Lord, but in the humiliation of England.
>
> . . . hereafter be our boast —
> Who hated Britons hated him the most.

To the Prince, who loathed improvisation and slap-dash consideration of weighty problems, the policy of Palmerston and his personality were anathema. Their clash was, however, far more serious than a mere personal squabble and sprang from certain constitutional and party difficulties of the time which have been insufficiently appreciated.[2]

Though Lord John's Government, with Palmerston as Foreign Secretary, lasted for five and a half years it was a weak Govern-

[1] Bernal Osborne.

[2] Mr. Lytton Strachey — though often regarded by pedants as unsound — was the first historian to see the full significance of these events.

ment led by one of the most upright and ineffably feeble statesmen who have graced the armchairs of 10 Downing Street. It is true that he never had a majority in the House of Commons and that at any moment the two wings of the Conservative Party — Protectionists and Peelites — might have combined to vote him out. To him Whiggery meant everything and the one disaster to be avoided at all costs was the disruption of his Government. He saw that if he shed Lord Palmerston who was popular with the Radicals and with the Protectionists it must lead — as it in fact did — to the collapse of his Government. Loyalty, which was Lord John's strongest quality, bound him to Palmerston and he told the Prince that he was most anxious to do nothing to hurt Palmerston's feelings since he had acted with Lord John ever since 1831 " in a most bold and spirited manner on all political questions ".[1] The Duke of Bedford told Greville that Lord John had a strange partiality for Palmerston, that he " is in fact fascinated and enthralled by him ".[2]

Having made allowances for all Lord John's partiality and loyalty, the observer would have to agree that his handling of Palmerston was inescapably damning. Greville, apprised of all the facts, called Russell's conduct " inexplicable as well as unpardonable ".[3] Over and over again he allowed his Foreign Secretary to flout his authority as Prime Minister and to trample on the scruples of his Cabinet colleagues — in fact to treat the sacred constitutional doctrine of collective responsibility with the same abandoned levity with which he treated the doctrine of the divine right of despots. Lord Grey, for example, only joined the Government on an undertaking from Lord John that he would control the Foreign Secretary and secure the Cabinet against any imprudences of Palmerston.[4] Another Cabinet colleague told Greville that " John Russell was not fit to be the *Head* of a Government." [5] Greville himself wrote, with ample justifica-

[1] *Letters*, ii, 235. [2] Greville, vi, 166.
[3] Greville, vi, 167. [4] Greville, vi, 73. [5] Greville, vi, 65.

tion, that Lord John suffered " his own post as Prime Minister to be degraded and insulted ".[1]

Judged in the light of these facts the Queen and Prince are seen to have been engaged not so much in a personal struggle with Lord Palmerston as in an effort — by straining their constitutional authority to the limit — to control a disorderly and irresponsible member of their Government. As they themselves expressed it in a letter to Lord John in 1850, " Lord John has the power of exercising control over Lord Palmerston, the careful exercise of which he owes to the Queen, his colleagues and the country ".[2]

[1] Greville, vi, 167. [2] *Letters*, ii, 272.

CHAPTER VII

"HE GOVERNS US IN EVERYTHING"

IN the excitement following Palmerston's unauthorised recognition of Napoleon's *coup d'état*, the Queen and Prince succeeded in forcing Lord John to act. But their triumph was short lived. Exactly two months after Lord Palmerston was dismissed, Lord John's Government was defeated in the House of Commons and passed into the wilderness to the accompaniment of the jeering catcall of "Tit for Tat" from Lord Palmerston. Thus driven downwards by the discords of its leaders fell the last purely Whig Government of England. For 150 years the most influential public men, the most benevolent and the most enlightened, had been proud to fight beneath the famous emblem of the buff and blue but in its death-throes Whiggery had evolved a feeble Government, united in the recollection of ancient triumphs and of family loyalties, but lacking the more substantial unity of a clear-cut policy.

This debility of the Whig Party, no less than the general confusion and weakening of parties, played into the hands of the Prince. Men of all parties were, for example, curiously indifferent to the squalor and injustice — those nimble train-bearers — which followed in the wake of the commercial prosperity of England. Lord Palmerston once observed, and all Whigs would have cordially agreed with him, that it would be a waste of time for working men to sit in the House of Commons. He went on to argue that if working men found their way to Westminster they would start raising matters outside the province of legislation like wages, the relations between capital and labour and " the grievances of journeymen bakers ".[1]

The Prince felt that this divorce between politics and social questions was a mistake and he was always anxious to show that the Crown was alive to the problem created by the steady industrialisation of England. In 1848 he spoke at a meeting of The Society for Improving the Conditions of the Labouring Classes, and in the course of his speech he said :

> To show how man can help man, notwithstanding the complicated state of civilised society, ought to be the aim of every philanthropic person ; but it is more particularly the duty of those who, under the blessing of Divine Providence, enjoy station, wealth and education.[2]

Lord John Russell made great exertions to prevent the Prince from attending the meeting. This was partly due to Lord John's indifference to social questions and partly to the revolutionary disturbances of 1848. The Prince, however, held his ground, writing to Lord John :

> I conceive that one has moreover a *Duty* to perform towards the great mass of the working classes (and particularly at this moment) which will not allow one's yielding to the fear for some possible inconvenience.[3]

It was in the same year that he first showed his concern over the housing of the working classes, when he made a detailed inspection of some houses which had been put up in Bloomsbury. A Chartist, standing on the fringe of the crowd when the Prince came out, was heard to say, " He'll upset our apple-cart."[4]

As a result of this visit to Bloomsbury, his practical interest was roused and he helped to design and arranged for the erection of a small block of houses known as Prince Albert's model houses for families. Built in pairs with a communal staircase these contained a living-room, scullery and W.C. on the ground floor, and on the first floor a parents' bedroom and two bedrooms

[1] Woodward, *The Age of Reform*. [2] *Speeches*.
[3] Royal Archives. [4] Hodder, *Life of Lord Shaftesbury*, 1886.

for children. They were first put up opposite the entrance to the Crystal Palace in Hyde Park and they now adorn the fringe of Battersea Park.

This understanding of the conditions and lives of the people put the Prince in a position of authority *vis-à-vis* the Whig potentates who cared for none of these things.

In another respect the weakness of the Whig Party played into the hands of the Crown. The death-throes of Whiggery led to a great confusion of parties and a great weakening of party ties. During the 1850's there were compact bodies of Conservatives on the right and of Radicals on the left but between these extremes was a tangled mass of Whigs, Liberals, Palmerstonians and Peelites which provided a marvellous field for Taper and Tadpole. This disorder of parties gave the Prince political openings which would not have been possible in a time of stricter party ties.

In that important memorandum, already quoted,[1] in which the Prince had defined the overriding duty of a constitutional sovereign to watch and even control the Government of the day, he gave it as his opinion that a sagacious sovereign "should interfere in Party organisations" to make certain that people congenial to the Crown were chosen to form the Cabinet.[2] In those days party organisations did not extend much beyond the libraries of party leaders and the drawing-rooms of their wives. In these agreeable surroundings reputations were made and unmade, political alliances were forged and discreet whispers were dropped into editors' ears. The Prince did not, of course, mean that he or his secretary should sport in these delightful waters, he really meant that the Crown should play its part with the Prime Minister in selecting the members of the Cabinet.

The extent to which the Prince practised this interference was first illustrated by the events of February 1851. At that time, which was ten months before the dismissal of Lord Palmerston, Lord John Russell was defeated in the House of Commons and

[1] See page 133. [2] Royal Archives.

resigned. After an abortive effort by the Conservatives to form a Government, the Queen and Prince exerted pressure on the Peelites to form a Coalition Government with Lord John and without Lord Palmerston. They frequently saw the Peelite leaders — Lord Aberdeen and Sir James Graham — at the Palace and discussed with them the propriety of granting a dissolution to the Coalition Government if one were formed. The stumbling-block to the formation of this Government was the Bill for combating Papal Aggression to which Russell was pledged and to which the Peelites took exception. The Prince proposed that if the Peelites joined the Government they should have the right to oppose the Papal Bill and to vote against it even though they were members of the Government responsible for that Bill.[1] But most remarkable of all these discussions was that which turned on the choice of men for the Cabinet. The Prince told Aberdeen and Graham " to state their wishes " on this question and " The Queen and myself will bear them in mind when Lord John makes his proposals for the construction of the Government." [2] A Stuart sovereign could have hardly asked for a greater degree of personal Government than this. The Peelites were really a nineteenth-century version of the King's Party.

For the time being these negotiations between Whigs and Peelites failed, and, since no other Government could be formed, Lord John continued shakily in office. However, as soon as Lord Palmerston was dismissed in December 1851, the question of a junction between Whigs and Peelites was again revived as the Crown felt it essential to strengthen Lord John's Government. In the middle of January 1852 the Queen wrote to her Prime Minister, " The Queen gives Lord John full permission to negotiate ".[3]

[1] See Martin, ii, 352, 353. This proposal forms an interesting precedent for the arrangement by which certain stout-hearted members of Mr. Ramsay MacDonald's Government were allowed to speak and vote against the protectionist policy of that administration.

[2] Royal Archives. [3] *Letters*, ii, 360.

On this occasion the obstacle to agreement between the two parties was no longer Papal Aggression but certain measures of Parliamentary Reform to which Lord John was committed and of which the Peelites were apprehensive. Lord John had outlined to the Queen his proposals for Reform before even submitting them to the Cabinet. Evidently, on his own judgment, the Prince decided to tell the Duke of Newcastle, one of the Peelite leaders, what Lord John's proposals were. "I thought it best", the Prince writes, "to show him the plan more in detail, in order confidentially to ascertain the views of the Peelites . . . the Duke expressed his great fear of the measure."[1]

The Prince then saw Lord John at Windsor and tried to persuade him to modify his Reform proposals, but here, on a patch of soil which was peculiarly his own kingdom, the worm at last turned. Lord John stiffly muttered, "I have been treating of the Reform question since 1819" and he kept on lugging out a massive gold turnip, murmured about a train and gave a general impression of the White Rabbit in a hurry.[2]

Nonetheless, these negotiations would probably have led to a fusion of Whigs and Peelites but for the unexpected defeat of Lord John's Government in February 1852. Since some of the Peelites voted against Lord John on this occasion there could be no question of re-forming Lord John's Government on a broader party basis at that time, and the narrative of royal cabinet-making is now interrupted by a short break of Conservative rule with Lord Derby as Prime Minister and Disraeli as leader in the Commons.

To this purely Conservative Government, formed in February 1852, the Queen and Prince (though they sought to be fair) were strongly antipathetic. Greville goes so far as to say that the Government was "detested by the Court". Derby was an accomplished scholar, whose translation of the Iliad was generally esteemed, a sharp and agile debater who was called by Lytton the

[1] Royal Archives. [2] Royal Archives.

Rupert of Debate, and above all else loyal to the Conservative tradition. But what blasted him in the eyes of the Court was that he was fashionable and that he was a racing man. Of his henchman Disraeli both Queen and Prince were bitterly scornful, never forgetting what the Queen called "his conduct to poor Sir R. Peel".[1] Their feelings were slightly mollified by his amusing accounts of proceedings in the House of Commons with which, as leader, he had to supply the Queen. "Mr. Disraeli (alias Dizzy) writes very curious reports to me of the House of Commons proceedings — much in the style of his books. . . ."[2] But their attitude to the Government was one of scornful superiority comparable to the treatment of the housemaid by an Edwardian governess.

They first subjected Derby, who had been in governments when they were rollicking with their dolls, to a severe lecture. The Prince started by telling him that it was no good driving a government out unless the party which did so was prepared to replace it. To this constitutional platitude Derby assented. Primed by Stockmar beforehand, the Queen chipped in with the astonishing remark that as she had always supported Liberal measures she would not expect Derby to make great divergences from Liberal policy, otherwise people might say, "I have changed my opinions with the change of ministers."

Derby was not John Russell, and at this curious travesty of the sovereign's constitutional position he "warmed up", in the Prince's words. He argued vigorously and correctly that "the Government was solely responsible for their measures to Parliament". The Prince then tried to smooth things down by saying that the Queen only wished him to bear in mind that "besides her constitutional position there was a personal one which had to be taken care of".[3]

As soon as Lord Derby had kissed hands the Prince had a further conversation with him, stressing that for the Household

[1] *Letters*, ii, 303. [2] *Letters*, ii, 386. [3] Royal Archives.

appointments two conditions were necessary, viz., "that the persons . . . should not be on the verge of bankruptcy and that their moral character should bear investigation ".[1]

A few days later Derby submitted his list of names for the Court appointments and the Prince noted with horror "the greater part were the Dandies and Roués of London and the Turf". Particular exception was taken to the names of Lord Munster, Lord De L'Isle, Lord Glengall, Lord Templemore and Lord Canterbury. He prepared a counter-list of twenty respectable names and he told Lord Derby that nothing had done the Orleans Monarchy more harm than the murder of his wife by the Duc de Praslin, one of Louis Philippe's courtiers. He had the grace to add, "I am not meaning to imply that your racing friends are capable of such acts," but the inference was obvious and it serves to show the deep gulf fixed between the Court and the Conservative aristocracy.[2]

However, a more serious issue quickly developed on which the Court felt that the Derby Government was lax — the question of National Defence. The Prince — in common with many far-sighted subjects of the Queen — was alarmed by the revival of Napoleonic martial glories in France. In particular he felt that Palmerston's policy had antagonised the whole of Europe and that if France attacked this country it would be with the muttered blessings of the other European powers. King Leopold, who felt himself nearer than his nephew and niece to the point of danger, maintained a running fire of whimpers and grumbles against Napoleon which were not without their effect. In writing of Napoleon to the Queen, King Leopold likened himself to a person "in a hot climate who had the misfortune to find himself in bed with a snake ".[3]

In the closing days of the Whig Government, the Prince wrote to Lord John asking him to prepare a statement for the Queen of the naval and military resources of the country, how Lord John

[1] *Letters*, ii, 371. [2] Royal Archives. [3] *Letters*, ii, 377.

suggested that these should be increased and giving some indication that the enlarged forces should be permanent. The Whig militia bill which was Lord John's reply and on which Lord Palmerston succeeded in turning the Government out, was regarded by the Prince as quite inadequate. Nor was he satisfied by Lord Derby's bill and he set out his own views which covered twenty manuscript sheets of paper. His views, which were broadly supported by the Duke of Wellington, were that a permanent Reserve Force should be built up and that the Government should not be contented with the establishment of a supply of volunteers. When Lord Derby read the Prince's views he was naturally alarmed at a project being set up in opposition to his own Government's bill. But the Prince was able to reassure him that no one except the Duke of Cambridge had seen it.[1]

Shortly afterwards he drew up a scheme for the defence of London making full use of the railways. Twenty-five thousand men were to be centred on the capital with advanced posts on the Great Western Railway at Reading, the South Western at Farnborough and the South Eastern at Reigate.

All this he enjoyed and the Queen noted apropos these military topics: " Albert becomes really a *terrible* man of business; I think it takes a little off from the gentleness of his character ".[2] There is, however, no doubt that his political activity slightly startled the Derby Cabinet and there is likewise little doubt that they began to gossip about the extent of the Prince's influence. Nor was their gossip wholly kindly, since complete confidence between the Court and Derby was lacking. Disraeli, with the polished servility of his tribe, could write to the Prince, " I shall ever remember with interest and admiration the princely mind in the princely person ".[3] These honeyed trifles, to which the Queen in widowhood was readily to succumb, did not deceive the Prince and he trounced him in writing to Derby by a reference to " the laxity of his political conscience ".[4] In

[1] Martin, ii, 444. [2] *Letters*, ii, 367. [3] *Letters*, ii, 417. [4] Royal Archives.

December 1852, after a life of ten months, the Conservative Government was defeated.

At last the road lay open for a Government broad based on Whigs and Peelites — that objective for which the Prince had fought with such tenacity. But the situation was confused because the second largest party in Parliament —that is the party next in strength to the Conservatives — was the Radical or Liberal Party with no outstanding leader and scant favour at Court. The Whig Party came next and the Peelites were the smallest with a mere fifty. In these circumstances there was no very obvious leader for whom the Queen could send and on resigning Lord Derby was undoubtedly right to tender his advice as to whom she should consult. He advised that Lord Lansdowne, a Whig of great experience and integrity who was widely trusted, should be summoned to give his advice. In recording this interview with Derby the Prince says, "I interrupted Lord Derby, saying that, constitutionally speaking, it did not rest with him to give advice." [1]

The Queen said that she thought of sending jointly for Aberdeen, the leader of the Peelites, and for Lansdowne. In the result Lansdowne, who had been Chancellor of the Exchequer half a century earlier, proved himself a worthy custodian of tradition by being confined to the house with one of those portentous attacks of gout which stamped a man as at once a nobleman and a Whig.

Lord Aberdeen was thus lucky and as it was known that he was strongly backed by the Court he had no difficulty in enlisting the support of the Whigs, both Lord John and Palmerston agreeing to serve under him. Not only did the Court choose the Prime Minister but they exercised a remarkable degree of control over the members of the Cabinet. They flatly vetoed any suggestion that Palmerston should lead in the House of Commons or go back to the Foreign Office. In recording the second inter-

[1] *Letters*, ii, 413.

view of Aberdeen with the Queen, Prince Albert writes, "I gave Lord Aberdeen a list of the possible distribution of offices, which I had drawn up, and which he took with him as containing 'valuable suggestions'".[1] There was a question of either Mr. Gladstone or Sir James Graham being appointed to the Exchequer. The Prince's memorandum says, "We argued the greater capabilities of Mr. Gladstone for the Finance — therefore Mr. Gladstone".[2] The Court successfully objected to Mr. Bernal Osborne who was very radical and had just fought a resounding election in London, where he had been called the Leader of the Pope's Brass Band, from being appointed as Under-Secretary at the Foreign Office.[3]

Three days after Christmas the Queen wrote in transports of joy to her uncle, "The formation of so brilliant and strong a Cabinet would, I was sure, please you. It is the realisation of the Country's and our *most* ardent wishes. . . ."[4]

Lord Aberdeen's Government could, without exaggeration, be called the creation of Prince Albert. It happily combined men of great talent with an emasculation of party loyalty — a type of coalition ever close to the affections of a constitutional sovereign. Above all it was a posthumous triumph for Sir Robert Peel; his men, his lieutenants, by flinging themselves into the arms of the Whigs had exacted a sharp revenge for the treatment which Peel received from the Conservatives in 1846. Brilliant and strong the Cabinet may have been, as the Queen asserted, but thinking men began to wonder on what political issue these mighty potentates had come together. Lord Palmerston and Lord Aberdeen who had been at each other's throats all their political lives were reduced to recalling their old schoolboy friendships sixty years before at Harrow, while Lady John Russell, over the tea-cups in her hideous house in Chesham Place,

[1] As this list would not appear to have survived, it is impossible to say how far Aberdeen was influenced by it. *Letters*, ii, 415.

[2] *Letters*, ii, 421. [3] *Letters*, ii, 423. [4] *Letters*, ii, 428.

began to grumble and whimper because Johnnie had not been given the first place. She had, as Greville well expresses it, just sufficient brains to be mischievous.[1]

Derby was sharply rapped over the knuckles by the Queen for daring to question how Lord Aberdeen was going to reconcile "the many and serious discrepancies, in matters both of Church and State" between himself and his colleagues.[2] Princess Lieven, even in the grip of antiquity a shrewd observer of the English scene, asked, "Who could have been so mad as to predict this Trinity?" In fact like many a Coalition Government, before and since, Aberdeen's Government had a great diversity and variety of talent but no concentration of purpose. In calm seas that might have proved a weakness which could have been concealed, but in the rough waters which it quickly met this lack of cohesion filled the public with panic in which it turned with a kind of savage good sense not only on the Captain but on that illustrious Prince who was known to be behind him.

The immediate occasion of the outbreak of public temper was on the Eastern question — a tangled and complicated issue for which temper was one of the worst possible introductions to a clear understanding of its rights and wrongs. For a dozen years it had loomed, threatening and oppressive, on the horizon, drawing many a puzzled and frowning glance from the statesmen of Europe. It was nearly ten years since the Emperor of Russia in Buckingham Palace, in those confident tours of autocracy, had pronounced the Turk a dying man. His longing to carve up the corpse only grew more obvious with the years. When the Turks gave certain rather unimportant concessions over the Holy Places in Palestine to the French, the Russians took more active steps to speed the invalid to the grave by invading what were called The Principalities.[3] The whole elaborate machinery of mid-nineteenth-century diplomacy, like a great broody hen,

[1] Greville, vii, 153. [2] *Letters*, ii, 419.

[3] These roughly correspond to modern Bulgaria and Roumania.

then settled on the dispute in the full feathers of conferences, special missions, protocols and *Projets de Notes*. By the late summer of 1853 the Prince noted, "The public here is furiously Turkish".[1]

The Cabinet, on the other hand, behaved rather like a dissenting minister caught in a drunken fight outside a pot-house. Good advice and general appeals for sweet reasonableness were accompanied by gestures of some bellicosity and much absurdity. Aberdeen, with the majority of his Cabinet bent on peace but with Palmerston mouthing out the Turkish sympathies of the moment, was more concerned with keeping his Government together than with a consistent policy. Lord John thought that a Reform Bill was really of far greater importance than the squabbles of these Eastern barbarians.

With affairs in this plight the Court moved up to Balmoral in September 1853, where the Queen and Prince were engrossed in the details of laying the foundation stone of the present castle. That important little ceremony — suggestive of the solidity of property — was characteristic of the age and made a peculiar appeal to the Prince. On September 28th the Queen laid the foundation stone, striking it with vigour and pouring over it a libation of oil and wine. In the cavity below the stone was placed a sealed bottle, inside which was a parchment with the signatures of the Queen, the Prince, the royal children (as many of them as could write) and the Duchess of Kent; also inside the bottle was a complete set of the coins of the Queen's reign.

"We should enjoy the stay here greatly, were it not for the horrible Eastern complication", wrote the Prince. A few days later came the startling news that Aberdeen, under pressure from Palmerston, had agreed that the British Fleet should enter the Black Sea. This move was hedged round with restrictions, the most important of which was that the Fleet should only be used

[1] Martin, ii, 513.

in defence of Turkish territory, but its significance was obvious. The Prince wrote that it was "morally and constitutionally wrong" for the Cabinet to take a decision of this magnitude without giving the Crown a chance to sanction it. He accordingly sent down the First Lord of the Admiralty, who was minister in attendance at Balmoral, to London to represent the Crown's point of view. Aberdeen could only say that if he had known the feelings of the Queen and Prince "which he had imagined to be of more animosity against Russia and leaning to war" than they in fact were, he might have stood out against sending the Fleet.[1]

The Court hurried back to Windsor and in a memorandum which was submitted to the Cabinet, the Prince made the sound point that by sending the Fleet Great Britain was committed as "auxiliaries to the Turks". He added, "we ought to be quite sure . . . that they do not drive at war whilst we aim at peace".[2]

This memorandum was widely circulated since it was seen by the whole Cabinet and not, as was usually the case, by the Prime Minister alone; in fact Palmerston rebutted the Prince's argument and undoubtedly whispered in the ears of his cronies that the Prince was decidedly pro-Russian.

Meanwhile the Russians declared war on Turkey and sank a large part of the Turkish Fleet, rousing England to a perfect frenzy of pro-Turkish feeling. This even spread to intelligent strata of society and that formidable old *Grande Dame*, Maria Josepha, Lady Stanley of Alderley, whose literary style as a girl had been commended by Gibbon, wrote, "If we do not take an active part now in the affairs of Europe, we may as well turn Quakers at once".[3] In fact the public was ready to rend anyone who appeared to be advocating caution or to be obstructing the path of honour.

1 *Letters*, i, 456, 457. 2 Martin, ii, 526.

3 *The Stanleys of Alderley* (edited by Nancy Mitford. Chapman and Hall, 1939), p. 83.

Lord John, however, cared for none of these things and was deep in his plans for parliamentary reform and for setting the crown of a vote on the £10 householder. This struck Palmerston as so utterly *mal à propos* that he suddenly resigned on December 16th, but finding that the Cabinet was not committed to Lord John's proposal he withdrew his resignation ten days later.

This resignation fired the public mind with the wildest fury because Palmerston was known to be the leader of the anti-Russian party. Two years before, Palmerston had been dismissed by the Crown: the public argued that what had happened then had happened again. The one man who was standing up to the Russian bully, the darling of the people, had been dismissed by the machinations of Prince Albert acting on orders from Moscow. Thus it was whispered in the clubs, in the public-houses and on the streets and so to the ears of newspaper men.

A few days after the news of Palmerston's resignation was made public and during the festival of goodwill towards men, the Radical Press — notably the *Daily News* and the *Morning Advertiser*, which was also the organ of the liquor trade, began to attack the Prince by name with a malignancy which daily increased in violence. On Christmas Eve the *Daily News* wrote, "Should the influence of a husband prevail to undo the work of sixteen happy years, the grief of the devotedly loyal would be great, but the hazard to all parties infinitely greater". A fortnight later the same paper was writing, "Above all the nation distrusts the politics however they may admire the taste, of a Prince who has breathed from childhood the air of courts tainted by the imaginative servility of Goethe". A few days later the paper flung sense and decency to the winds in a comparison between the Prince and Piers Gaveston — the toady of King Edward II — and Mary Ann Clarke, the mistress of the Duke of York, who had done a brisk and profitable trade in the sale of commissions in the Army.

Pamphleteers took up the story where the newspapers left off, and readers were found for the following trash :

Last Monday night, all in a fright,
Al. out of bed did tumble,
The German lad was raving mad,
How he did groan and grumble !
He cried to Vic. " I've cut my stick :
To St. Petersburg go right slap."
When Vic. 'tis said, jumped out of bed
And wopped him with her night cap.

The public believed the remarkable story that the Home Secretary, with the agreeable curiosity of holders of that high office, had steamed open the Prince's letters and found him in treasonable correspondence with the Russians. A gullible crowd collected on Tower Hill to watch " the German lad " led captive in chains to expiate his awful crimes in company with the shades of Perkin Warbeck, Lady Jane Grey and the Duke of Monmouth.

At the same time less disreputable sources were directing their fire at the Prince. In January, *Punch* had a cartoon of the Prince nervously skating by a board labelled, " Foreign Affairs very DANGEROUS ". A terrified procession of crowned sovereigns follows behind him, while Palmerston with great verve and dexterity is executing figures of eight in the background. Then the Conservative Press — principally the *Standard* and the *Morning Herald* — took up the hue and cry, concentrating on the point that the political influence of the Prince was unconstitutional and abounding. The *Morning Herald*, which was Lord Derby's organ, was especially searching. In a letter published in this paper an authoritative statement about the Prince being present at interviews between the Queen and her Ministers was made. This was not generally realised by the public and caused a stir, especially as the writer averred :

His Royal Highness is not at such times a silent listener, but takes an active, often a leading, part in the deliberations. . . . It is too much that one man, and he not an Englishman by birth, should be at once Foreign Secretary, Commander-in-Chief and Prime Minister under all administrations.

The letter was simply signed "M.P." but against the copy which he filed the Prince has written "Lord Maidstone". Maidstone was a bitter and virulent Tory whose father had fought a duel with the Duke of Wellington over Catholic Emancipation. He married a daughter of the Prince's old enemy, Lord Uxbridge,[1] and this probably explains the reference in the letter to Lord Melbourne, who never allowed the Prince to be present when he saw the Queen on business, "and by his prohibition incurred the lasting though ineffectual displeasure of the Prince".

Accompanying the letter was a leading article which said, "We implore him to dismiss such men as Baron Stockmar from his counsels and to employ honest Englishmen". This was, of course, a serious attack because, unlike much which had appeared, it was informed and accurate.

At the same time the Prince was roundly accused by the Conservative papers of interference at the War Office, where there had been one of those personal squabbles — one of those prolonged battles of stiff politeness and formal cuts, with deeply wounded feelings on all sides, in which English Generals delight. The Adjutant-General (Sir George Brown) had an unseemly tiff with the Commander-in-Chief over the weight of knapsacks and resigned his office. Immediately the public fastened on him as a true Englishman who, like Palmerston, had been jockeyed out of place by the machinations of the German lad. This story was fomented and magnified in "the Senior United Service Club with all its grumblers",[2] where veterans of the old Duke's campaigns, fortified by liberal doses of spirit, gnashed their massive Victorian dentures with rage and fury against the Prince. So serious was

[1] Lady Constance Paget — one of the Queen's closest friends before her marriage. [2] The Prince to Stockmar. Martin, ii, 558.

this side of the storm that the Commander-in-Chief, Lord Hardinge, strongly advised the Prince to make public the correspondence which he had with the Duke when the latter had been anxious for the Prince to succeed him as Commander-in-Chief. In reply the Prince wrote :

My dear Lord Hardinge

I have to thank you for your kind communication. The nonsense and lies, which the public have had to swallow with respect to my humble person within these last three weeks, have really exceeded anything I could have imagined. . . . I do not think it would be advisable to make any use of what was certainly written for the Duke alone, nor could I admit of anybody sitting in judgment on the nature of my personal relations, services and duties to the Queen — duties of which no authority or law on earth could absolve me.

Ever yours truly,

Albert.

Windsor Castle, *17.1.54.*[1]

Many people, including the editor of *The Times*, thought that the whole attack was so deeply mischievous and alarming that the Government should publish an inspired defence of the Prince in the newspapers. Against this the Prince was adamant, holding that the proper place for his defence was in Parliament. However, some letters and pamphlets were published in his defence and the force of the attack was spent when Parliament met on January 31st. In driving to open Parliament the Queen and Prince were given a gratifying and tumultuous ovation, though the crowd reserved its greatest effort for the Turkish Minister. That evening, in a few dignified sentences which met with the general endorsement of the House of Commons, Lord John, as leader of the House, referred to the base calumnies with which the Prince had been assailed, adding, " the people of this country, always just in the end, will, as a result of this experience, give a firmer and stronger foundation to the throne." [2]

[1] Royal Archives.

[2] Hansard, cxxx, 191.

On the following day the Prince wrote to Lord John:

My dear Lord John

You must allow me to thank you for the admirable manner in which you carried out my defence in the House of Commons against the many slanders brought against me within these last weeks. Nothing could have been more clear, complete and dignified. . . .[1]

In the House of Lords things went less smoothly. All parties were united in deploring the wanton attacks on the Prince but Lord Derby bitterly resented the suggestion that the Conservative Party had been behind them. Seeing the figure of Greville listening to the debate behind the throne, who under the pseudonym of C. had written to *The Times* attributing these attacks to the Conservatives, Derby rounded on him, to the delight of his henchmen, saying, "he has stated distinctly 'the thing which is not'." The Tory Peers cheered with glee at the discomfiture of Greville, who was known in the Carlton Club as "this airified clerk",

> Ever plotting, ever peddling
> Master of all modes of meddling.

Lord Harrowby intervened later in the debate with a scornful allusion to the newspapers of the gentlemen of England who should have stopped the venomous slanders of their jackals. Lord Malmesbury, who had been Derby's Foreign Secretary and was thought to have been the author of one of the anonymous letters in the Tory Press, said, "I have never heard a more offensive speech spoken in this House in my life".[2] However, these statements in both Houses stopped the attacks with the same mysterious suddenness with which they had started.

As may be imagined, the feelings of the Queen and Prince were those of anger, surprise and injured innocence comparable to the sensations of Mr. Pooter in the *Diary of a Nobody* when his wife unexpectedly lost her temper with him after the ball at

[1] Royal Archives.

[2] Hansard, cxxx, 107.

the Mansion House. Only a few months before the outburst the Queen had written, in her gay and lively style, of the Prince, "And this nation does appreciate him, and fully acknowledges what he has done, and does do daily and hourly for the country".[1]

To have these words, as it were, flung back in her teeth was particularly mortifying, and as the Prince wrote to Stockmar, "Victoria has taken the whole affair greatly to heart, and was excessively indignant at the attacks".[2] To the Princess of Prussia the Queen characterised the attacks as "shameful and infuriating slanders",[3] and to Stockmar she wrote that the country "is a *little* mad".[4] The Prince, though startled and wounded, took it more phlegmatically, but like all men of a nervous, highly strung temperament his stomach and digestion suffered from the anxiety "as they commonly do where the feelings are kept long upon the stretch".[5]

Many ridiculous suggestions were laid before the Prince to account for the attacks. Some argued that they were inspired by the Czar. The King of the Belgians believed that they were all prompted by Napoleon III, who had just received a dynastic rebuff from the English Court. The Emperor's cousin, Prince Jerome, had wished to marry Princess Mary of Cambridge. King Leopold, in a sly allusion to the *embonpoint* of the Princess and to her natural reluctance to be sacrificed to this rather unattractive Bonaparte, referred to her to the Queen as "our fat Iphigenia".[6]

He had always argued that the Princess would make a good wife and that she would strengthen the bonds between England and France, but the Prince and Queen, with some show of scorn, refused even to hear of such a marriage. They were both devoted to this accomplished Princess who, in later life, as the Duchess of Teck, was to command the affection and admiration of the whole country. Napoleon had been extremely offended at the con-

[1] Martin, ii, 461.
[2] Martin, ii, 562.
[3] *Further Letters of Queen Victoria*, p. 41.
[4] Martin, ii, 542.
[5] Martin, ii, 562.
[6] Royal Archives.

temptuous manner in which the English Court had rejected Prince Jerome's suit and King Leopold firmly believed that the attacks were his revenge.[1]

For his own part the Prince believed that Lord Palmerston was solely responsible for them.[2] Echoing his master's voice, the Prince's private secretary, Grey, said, "I wish I could acquit him (Palmerston) of being the secret instigator of the ignorant, disgraceful and unjust attacks upon the Prince."[3]

There seems no proof that Palmerston instigated them—indeed such a proceeding was scarcely in keeping with a character whose animosities were never more than skin deep. He could unquestionably have stopped them almost as soon as they started by making it clear that the Prince had nothing to do with his resignation, which had in fact surprised the Court as much as the general public. Not till the attacks had been going merrily for several weeks did Palmerston make it clear in the *Morning Post*, which was his paper, that "his retirement had nothing to do with *me*".[4] But this, which was probably due to slovenliness, is not a proof that he instigated them.

It appears most likely that there were no malignant influences behind the attack on the Prince but that it sprang from a curious concatenation of circumstances which all came into operation in the late autumn of 1853.

The most important of these was his memorandum to the Cabinet in October 1853. This gave the impression that he was pacific even to the point of abandoning the Turk, and the bellicose section of the Cabinet undoubtedly whispered outside that the Court was opposed to the full rigours of an anti-Russian policy. Simultaneously there was much tittle-tattle in Conservative clubs and social circles about the degree of political power enjoyed by

[1] It is certainly true that the Emperor encouraged the French Embassy in London to maintain close relations with pressmen.

[2] Royal Archives.

[3] Lady Minto, *Myself when Young*. Muller, 1938.

[4] The Prince to Stockmar. Royal Archives.

the Prince, which had undoubtedly startled Derby and his Cabinet when they were in office. In an interview with Derby when he was first Prime Minister, the Prince had urged on him the importance of not divulging outside any question discussed between him and the Queen and Prince.[1] No doubt this was obeyed while they were in office, but as the Conservatives felt aggrieved by the lack of confidence shown to them by the Court they would have been less than human if they had not animadverted unfavourably on the political power of the Prince after their Government fell. Certainly Derby was very gossipy and indiscreet. When, in 1855, he was told in the strictest confidence by the Prince that Napoleon III had attempted to influence the Court during an English ministerial crisis, he immediately told one of his political associates.[2]

The Bishop of Oxford, who drafted, but did not publish, a pamphlet in defence of the Prince, was convinced that "some of the higher circles of the Derby party" were behind the attacks.[3] Certain it was that there was much critical chatter against the Prince in informed circles of the Right, among Palmerstonians and among Radicals howling for a war with the tyrannical Czar. As often happens in English history something petty and irrelevant gave it that extra twist so that it came flooding over the bounds of private gossip into the newspapers.

In November 1853 the Lord Mayor of London suddenly suggested that a statue should be put up to the Prince to mark all that he had done for the Exhibition. The suggestion was warmly supported by the Bishop of Oxford but was frowned on by the Prince himself. It so happened that just at this time the Corporation of the City, which was compounded of an absurd crew of bibulous and guzzling aldermen, was held up to constant scorn and ridicule in the newspapers as hogs who were gorging and

[1] *Letters*, ii, 371.

[2] See *Juridical Review* for December 1936. Article by Mr. Gavin Henderson.

[3] *Life of Wilberforce*, ii, 231.

swilling themselves at the expense of the poor ratepayers. Their unpopularity quickly and publicly attached itself to the Prince. *Punch* voiced feelings which were general in a poem called " Prince Punch to Prince Albert " which ended :

Then silence your civic applauders
Lest better men cease from applause,
He who tribute accepts from marauders,
Is held to be pledged to their cause ;
Let no corporate magnates of London,
An honour presume to award :
Their own needs, till ill-doings be undone,
Little honour to spare can afford.[1]

It was these circumstances — the rumours that he was pro-Russian, the gossip in Conservative and military clubs and the ridiculous affair of the statue — which laid the train leading to the alarming combustion which broke out so soon as Palmerston's resignation was announced. Yet, if, as seems clear, the outbreak was not fanned by the malevolence of the Prince's enemies, it remains one of the most unexpected and least creditable manifestations of English hysterics. Macaulay went so far as to observe that there had been " nothing so shameful since the warming-pan story ".[2] As was only to be expected, Sir Theodore Martin indulged in lamentations worthy of the Psalmist at his most abject. " No man bore calumny better than the Prince " — he wrote — " but to be misunderstood is to suffer not only in the moral shock but in the angry soreness of wounded affection." He goes on to say that the Queen was struck deeply in " her yearning regard " for her people.[3]

To Stockmar, safe in Germany, the whole affair was vastly enjoyable. Life had been far too easy for the Prince, and this was just what was wanted to temper his character. Into the ink-pot went the quill and off flowed those airy pomposities so delightful

[1] *Punch*, November 26th, 1853.
[2] Trevelyan, *Life and Letters of Lord Macaulay*. Longmans.
[3] Martin, iii, 2.

to write, so frustrating to read. "A mere garrison-life never makes a soldier", he began. "You have led nothing but a peaceful, comfortable, pampering and enervating garrison-life . . . never the manly thinking, the vigorous feeling which alone will stand the test when brought into conflict with the actual perils of life." [1]

In fact few men's lives can have been less pampered and enervating than that of the Prince. While the attacks were at their height there was a snap of cold weather and he worked off his spleen by vigorous games of ice hockey at Windsor with his elder sons and a team of Guards officers. Though he had grown fat he had lost none of his graceful skill on the ice, keeping goal to the admiration of the field. But brooding in the privacy of his own rooms at the Castle over the public clamour against him he could not understand it. With a consciousness of virtue which was characteristic he wrote, "I may say with pride that not the veriest tittle of a reproach can be brought against me *with truth*".[2] The fault was not his and therefore it lay — or so he argued — with the public. The Englishman was not educated, even a Cambridge undergraduate read no constitutional law or history. "This affair has made this very clear to me and I shall give Cambridge no rest until the gap has been filled in." [3] Perhaps the sense of justice was somewhat rough which sought to make the unhappy Cambridge lads with their bull pups, nags and wine-parties pay for the shortcomings of Grub Street.

The Prince had once written to Stockmar shortly before the outburst against him, "constitutional Monarchy marches unassailably on its beneficent course".[4] Yet no one who figured so largely as the Prince had done in nineteenth-century politics could hope to be unassailable. What the Prince never saw was that his actions may have been perfectly good, may have been, in his own words, safe "from the veriest tittle of a reproach", but

[1] Martin, ii, 545.
[2] Martin, ii, 561.
[3] Royal Archives.
[4] Martin, ii, 470.

yet their very existence was an offence to many. To him the smooth and measured tread of constitutional monarchy may have seemed beneficent, but to some it seemed dangerous, provocative and continental.

No sooner had the clamour died down than the long-expected outbreak of war with Russia widened the Prince's field of political action.

Never has England unsheathed her rusty sword in a more fumbling fashion than when Lord Aberdeen led her to war for the defence of the Sultan of Turkey. Admittedly the object of the war — a dusky and shifty Eastern potentate — was scarcely calculated to inspire the finest flights of chivalry, but as the newspapers quickly elevated the Czar into a monstrous ogre, the war was not unpopular. Aberdeen himself, who had been in the thick of politics in the days of the great Napoleon, seems to have laboured under some confusion as to whom we were fighting. Certainly the war had been going on for some months when he made a remarkable and spirited defence of the Czar in the House of Lords. The Court was understandably horrified at this display and the Queen wrote to him to express the hope that he would not again " undertake the ungrateful and injurious task of vindicating the Emperor of Russia ".[1]

The leader of the House of Commons, Lord John, was only constrained to abandon his Reform Bill, in the face of the peril to the nation, under pressure from his colleagues and the Court. He announced the withdrawal of his favourite measure to the House of Commons in a voice choked with sobs. Aberdeen's personal followers in the Cabinet, who included the War Secretary, were as half-hearted about the prosecution of the war as he was.

The attitude of Prince Albert to the war was interesting and different. Like Aberdeen he had favoured compromise and had incurred much odium in pursuing that policy, but once battle was joined there was no stronger advocate for its vigorous

[1] *Letters*, iii, 35.

prosecution than the Prince. He always hoped that Prussia and Austria would join the Western Powers (France and England) against Russia, eventually reducing her "to a purely Sclavo-Asiatic state".[1] The neutrality of Austria he could just understand but the neutrality of Prussia he never forgave. He felt that a braver policy by Prussia could have avoided the war, and as he expressed it to his stepmother, "If there were a Germany and a German sovereign in Berlin, it could never have happened."[2]

The Queen and Prince had considerable difficulty with their uncle Leopold, who greatly disliked the Anglo-French alliance and the growing friendship between Napoleon and the English Court. The Queen was excessively annoyed to find the King in correspondence with Aberdeen emphasising the peace-loving nature of the Czar, and she sent him a firm rebuke. For his part the Prince sent King Leopold a careful appraisement of the English point of view. After saying that it is a mistake to ascribe English foreign policy to a material basis or to one of cold calculation, he says, "Her policy is one of pure feeling and therefore often illogical. The Government is a popular Government, and the masses upon whom it rests only feel and do not think."[3]

For the Queen and Prince — as indeed for all far-sighted English people—the Crimean War was a period of great strain and constant intense anxiety. A shade cruelly, Lytton Strachey says of the Queen at this period that "it was pleasant to be patriotic, and pugnacious".[4] Her Journal, which was not available to Strachey, shows not only the depth of her feelings over the casualties (natural to one of her warm and sympathetic nature), but the way in which both she and the Prince were kept on the rack of anxiety for days on end. They realised — and it was this which alarmed them—that war with Russia was something more serious than a mere filibustering adventure and that the country was fighting a formidable enemy with the flimsiest resources.

[1] Martin, iii, 13.
[2] Martin, iii, 61.
[3] Martin, iii, 21.
[4] Strachey, 196.

At first things went tolerably well. In the summer of 1854 the Crimea was invaded, the Battle of Alma was won and Sevastopol was invested. Unhappily it was not captured and it became clear that the British Army under Lord Raglan would have to maintain their precarious footing on Russian soil throughout the ardours of a winter campaign. When this became apparent the Prince wrote at once to the Prime Minister :

My dear Lord Aberdeen

This morning's accounts of the losses in the Crimea etc. the want of progress in the siege with an advancing adverse season and the army of the enemy increasing, must make every Englishman anxious for his gallant brothers in the field, and the honour of his country.

The Government will never be forgiven, and ought never to be forgiven, if it did not strain every nerve to avert the calamity of seeing Lord Raglan succumb for want of means. . . .

The time has arrived for vigorous measures and the feeling of the country is up to support them, if Government will bring them boldly forward.

He then proposed that the Militia should be brought up to strength and used to relieve units of the Regular Army in the Mediterranean, thereby releasing trained men for the Crimea. He urged that a foreign legion should be enlisted and that militiamen should volunteer into the Line regiments. He ended :

These measures might be taken on the responsibility of the Government, awaiting an Act of Indemnity, or might be laid before Parliament convened for that purpose. Pray consider this with your colleagues.

The Queen would wish you to come down here this evening to stay over night. The Duke of Newcastle [1] will be here, and we should like to talk these matters over with you.

Ever yours truly,

Albert.

Windsor Castle, *11th November 1854.*[2]

[1] Secretary of State for War. [2] Martin, iii, 145-7.

This letter was almost prophetic. The Aberdeen Government avoided the Prince's suggestions until they were forced by Parliament to put them all into effect. Indeed the impression of reluctance to reinforce the Army which they gave was one of the principal causes of their downfall in February 1855. Thus after two years of inglorious life the Aberdeen Government shuffled from the stage leaving Lord Palmerston as head of the new Government.

When it was clear that no political combination which excluded Palmerston from the first place could endure, the Queen accepted " the poor old sinner ".[1] Lytton Strachey says that she sent for Palmerston " without reluctance ", but this is not correct. At the time she wrote that his appointment was " personally not agreeable to me, but I think of nothing but the country, and the preservation of its institutions, and my own personal feelings would be sunk if only the efficiency of the Government could be obtained ".[2]

As a distinguished historian[3] has observed, this memorandum does great honour to the Queen. That the Court completely subordinated private feelings to public duty is shown by Palmerston writing to his brother, " I have no reason to complain of the least want of cordiality or confidence on the part of the Court ".[4]

The chances and changes of politics no less than the peril with which the country was faced brought the Court and Palmerston together. For four years, from 1848 to 1852, they had fought to the limit of their power to avoid this, but experience of Palmerston as Prime Minister taught them to welcome what they had feared. A year later, in 1856, the Queen was writing to Lord Palmerston to offer him the Garter as a mark of appreciation of the manner in which he had maintained " the honour and

[1] The Queen to King Leopold. Royal Archives.

[2] Royal Archives.

[3] Mr. Gavin Henderson, to whose article on " The Influence of the Crown, 1854–1856," in the *Juridical Review* for December 1936, I am deeply indebted.

[4] *Life of Lord Palmerston*. Ashley, ii, 306.

interests of the country". In a graceful reply Lord Palmerston observed that his task had been "rendered comparatively easy by the enlightened views which Your Majesty has taken of all the great affairs in which Your Majesty's Empire has been engaged".[1]

But in spite of this new twist in events the Prince always felt that the Court had a peculiar responsibility for Aberdeen and the Peelites. This explains a remarkable letter which the Prince sent to Aberdeen in the summer of 1855 when he learned that Aberdeen's followers were to advocate a negotiated peace with Russia. He wrote:

My dear Lord Aberdeen

I had sent Colonel Phipps to your house to know whether you were in town and whether it would be convenient for you to come here for a few minutes before dinner. He has not found you at home, and I am therefore compelled to write to you upon a subject which would have been much better treated in conversation than it can be in a hurried letter; I mean the line which your former friends and colleagues (with the exception of the Duke of Newcastle) have taken about the war question. It has caused the Queen and myself great anxiety, both on account of the position of public affairs and on their own account.

He continued by saying that they would damage themselves in the eyes of the public and that they were striving as Americans would say to "'realise the whole capital of the unpopularity' attaching to the authors of our misfortunes. . . ."

However much on private and personal grounds I do grieve for this, I must do so still more on the Queen's behalf, who cannot afford in these times of trial and difficulty to see the best men in the country damaging themselves in its opinion to an extent that seriously impairs their usefulness for the service of the state. . . .

Ever yours truly

Albert.

Buckingham Palace, *3rd June 1855*.[2]

[1] *Letters*, iii, 186, 187.

[2] Royal Archives. Quoted with trivial emendations in Martin, iii, 289.

In writing to Stockmar the Prince refers to this as " a fiery letter " and it certainly seems a dangerous attempt to influence the opinions of private members of Parliament. An anonymous pamphleteer said with some force, when this letter was first published, that it was " lacking in respect for the usage and rights of the House of Commons ".[1]

The reasoning in that letter is indubitably sound and while posterity may hold that Gladstone and the Peelites were right in seeking to end the war in 1855, they were wantonly inviting the anger of the public in seeking to slide out of a war which only four months earlier they were responsible for waging. However, the fact that the Prince could, without causing offence, write such a letter shows the degree of influence which he had won. Indeed, the increase in the power and importance of the monarchy during the two years of the Crimean War was unbounded.

To modern eyes one of the oddest things about the war was the dearth of information reaching England from the front. For days after the victory of Alma the Court and Government had to rest content with a miserable version of the battle — garbled and suspect — which came from Bucharest. Writing to King Leopold the Prince said, " we get nothing but Russian news, and our own comes so late and in such fragments that it is difficult to make head or tail of it ".[2] What was even more serious than the suspense for those waiting for authentic news was the lack of any precise information about the requirements of supplies and reinforcements needed by the Army.

At the end of 1854 the Prince wrote to the Secretary of State for War saying that the want of system in the Army in the field " has much distressed and occupied me ".[3] To meet this he urged the adoption of a system of returns — the only remedy " where people are not born with the instinct of method, and are prevented by want of time or inclination from writing ". He

[1] *The Crown and the Cabinet*, by Verax Manchester, 1878.
[2] Martin, iii, 143. [3] Martin, iii, 177.

enclosed a complete system of tabulated returns drawn up by himself. After the fall of Aberdeen's Government this proposal of the Prince's was adopted. The Queen, more domestically-minded, wrote to Lord Raglan to complain that the men were being given unroasted coffee, adding, "Lord Raglan cannot think how much we suffer for the Army".[1]

On major questions of Army organisation — such as the development of the camp at Aldershot and the selection of the site — the Prince played a decisive part. In connection with the command in the Crimea he summoned a meeting at Windsor of the Prime Minister, the Commander-in-Chief and the Secretary of State for War, whom he persuaded to agree to his plan for the reorganisation of the army in the Crimea, its division into two *corps d'armée* under one chief. Well informed by officers in the Guards of the state of affairs in the Crimea, he complained to the Secretary of State that convalescent soldiers were being sent back into the line before they had fully recovered. He urged that a convalescent camp should be established at Corfu.[2] A visit to Portland and the sight of 1500 "strong and stout-looking convicts" in the Quarries suggested to his fertile mind that they ought to be sent out to the Crimea to build roads.[3]

The following letter is characteristic of his general supervision of the War Office:

MY DEAR LORD PANMURE

A conversation with the Chancellor of the Exchequer yesterday has convinced me that the notion exists in some quarters that the sum of money taken this year for Works (Barracks, Fortifications etc.) is too large, and that it may be desirable not to spend it and to reduce the Works! This renders it the more necessary to go vigorously ahead in your Department.

I wish to remind you that the Queen has not yet had submitted to her the plans for the new Barrack at Gosport nor of that for Dover. This is the proper season for the works and it is very important to push them. . . .

[1] Martin, iii, 180. [2] Royal Archives. [3] Royal Archives.

I have not been able to go to Colchester, but on enquiry I find that although a camp for 3000–4000 men has been erected there, there is not drill ground there even for a complete Battalion. On whose recommendation was this spot selected? The Horse Guards disclaim all knowledge of it. You will not suppose that I put this question in fault-finding spirit — but merely to assist in guarding against mistakes which must defeat the object the Government, and you in particular, have in view. . .

ALBERT.[1]

Over military matters during the war the Prince exercised a close and constant supervision. In the early months he was primarily concerned with man-power and with efforts to bring the Army up to full fighting pitch. In November 1854 he wrote to the Secretary at War, Mr. Sidney Herbert,[2] urging that reserves for the Crimean army should be built up in Malta and Gibraltar, invoking the precedent of Napoleon who "always had reserves for his army between it and the home depots".[3] It was known that the Commander-in-Chief was anxious to build up reserve battalions in England for each one out in the East, and in writing to Sidney Herbert, the Prince hoped that he would

nip in the bud this new attempt at converting the augmentation so much needed by the Battalions in the East into the formation of those detestable second battalions which Lord Hardinge (the Commander-in-Chief) will cling to through good and evil report . . . trust you will both (Newcastle and Herbert) be stout in the matter and prevent what I call Horse Guards tinkering.[4]

Previously he had written to congratulate Sidney Herbert on his energetic measures, complimenting him on trying to get what we want, "not office organisation—but *soldiers* and plenty of them. The Campaign will have sufficiently proved that no slashing articles in *The Times* or speeches in the House of Commons can

[1] Royal Archives.

[2] Sidney Herbert was Secretary *at* War and the Duke of Newcastle was Secretary *for* War. The two offices were blended at the end of 1854.

[3] Martin, iii, 169.

[4] Royal Archives.

make up for the want of *Men*."[1] Broadly speaking, the suggestions of the Prince were carried out, resulting in a steady flow of troops for the fighting line.

He was no less busy about the actual conduct of military operations. In the early weeks of the war he wrote to the Duke of Newcastle urging an attack on Varna — a port on the Black Sea now in Bulgaria. In his letter to the Duke he said, "Have you considered the propriety of ordering a portion of our force, assisted if possible by a portion of the French, to Varna forthwith?" After outlining the advantages he said that "throwing a division into Varna would not in the least interfere with ulterior operations, as it is a seaport, giving every facility for embarkation threatening Odessa, Sevastopol, the Caucasus etc."

The Duke was away from London "attending to my own affairs", but he wrote a private letter to Lord Raglan urging him to carry out the Prince's suggestions.[2]

From the south the Prince's roving eye wandered to the north and he wrote to the First Lord of the Admiralty urging a naval attack on Bomarsund in the Gulf of Finland.[3]

Later in the war, when the siege of Sevastopol was at its height, he was writing to the Duke of Newcastle's successor — Lord Panmure.

> Would it not be well to put the following question by telegraph to General Simpson "Have you and the Admiral thought of the use of rafts or gunboats in the harbour of Sevastopol to destroy the fleet or to take the batteries in flank?"

This telegram was sent.[4] After the fall of the town he drew up a long memorandum drawing attention to the mistake of locking up 50,000 Allied troops in the fortress. He thought that 20,000 would be ample for purposes of defence. He asked that his memorandum should be circulated to the Cabinet and he also sent a copy of it to the Commander-in-Chief in the Crimea.

[1] Royal Archives. [2] Royal Archives.
[3] Royal Archives. [4] Royal Archives.

Lord Panmure, reasonably enough, objected to this and telegraphed to the Commander-in-Chief asking him to destroy the covering letter and "note the communication as having come through me".[1] But the Government — even Lord Palmerston's Government — seem to have welcomed the Prince's ideas and suggestions, only safeguarding him from the possibility of attack if the range of his activities became known.

Ever anxious to encourage new and unorthodox means of waging war, he wrote to Lord Palmerston, strongly supporting a somewhat wild idea of attacking Cronstadt by submarine.

MY DEAR LORD PALMERSTON

I write to remind you of Mr. Scott Russell's submarine ship.[2] I have seen the report of the Committee of officers who, after having been beat out of all their former positions that the thing was *an impossibility* now fall back that it won't be applicable at Cronstadt. . . .

I sincerely trust you will order some more machines. . . . It is *a priori* impossible that so important a new fact as submarine navigation should be useless in the hands of men of genius.

Ever yours truly,

ALBERT.

WINDSOR CASTLE, *January 9th, 1856*.[3]

Though they belong to a later date the Prince's views on the possibilities of flight are likewise interesting. Writing to the Duke of Argyll in 1859 he says:

You seem to have absolutely mastered the nature of birds' flight, and the causes which stand in the way of aerial navigation succeeding on the principles as yet followed. I am not sure whether the flight of some insects would not throw additional light on the question. Take the heavy beetles — for instance the cockchafer etc. Their wings are very small in proportion to the body; the body is very heavy; they have no tail, no plumage, nothing to support them in the air but muscular action . . . their power is obtained by velocity of stroke.[4]

[1] Royal Archives.
[2] Scott Russell had been closely associated with the Prince in the Exhibition.
[3] Royal Archives.
[4] *Autobiography of Eighth Duke of Argyll*. John Murray, 1906.

It is clear that the Prince had no very high opinion of either the War Office or the Horse Guards (the Headquarters of the Commander-in-Chief), and it is indicative of the true feelings of the Court that the Queen, after meeting Florence Nightingale, observed " such a *head* ! I wish we had her at the War Office." [1] Apart altogether from the large questions of strategy and military organisation he felt that the War Office was slovenly on questions of discipline and welfare. After a visit to Aldershot he wrote to complain of the clothing of the Rifle Brigade, " which was very badly made up ", and he was also shocked by the appearance of a junior officer slouching up to him in a shooting-jacket.[2] That he had no great confidence in the efficiency of the Quarter-Master side of the War Office is implied by his sending out to the Crimea a present of fur great-coats to all his brother officers in the Brigade of Guards.

He was also strongly dissatisfied with the awards for valour and the proposal for the Victoria Cross sprang from his fertile mind. At the beginning of 1855 he drew up the following memorandum :

1. That a small cross of merit for personal deeds of valour be established.
2. That it be open to all ranks.
3. That it be unlimited in number.
4. That an annuity (say of £5) be attached to each cross.
5. That it be claimable by an individual on establishing before a jury of his Peers, subject to confirmation at home, his right to the distinction.[3]

From these proposals emerged the Victoria Cross which was first awarded in the following year. Though old-fashioned officers were apt to grumble that it was a part of every soldier's profession to be brave, the creation of the Victoria Cross was timely — filling a serious gap in English service decorations.

[1] Quoted by Lytton Strachey in *Eminent Victorians*.
[2] Royal Archives. [3] Royal Archives.

The Prince, who was always critical of the English Press, felt that during the war they passed all bounds and that their revelations from the front helped the enemy. In a speech at the annual dinner at Trinity House in 1855 he contrasted the advantages in war of "uncontrolled despotic power" compared with those of a parliamentary power when every project was discussed and revealed and every mistake was "publicly denounced, and even frequently exaggerated, with a morbid satisfaction". He ended his speech by saying, "Gentlemen! Constitutional Government is under a heavy trial and can only pass triumphantly through it if the country will grant its confidence — a patriotic, indulgent and self-denying confidence — to Her Majesty's Government."[1]

This was a plain allusion to *The Times* and to its turbulent correspondent in the Crimea, W. H. Russell, whose despatches, though fully justified, were reckless in their revelations. As a British General expressed it, the Russians had no need of espionage, they could "get it all for 5d. from a London paper".[2] To the Secretary of State for War, in a reference to Russell, the Prince expressed himself more openly. "The pen and ink of one miserable scribbler is despoiling the country of all the advantages which the hearts blood of 20,000 of its noblest sons should have earned."[3]

In one so precise and restrained as the Prince, this outburst shows how the anxieties of war had played on his nerves. This was also shown when the news — so long expected — at last came that Sevastopol had fallen. The Court was staying at Balmoral at the time, and the news arrived while the Queen and Prince were at dinner. Immediately afterwards the Prince rushed up a precipitous hill, lit a huge bonfire, cheered lustily and fortified himself with nips of whisky. His private secretaries, who were both fagged by work, panted behind, grumbling at this

[1] *Speeches*, p. 157. [2] *History of "The Times"*, p. 188.
[3] Royal Archives.

curious display of undergraduate spirits. Round the bonfire they were joined by the Highlanders who, having drunk copiously of whisky, were — in the carefully chosen language of Queen Victoria — " in great ecstasy ".[1] To the Prince the evening was " wild and exciting beyond everything ". This was almost the last display in his life of those crackling high spirits which had made him in his young manhood an entertaining companion, and in the manifestations of which the Queen ever delighted.

But events at home — the celebrations of victories or the prods at the War Office — were the least important part of the Prince's tasks during the war. For it was during these years, with the full connivance of the Government, that he became something of a European personality. It was of the first importance that the alliance between Great Britain and France — rather shakily constructed out of fear of Russia — should be deepened and strengthened. The Government saw that the first step to this was by an understanding between the English Court and Napoleon. In the summer of 1854 the Emperor was to be at St. Omer, in camp, and it was urged on the Prince that he should go to meet him there. The British Ambassador in Paris emphasised the great advantages which would flow from the influence of the Prince's " sound understanding " on the Emperor.

Accordingly, at the beginning of September, the Prince spent four days at Boulogne with the Emperor. As they drove to and from the various camps or chatted in the evenings (though these were somewhat marred for the Prince by the endless smoking and the general *ton de garnison*) they discussed every topic of the day. Dickens, who was at Boulogne finishing off *Hard Times*, saw them riding through Boulogne and in response to his greeting the Emperor took off his cocked hat and the Prince raised his plumed field-marshal's head-dress.[2] Dickens thought that they

[1] Journal.

[2] This was the customary salute of the period. It explains why the Prince, in his statue in High Holborn, is portrayed doffing his field-marshal's hat.

were jogging along in the pleasantest way and he noted that they were talking extremely loudly about the view. It was perhaps characteristic of the simplicity of English royalty that the Prince was attended by a couple of grooms in scarlet liveries who looked very bizarre in the middle of a posse of French generals who were in attendance on the Emperor.

The Prince quickly fell a victim to the charm of the Emperor, and he was touched to the heart by the openness and want of reserve with which Napoleon broached every subject. Certainly they discussed the most delicate matters, including the *coup d'état* which the Prince called " une affaire *douteuse* dont personne ne pouvait prévoir les conséquences ". They discussed their respective systems of Government, the Prince explaining that the Queen controlled affairs by seeing all important despatches before they were sent, while the Emperor admitted that he relied on the reports of private agents whom he employed to report on his diplomats. The Prince expatiated on the whole of English foreign policy since the days of Canning which he followed up by " going cursorily through Mr. Gladstone's Budget speech ".

The Prince noted with distress the eagerness with which the Emperor devoured reports from his agents and from the police while scarcely troubling to read official papers or the newspapers. Even at this early period the Prince put his finger on the flaw in the Napoleonic régime which within twenty years was to bring the whole frail structure tinkling down. " He is bound to keep up the 'spectacle' and, as at fireworks, whenever a pause takes place between the different displays, the public immediately grows impatient." [1]

This meeting between the two royalties was followed by a state visit to Paris in 1855 by the Queen, the Prince and their two eldest children. To the accompaniment of shrill cries of "Vive la Reine ", " Vive le Prince Albert ", they closed the ancient feud between England and the Bonaparte family which had lasted for

[1] Martin, chap. lvi.

sixty years. In the following autumn the Emperor came to stay at Windsor and was invested with the Garter. They thus set the seal of respectability on the Emperor and his dynasty. But the Emperor was a difficult customer and not an easy ally, and the English Government had cause to be grateful to the Prince for deflecting him from some serious breaches of loyalty and many acts of folly. In fact, so close were the relations between the two Courts that when Aberdeen's Government fell the French Ambassador wrote to the Prince to say that any Government which did not include Palmerston and Clarendon would imperil the stability of the Franco-British *entente*. The Prince sent no reply to this letter, merely forwarding it to the acting Foreign Secretary with the request that he would point out to the French Ambassador the constitutional impropriety of what he had done.[1]

In fact, the war and the French Alliance drew Palmerston, Clarendon and the Prince into harmonious accord. On all major questions of foreign policy — especially those affecting Austria and Prussia — the English statesmen entirely deferred to the judgment of the Prince. One important example shows how far this went. In 1856 Clarendon drafted a despatch for the Prussian Government which ended up, "the neutrality which Prussia professed to maintain is now considered by H.M.'s Government to be at an end". The Prince at once pointed out that this was tantamount to a declaration of war and insisted on its being modified. Certainly it is somewhat remarkable that a foreigner by birth should have had to point out to an English Foreign Secretary the full implications of the language which he was using.[2]

From the Crimean War may be dated the attainment of full political power by the Prince. For the early years of his life in England he had to struggle for the Queen to include him in political partnership. For the middle years of his life he had to struggle with the politicians to accord to the Crown the position

[1] Royal Archives. [2] Royal Archives.

THE PRINCE AND NAPOLEON III AT BOULOGNE, 1854
From the picture by George Thomas

in politics to which it was entitled by ability and tradition. From 1855 onwards that position was fully recognised and enjoyed. From now onwards the pupil of Stockmar had outsoared the tutelage of his master. Although the Queen and Prince remained devoted to their old friend, his neat, black figure no longer haunted the corridors of Windsor and was no longer to be seen peeping from a window at the hills round Balmoral. " My dear Lord " — he once said to Lord Granville — " have you yet to learn that in the case of Royalties, so soon as one is neither useful nor amusing, one's only course is to disappear ? "[1]

England knew the political doctor no more, and whatever reason he may have given for this to Lord Granville, there was in his case no diminution of royal favour. Both the Queen and the Prince begged him to come back, never lost their affection for him and maintained a regular correspondence with him. Advancing years and nervous apprehensions about his health were the cause of his leaving the English Court, but he had the satisfaction of knowing that his work lived on. He would have been profoundly gratified if he could have known that a shrewd observer of the political scene remarked of the Prince, " I take it that he governs us really in everything."[2] He did.

[1] *Personal Papers of Lord Rendel.* Ernest Rendel, 1931.
[2] *Miss Emily Eden's Letters.* Macmillan, 1919.

CHAPTER VIII

BISHOPS AND DONS

An Englishman's politics the Prince found difficult to understand, but by application and perseverance he mastered them. An Englishman's religion he found impossible of comprehension, and the more closely and deeply he studied the question, the more impenetrably cloudy stood "the mountain tops where is the throne of truth". For a just appreciation of the religion of the English he started with one fatal disadvantage — he was no churchman. Tolerant and broadminded as he was, he betrayed a curious narrowness and bigotry in matters ecclesiastical. He brought to this country a continental horror of clericalism and the Church of Rome which frequently betrayed themselves in ordinary conversation. He said, for example, "Generally one cannot augur favourably of a man educated by the Jesuits."[1] In a public speech he caused some offence by a reference to the Reformation as "our ancestors shaking off the yoke of a domineering Priesthood",[2] and he observed privately after attending a meeting of the S.P.G. that the secretary "struck me antipathetically as an unctuous priest".[3]

After attending a Roman Catholic wedding he wrote to his eldest son that the religious part was "perfectly ludicrous", adding that when the congregation is at close quarters "all the nonsense becomes apparent".[4] In a reference to these papal prejudices of the Prince Mr. Gladstone used a phrase which,

[1] *Memoirs of Prince Hohenlohe*. Heineman, 1906. [2] *Speeches*, p. 146.

[3] Royal Archives. In spite of the Prince's strictures he was an outstandingly successful secretary of the society. [4] Royal Archives.

coming from him, must be interpreted as a severe condemnation — " His views of the Church of Rome must, I think, have been illiberal ".[1]

" He had no natural piety ",[2] wrote his brother, and like many observations of that most malicious and wicked man this fell perilously near the truth. His mind was far removed from the simple aspiration of the English churchman expressed by the poet,

> And I could wish my days to be
> Bound each to each by natural piety.[3]

Piety as meaning reverence for God was the distinguishing mark of the Church of England even in the dark days of the eighteenth century.[4] Piety in that sense the Prince never understood and in his early days Anson had to warn him to be more circumspect in his criticisms of the Church of England.[5] The Prince was certainly no atheist or agnostic for he believed in life after death and in the existence of a Beneficent Creator. But his religious opinions were loose and unconfined by dogma.

In 1860, when he was instructing his second son in religious matters, he set down his views thus :

> I was most anxious to root up the Covenant theory that man's nature is sinful — that he must therefore sin and that Christ by his Death has freed him from punishment for sin — and in its stead to establish as a conviction the right theory that sin is not positive, but something transitory, the struggle between the animal nature and the moral law, which begins with the knowledge of the Law, and ends with its victory over mere impulse in ethical freedom — which freedom Christ has won for us by his teaching, life and death if only we follow him.[6]

It was doctrines of this kind, based rather on specious morality than on the teaching of the Churches, which led the wife of one

[1] Morley, ii, 91. [2] *Memoirs of Duke of Saxe-Coburg-Gotha*, i, 25.
[3] Wordsworth, " My heart leaps up ".
[4] See *Eighteenth Century Piety*, by W. K. Lowther Clarke, S.P.C.K.
[5] Royal Archives. [6] Royal Archives.

of his secretaries to say, "Churchmen could not but distrust him."[1]

This would not have been so serious if the Queen had not largely shared his prejudices. She might have been expected to have been sounder than she was on ecclesiastical matters since she belonged, in the jargon of the day, to a good church family. The old Royal Family — the sons and daughters of George III — were very stout church men and women, and King William IV on his deathbed (after a life which had not been outstanding for Christian endeavour) startled his attendants by ejaculating in his pop-gun fashion, "The Church! The Church!" But unluckily the Queen's religious upbringing was outside the control of her father's family, and, as the Prince expressed it, "She received no very high opinion of religion from her mother and the Baroness."[2] Both the Duchess of Kent and Baroness Lehzen — nurtured in the harsh and dreary doctrines of Luther — were ill-equipped to instruct anyone in the teaching of the Church of England. The first glimmering of the truth was realised by the public before the Queen's marriage. In 1838 the Vicar of Leeds, Dr. Hook, preached a remarkable sermon in the Chapel Royal called, "Hear the Church". He ended his discourse, fixing his eyes on the small occupant of the splendid, plush pew, with these words:

> May the great God of Heaven, may Christ, the Great Bishop and Shepherd of Souls, who is over all things in the Church, put it, my brethren, into your hearts and minds to say and feel as I do. "As for me and my house we will live in the Church, we will die in the Church, and if need shall be, like our martyred forefathers, we will die *for* the Church."[3]

The Queen was said to have marked her disgust at the prospect of martyrdom and her disapproval of this eulogy of the Church by drawing the curtains in front of her pew with a sharp and

[1] *Life of Lady Ponsonby*. [2] Royal Archives.
[3] *Life of Hook*, by Prebendary Stephens. Bentley, 1878.

decisive rattle. Certain it is that she was very angry and it was generally believed that never again was Hook to offend the ears of royalty with such simple truths.[1] Guile and deception were completely lacking in the Queen's character and she never made the least pretence to beliefs which she did not hold. "You know I am not much of an Episcopalian," she once told her Prime Minister. "No, Ma'am, I know that well," Mr. Gladstone drily replied.[2]

Neither the Prince nor the Queen were able to accustom themselves to the importance which English churchmen attached to the act of kneeling. When the Princess Royal learned her first prayer, her governess, Lady Lyttelton, insisted that she should go to her bedroom and say her prayers kneeling down. The Queen, who was devoted to Lady Lyttelton, and would have taken her advice on any other topic, could not understand her insistence that the child should kneel and contested it violently, even writing to her half-sister to find out if she made her children kneel.[3] The Prince thought that the insistence on kneeling seemed "stiff and cold — a peculiar feature of English religiosity". He saw Lady Lyttelton and argued with her that in Germany kneeling "had gone out with the Reformation, I do not do it". But Lady Lyttelton was adamant and told the Prince that she thought "sitting highly irreverent". Eventually, the Prince agreed that as the Princess was to be "brought up in England her prejudices must be those of the English Church".[4]

Against this background the decision of the Queen and Prince to become Presbyterians when they crossed the Border into Scotland appears natural and seemly. But some of the Queen's subjects — especially those familiar with the glorious history of the Episcopal Church of Scotland — were outraged by the spectacle of the Defender of the Faith indulging in the familiarities

[1] *Life of Bishop Wilberforce*, i, 124. John Murray, 1880.

[2] *Personal Papers of Lord Rendel.*

[3] *Letters*, i, 509.

[4] Letter to Stockmar. Royal Archives.

towards the Almighty encouraged by the Presbyterians. Dr. Routh, the learned President of Magdalen who had known Dr. Johnson and enshrined the finest Anglican traditions of piety and scholarship, cheeped out at a dinner-party held to celebrate his ninety-fifth birthday, " The Church is in great peril from a Kirk-going Queen and a Prince who betrays his rights."[1] Although he had reached such a prodigious age neither courage nor sense had deserted him.

It should not for a moment be imagined that either the Queen or the Prince were lacking in personal religious feelings of great depth and sincerity. They clung to the old-fashioned habit of very rare communions for which they prepared themselves closely, living in retirement the previous day.[2] On Sundays they usually read out loud from Dr. Arnold's *Sermons*, Thornton's *Family Prayers* and other religious books of a strongly low church and evangelical flavour. As soon as the private chapel in Buckingham Palace was finished, they went in for prayers each morning on their way out to walk in the gardens. But what Dr. Routh sensed and criticised was that they were out of sympathy with the most vigorous — even if it was the most turbulent — side of church life, the High Church Party, which sought to revivify Anglicanism by drawing out of cold storage the Catholic traditions of Laud and the early seventeenth century.

The average clergyman at the beginning of the nineteenth century was scholarly and humane but far removed from the mind and interests of the majority of his flock. " They are constant readers of The Gentleman's Magazine, deep in the antiquities of signs of inns, speculations as to what becomes of swallows in winter, and whether hedgehogs or other urchins are most justly accused of sucking milch cows dry at night."[3] In the pursuit of those important and fascinating researches they failed to appreciate that a new population was springing up in the

[1] *Dr. Routh*, by R. D. Middleton. Oxford Press, 1938.
[2] Royal Archives. [3] *Life of Hook*, previously quoted.

industrial towns which was untouched by the Church. The High Church Party, conscious of the danger, and drawing new strength from the spiritual and Catholic doctrines engendered by the Oxford Movement, attracted the liveliest and noblest minds of the youth of the early Victorian Age. Religious topics dominated the conversation of Army Officers and of Civil Servants, of masters and boys at public schools and, above all, of dons and undergraduates at the University. Indeed, to such lengths did this go that an undergraduate was obliged to prepare a friend for the appalling news that one of their number had doubts about the Blessed Trinity.[1] "All the young people are growing mad on religion," growled Lord Melbourne.[2]

Naturally this intellectual activity was impossible without friction and controversy; in fact during the 1840's and 1850's religion cold-shouldered politics from the front rank of public controversy. The bitter wrangles of party were transferred from the hustings to the pulpit and from Parliament to the Chapter House.

Of the frenzy and fury of these religious disputes the Queen and Prince profoundly disapproved. Not understanding the principles from which these quarrels arose, they made the mistake of attributing the blame for their existence to one side — the Oxford Party, whom they regarded as solely responsible for the mischief. When the Prince appointed Dean Liddell his domestic chaplain he explained that he was anxious to attach to his person "one who has kept the even tenor of his ways amid the perils by which his path at Oxford was beset."[3]

Yet it might have been supposed that the Prince's friendly association with Wilberforce, his chaplain and the most accomplished churchman of his age, would have done something to correct the balance. The two men understood each other —

[1] Mr. G. M. Young, *Portrait of An Age*. Oxford, 1936.

[2] Bunsen, i, 499.

[3] *Henry George Liddell*, by Reverend H. Thompson. Murray, 1899.

they had heated religious discussions, enjoyed their games of chess and in winter skated together. The Queen triumphantly records in her Journal that she went to watch them skating at Claremont and that the " Archdeacon got two falls ".[1] In the pulpit the Archdeacon was on less treacherous ground and he did endeavour to set before his royal congregation views on the Church which were in conformity with the spirit of the times. The Prince always listened most intently to his sermons (though he sometimes complained of their length) and invariably discussed them with Wilberforce afterwards. On one occasion the Archdeacon had preached on the subject of Christ's intercession for the sins of the world with the Father. The Prince told Wilberforce that this was an entirely new idea to him, that he would give it his most serious reflection and that at least he now understood why the Church of England always ended her prayers with the words " through Jesus Christ our Lord ". The Archdeacon was not, however, always discreet, and Stockmar had to warn the Prince not to discuss Church matters with anyone.[2] In correspondence with a friend, who had criticised the Prince's lax observance of Sunday, Wilberforce correctly said that " he was a thoroughly sincere Lutheran ", believing that Sunday should be a day of relaxation. He was able to reassure his correspondent that cards were always banished at Court on Sundays, but he had to admit a German game of four-handed chess was indulged.[3]

Many churchmen felt that Wilberforce had not been wholly successful in weaning the Queen and Prince from these Lutheran predilections. When he was made Bishop of Oxford in 1845, his place at Court was offered to Manning, who was then still faithful to the Church of England ; Manning observed that he realised that this appointment would draw him into the atmosphere in which he had seen Wilberforce wither.[4]

[1] Journal. [2] *Life of Wilberforce*, i, 377.
[3] Royal Archives.
[4] Purcell, *Life of Manning*. Macmillan, 1895.

When Wilberforce was made a Bishop, the Prince wrote to him defining his ideas of the position of a Bishop in the House of Lords. With engaging modesty he said that after starting to write he had abandoned the attempt for fear of seeming presumptuous. Anson had, however, encouraged him to persevere. He started with the obvious point that a Bishop should abstain completely from politics but that he should speak " boldly and manfully " on the interests of Humanity. These he specified as Negro Emancipation, Education, improvement of the health of towns, measures for the recreation of the poor, against cruelty to animals, for regulating factory labour. This shows the extent to which, in the 1840's, " the condition of the people question " was regarded as being outside politics. The Prince went on that in religious affairs the Bishop should always take the " part of a Christian not of a mere Churchman ". A Bishop ought likewise to be ready to admonish the public, and the Prince instanced the duty of Bishops to reprove the wickedness of railway speculators. In these ways he felt that Bishops could become a powerful force in the House of Lords affording great protection to the people.[1]

In ecclesiastical appointments the Prince took a lively interest and Wilberforce owed his bishopric to royal intervention. In these matters Lord John seems to have allowed the Prince to do pretty much as he liked, and he was directly responsible for one appointment which gave rise to a good deal of controversy — that of the first Bishop of Manchester, Dr. Lee, in 1847. He wrote to Lord John, " I am convinced you would not repent of your choice were you to recommend Dr. Lee for the Bishopric of Manchester ".[2] Dr. Lee, a pronounced low churchman, had been a master at Rugby under Arnold and had recently been headmaster of King Edward's School, Birmingham. The appointment was very generally criticised and Dr. Hook went so far as to say that an ecclesiastical body should be set up to advise the Prime

[1] Martin, ii, 132 ff. [2] Royal Archives.

Minister to prevent him from making appointments in order to propagate certain religious principles.

But the outcry over the Bishop of Manchester's appointment was as nothing compared with that over the appointment of the Bishop of Hereford in which the Prince again played a leading part. For this position Lord John selected Dr. Hampden, another low churchman of the Arnold school, who had already been censured by the University of Oxford for his Bampton Lectures in which he declared that the authority of the Scriptures was of greater weight than that of the Church.[1] The appointment was an astounding one and *The Times*, very friendly at that period to Lord John, observed, " We cannot imagine on what principle or motive it has been adventured ".

The outcry against the appointment was instant, formidable and loud. The lion-hearted Bishop of Exeter plunged headlong into battle, organising, with the help of Bishop Wilberforce, a Remonstrance among the Bishops. Lest the Prime Minister should show signs of weakening as the lawn banners of his critics were unfurled, the Prince, according to Greville, wrote to him every day espousing the cause of Hampden. Certainly he entered the struggle with characteristic enjoyment and ease. Writing to Stockmar he says, " We are in the midst of a fierce ecclesiastical controversy over Dr. Hampden and for the last six weeks I have studied nothing but theology ".[2]

The fruits of this study were showered on the poor Bishop of Oxford who, in addition to signing the Remonstrance, had urged the Prime Minister to arrange for Hampden's examination by a tribunal of the Church. The following letter from the Prince to Anson, which was to be shown to Wilberforce, showed how strongly the Prince felt :

the History of the Christian Church in all parts of the Globe shows the objectionable nature of such judgments by divines upon others

[1] There were many other causes of complaint against Hampden who had been a stormy petrel in Oxford ecclesiastical circles since 1832.

[2] Royal Archives.

upon points of doctrine. Why ! the greatest crimes and abominations, bringing disgrace upon the name of christianity, have been perpetrated in all times by such Councils of Divines.

He then ran through the Nicaean Council, the persecutions of Arians, Albigenses and Waldenses, of Huss, Savonarola, Wycliffe and Servet. He went on

If the spirit of the times allowed it, the Bishop of Exeter might not be disinclined to have Hampden burned.[1]

The Prince's vehement language indicated the strength of his feelings against Wilberforce. He referred to him as having "shown us the cloven hoof" and in a letter to Stockmar he writes:

Our little Oxford has flung himself into the controversy on the side of the Zealots and is fighting with Henry of Exeter. I dissected anatomically a jesuitical letter of his to Anson and wrote a memorandum showing jesuitism and absurdity to be its chief content. Anson took it to him and since then Oxford has remained in bed and been most uncomfortable.[2]

The poor Bishop could only reply that he had been actuated by an imperious sense of duty to God and the Queen.[3]

One other ecclesiastic was to come under the Prince's grave displeasure and that was the Dean of Hereford. An elderly gentleman who had long coveted a bishopric, he sent a memorial to the Queen asking that he should be appointed instead of Hampden. He advanced as arguments for his appointment that he had been high in favour with King William, who would never receive the communion wine from anyone else and who had promised him a bishopric on his deathbed.[4] Shortly after this the Dean wrote to Lord John saying that he proposed to vote against Hampden in the Chapter. The Prince at once wrote to the Prime Minister :

I see in the papers a letter from the Dean of Hereford to you, which is the climax of the bigotted warfare about Hampden, and

[1] Royal Archives.
[2] Royal Archives.
[3] Royal Archives.
[4] Royal Archives.

calculated to do much mischief. . . . I send you herewith a specificum which if administered now at the height of the fever-paroxysm may act as a sedative.[1]

This specificum was the Dean's memorial to the Queen, which the Prince urged should be published without comment. This was not in fact done and Russell simply replied to the Dean, "I have had the honour to receive your letter in which you intimate to me your intention of violating the law".

The dust of the Hampden case had scarcely settled when the Archbishop of Canterbury, a benign Churchman, who had devoted his life to gardening, died. Unquestionably the Prince would have pressed for Wilberforce's appointment before his polemics against Hampden, but his offence was never forgiven and the most acute and versatile mind in the Church of England was doomed to beat itself out in the routine of a provincial bishopric. Royal displeasure blocked his preferment. As it was, the Prince wrote to Lord John, "The appointment of a successor will be very difficult. How old may the Bishop of Chester be? It would be important that a liberal Archbishop should hold the place for some time to come."[2] The Bishop of Chester was sixty-eight and Lord John acquiesced in his appointment. It was a shocking appointment, because the new Archbishop, though good and amiable, was incapable of giving the Church the leadership which it sorely lacked and which it would certainly have been given under the sagacious guidance of Wilberforce.

The ecclesiastical appointments of Lord John — the most controversial of which were abetted and even inspired by the Prince — did great harm to the Church, helping to swell the steady stream of converts to Rome which marked the 1840's. Judged by any standards, Lord John — who was streaked with the obstinate agnosticism of the Russell family — was wrong to make appointments suitable to his own feelings or, as Hook expressed it, "in order to propagate certain *religious* principles".

[1] Royal Archives. [2] Royal Archives.

The religious partialities of the Prince, which, like Lord John, he allowed himself to indulge, reveal a curious flaw in his mind. He held that there was a line in ecclesiastical matters on one side of which all was wrong and on the other side of which all was right. It was only necessary by argument and memoranda to marshal all the facts and each issue would fall naturally into place on one side or other of the line. This left out of account the broad tolerance in which the Church was rooted and from which it drew its strength. For in spite of all the angry squabbles and bitter wrangles of the 40's there sprang from the Church an intellectual class firmly based on Christian scholarship which is seen to have been " the culminating achievement of European culture ". In the splendid language of the finest and most acute historian of the period :

> Yet in the far distance I can well conceive the world turning wistfully in imagination to the life of the University-bred classes in England of the mid-nineteenth century, set against the English landscape, as it was, as it can be no more, but of which nevertheless some memorials remain today . . . in that walled close where all the pride and piety, the peace and beauty of a vanished world seem to have made their last home under the spire of St. Mary of Salisbury.[1]

That world the Prince never entered, its dignity and beauty he never understood. He hungered for the society of intellectuals, but all the most lively minds of his contemporaries in England were cramped beneath those shovel hats by which he was instinctively repelled. In the more speculative era which followed his death he would have been welcomed and understood, but the twenty years' period of his sojourn in England was an almost exclusively clerical age which, by itself, created a barrier between him and the English. He sought to make up for what he was missing by cultivating the society of artists, historians and scientists, but many people would have agreed with the second Lord Lonsdale who, with the sturdy sense of his family, was overheard

[1] G. M. Young, *Portrait of An Age*.

in the Library of the House of Lords referring to the Prince's friends as " these damn'd scientific blackguards ".[1]

He also sought to make himself known in university circles. Himself a university man, he began to show an interest in English universities from the start of his life in this country. He visited Oxford in 1841, but he was much disgusted when the undergraduates, in his presence, set up a violent, anti-Whig caterwauling. He was likewise antipathetic to Oxford as the home of the High Church Movement and he was in consequence thrown into the arms of Cambridge, which was less representative of the prevailing intellectual fashions of the day. At Cambridge all was mathematical, precise and evangelical, confined in the icy grasp of a peculiar kind of country conservatism. In the autumn of 1843 the Queen and Prince made a sudden decision to visit Cambridge and to exercise their right of staying in Trinity. They gave less than a fortnight's warning of their intention and the college authorities were thrown into a fever of painting and cleaning, and dons rushed to their tailors to order knee-breeches.

After a night of wind and rain, followed by clear skies, the Queen and Prince drove down from London in a new post-chaise, reading out loud to each other from a German novel.[2] On arriving at Trinity they were given a respectful but tumultuous welcome by the undergraduates and it was during this visit to the college that the undergraduates spread their gowns for the Queen to walk across; one of them, afterwards Bishop of Exeter, recalled more than fifty years later the graceful mirth with which she thanked them.[3] Dons, long accustomed to the brutalities of Common Room life, brushed up their manners and practised walking backwards, but everyone remarked, and was slightly disconcerted by, the speed with which the Queen moved.[4] The

[1] Royal Archives.

[2] Journal. The book was *1812*, by Louis Rellstab.

[3] *Life of E. H. Bickersteth*, by F. K. Aglionby. Longmans, 1907.

[4] *Life of Adam Sedgwick*, by Clark and Hughes. Cambridge Press, 1890.

impression made by the Prince was most favourable. He flattered the dons by asking intelligent questions, and when he and the Queen went round Sedgwick's geological museum he won golden opinions by pointing out the rarest specimens in the collection, and his final courtesy to the University was to insist on climbing the roof of King's College Chapel.

So favourable was the impression which the Prince made that when, three and a half years later, the Chancellor of the University died, the Master of Trinity, backed by other Heads of Houses, asked the Prince to let his name go forward for the Chancellorship. The Prince agreed to this, provided that there was no contest. Unluckily, St. John's, next to Trinity the most powerful college, was already in the field with a strong Tory and Church candidate, an old Johnian, Lord Powis. It is surprising and indicative of the feeling against the Prince in Tory Church circles that Lord Powis declined to withdraw. The Prince's supporters had already started their campaign and they used every effort to persuade the Prince to go on. The Vice-Chancellor went up to Buckingham Palace and saw the Prince, having arranged with his Cambridge friends that he would telegraph the verdict in a simple code — A for acceptance, C for conditional acceptance and R for refusal. The same afternoon the Prince's Cambridge friends received the telegram with the single letter R.[1]

After further discussions, notably with Peel, the Prince consented (and this emphasises his great anxiety for an official connexion with the University) to allow his supporters to let his name go forward for election though he himself would remain entirely passive and outside the fray.

No academic election has ever aroused similar feeling. Considering that Lord Powis could only muster two Heads of Houses and that all the rest were solid for the Prince, there were good

[1] For all these details of the Prince's connexion with Cambridge I have relied entirely on Mr. Winstanley's book on *Early Victorian Cambridge*. Cambridge Press, 1940 — a book of the first importance and distinction.

grounds for believing that the Prince would win comfortably. However, in more bustling parts of the British Isles than Cambridge, where Heads of Houses were of less account, the support for Lord Powis was strong. The London Press was solidly behind him and *Punch* held up to ridicule the gushing loyalty with which the academic leaders avowed their support of the Prince. It was even suggested that if H.R.H. were elected all members of the Senate would have to kneel during the installation, "the Heads of Houses remaining entirely prostrate".[1] Many voters seem genuinely to have felt that the true dignity and independence of the University demanded that the Prince should not be elected.

The poll was held on February 25th, 26th and 27th, 1847. Lord Powis ran special trains from London for his supporters and he started well, but the spectacle of two members of the Government (Lord Palmerston and Lord Lansdowne) and an ex-Lord Chancellor (Lord Lyndhurst) voting for the Prince, steadied opinion. The undergraduates showed their partiality for the Prince when Lord Fitzwilliam, resplendent in scarlet gown, voted for Lord Powis, by calling out, "Here she is — the Lady of Babylon."

In the result, the Prince had a majority of 80, which, out of a total poll of 1791, was not large. All the church bells in Cambridge were set ringing, but Lord Powis's supporters comforted themselves with the reflection that many of their clerical supporters had not voted because one of the polling days was a Friday in Lent. The most perfervid of the Prince's supporters was not daunted by the smallness of the majority, and loyally noted in her Journal, "all the cleverest men were among those on my beloved Albert's side".[2]

The letter announcing the Prince's election was drafted by the Public Orator, one of Lord Powis's leading supporters, and bade the new Chancellor "look carefully after the interests of the

[1] *Punch*, xii (1847), 88. [2] Journal.

Church ". The installation ceremony, which was held at Buckingham Palace, was attended by a deputation of leading members of the University. They were afterwards entertained to dinner by the Prince, who must have found their manners a trifle odd. On being offered claret or sherry the Master of Caius startled the company by brusquely replying, " Port, if you please." The Master of Sidney Sussex made a beast of himself on turtle soup and punch. As a result of this rich combination his fellow dons had to bustle him out of the room.

At the beginning of the following July the Queen and Prince again stayed in Trinity for the formal ceremony of installation at the Senate House. They travelled by the Eastern Counties Railway, " the great railway king, Mr. Hudson himself, going with us ",[1] accompanied by a fine posse of princes, noblemen and ladies. On arrival at Trinity, the Prince, at the head of a vast retinue of dons, had to read a formal address of welcome to the Queen. Not unnaturally they had some difficulty in keeping their countenances, for, as the Queen expressed it, such formality between husband and wife was " almost absurd ". However, they managed admirably, except they could not wholly hide their mirth when the Heads of Houses kissed the Queen's hand, which they accomplished " with an infinite variety of awkwardness ".[2]

At the Senate House a somewhat woolly ode by the ancient poet laureate, Wordsworth, was sung. Himself a Johnian and Tory he would perhaps have done better had he been asked to sing the triumphs of Lord Powis. Not altogether judiciously he referred to the Prince as " the chosen lord " of Cambridge and ended :

Resound, resound the strain
That hails him for our own !
Again, again and yet again,
For the Church, the State, the Throne !
And that Presence fair and bright,
Ever blest wherever seen,

[1] Journal. [2] Bunsen, ii, 136.

Who deigns to grace our festal rite,
The Pride of the Island, Victoria the Queen.

In describing the presence of Queen Victoria as "bright", Wordsworth had used an adjective peculiarly appropriate to the occasion, for the dignitaries of Cambridge, accustomed to the gloom and dirt of college rooms, were quite blinded by the flash and sparkle of her diamonds, with which, as the Vice-Master of Trinity observed, she was "almost covered".[1] During all their visit the sun shone with unrelenting, East Anglian glassiness, and on the last evening the Prince and Queen were thankful to slip out for an informal stroll through the Backs after dinner. The Prince wore his Chancellor's cap, and a mackintosh over his dress-coat, and the Queen was in evening dress "with a veil over my diadem".[2] The Queen's knowledge of the Cambridge vernacular was not strong and she alluded to the Backs as "the waterside". Listening to the distant hum of Cambridge town they thought that the only thing lacking was singing, which, they agreed, would have been heard in any other country than England.

The Prince's connexion with Cambridge was, however, far more real and deep than that of a mere ceremonial figurehead. The years of his chancellorship were among the most critical in the history of the University. Like a rooster on a frosty night which draws the marauding fox, Cambridge, black with clergy, rich and helpless, attracted the greedy gaze of reformers.

At this time all power in the University rested with the Heads of Colleges. They used to forgather in the vestry of Great St. Mary's after church service on Sunday and from there the University was governed. All clergy, wearing wigs and only deigning to mix with themselves or professors, they were like a close corporation of minor bishops, with the power and un-

[1] These were doubtless the family jewels which legally belonged to the Queen's uncle, the King of Hanover. "I hear the little Queen was loaded with my diamonds," he once complained.

[2] Journal.

popularity of that species of mankind. Naturally, there were able and enlightened men among them, but for the most part they took their stand on the privileges of their order. The most far-sighted of them realised that a measure of reform was inevitable but all their exertions were directed to preventing this from being imposed from without. In this manœuvre they had the whole-hearted sympathy of the Prince. In the autumn after his election, the Master of St. Catharine's went to stay with him at Windsor and the two men discussed the possibilities of reform. The Prince made it clear that he thought it deplorable that "geography, modern languages, the history of art and aesthetics" found no place in a Cambridge education. The Master agreed and the Vice-Chancellor was likewise thought to be sympathetic to change, but all warned the Prince that the Heads of Colleges were "such a nervous body" that it would be necessary to proceed with the utmost caution. At the same time, the Prime Minister made it clear to the Prince that he was about to advise the Queen to set up a Commission of Enquiry into schools and colleges. The Prince persuaded him to put this off while they waited to see what the two reforming Masters could achieve.

The Prince worked hard behind the scenes at these reforms and in the autumn of 1848 he was able to note in his diary, "my plan for a reform of the studies at Cambridge is carried by a large majority". The execution of the plan was slow and eighteen months later, without a word of warning to the Prince, Lord John agreed to the appointment of a Royal Commission to enquire into the state of the universities. Both Queen and Prince were understandably annoyed and in a letter for publication to the Vice-Chancellor the Prince made it clear that he disapproved of the Cabinet's decision, but he pointed out that as Ministers could not go back on their word, the University should do all it could to help the Commission. Dons, though sometimes old-maidish in their personal habits, are fearless and bellicose in controversy and they were disappointed that the Prince's letter was not more of a trumpet-call to battle. Yet the Prince could hardly have taken a stronger line against the head of the Queen's Government, and as it stood his letter was indubitably courageous.

The Prince personally intervened to persuade Sedgwick to serve on the Commission and he did everything he could to make what was inevitable palatable to the University. Unhappily, the Vice-Chancellor at this time, the Master of Jesus, was a nervous, encrusted Tory with the mind of a scholar but the political views of a backwoodsman. The Prince invariably asked the Vice-Chancellor to dinner and the Master of Jesus took great pride in being "the first to *decline* the *invitation*. Represent to our Prince Chancellor" — he scornfully wrote — "that I would rather not that any invitation should be given."[1] Supported by an equally fusty creature, the Master of Clare, he refused to answer any of the Commissioner's questions, basing his refusal "on a sense of public duty". When a prominent member of the University died, the Prince had to confess to Lord John that he had not heard of it, "the present Vice-Chancellor withholding all information from me on principle".[2]

In all Cambridge matters the Prince took the most meticulous interest, even down to seeing the examination papers on subjects in which he was particularly interested. In 1849 he suggested that the Chancellor's medal for English poetry should be given to the best elegiac poem on the late Queen Adelaide. This pious and ancient widow was hardly calculated to infuse the manly youth of Cambridge with poetic ardour, but the Vice-Chancellor dutifully replied to the Prince that "the subject is admirably calculated to give scope to the expression of noble and poetic sentiment".[3]

To a man educated abroad as the Prince had been, some aspects of Cambridge life seemed archaic and nonsensical. He could not understand the narrowness of the curriculum (which was, at that

[1] Royal Archives. [2] Royal Archives. [3] Royal Archives.

time, confined to mathematics and classics), the relative unimportance of professors and the exaltation of college life. His conception of a university was at once large and liberal. In 1853 he wrote to Lord John :

> On the whole the Universities should not only be considered as schools and places for teaching and being taught, but also as seats of learning where the *savants* of this country may find a home which at present is absolutely denied to them, and they themselves being driven to join the mere money-making pursuits or to starve.[1]

In no sphere of his work in England did the Prince show to better advantage than in his careful guidance of Cambridge University. His progressive mind, firmly buttressed by common sense, shines with refreshing lucidity in contrast to the narrow political partialities of the extreme reformers on the one hand and the clerical backwoodsmen, steeped in port and parchment, on the other. His liberal views of what a university should be have largely been endorsed by posterity, but perhaps more praiseworthy than being right was his guidance of the University into the path of reform without hopelessly antagonising the dons, who as a class were at that time more impressionable than children — more crotchety than maiden aunts. Choosing his confidants at the University with great judgment and discretion — they were principally Sedgwick, the Master of St. Catharine's, and later Bishop Lightfoot — and seeking advice from men of judgment outside the University, like Sir Robert Peel, Lord Lansdowne and Baron Bunsen, he proved an invaluable leader to Cambridge as it gingerly set its foot on the awkward paths of reform. Certainly the Prince can have no higher encomium than that bestowed on him by Mr. Winstanley — the more valuable coming from one who never needlessly indulged in panegyrics and from one who was, through his knowledge of Cambridge and its traditions, peculiarly qualified to judge.

[1] Royal Archives.

For him the Chancellorship was no sinecure but a charge both sacred and onerous. An ancient seat of learning had entrusted itself to his care, and he intended to guide it along the path of educational reform. Therefore, he was determined . . . to make his influence felt . . . for a completely unselfish purpose. It was a difficult task but . . . he succeeded in accomplishing it.[1]

[1] *Early Victorian Cambridge.*

CHAPTER IX

THE GREAT EXHIBITION

MANY people — both among the Prince Consort's contemporaries and among those who only know him from the pages of history — too readily dismiss him as ponderous and dull. Even Lytton Strachey fell perilously near this prevailing mistake when he likened him to a butler.[1] Certainly his mind, which was well and neatly stocked, and his temperament, which was tenacious and argumentative, opened the way to the road down which travel that melancholy company — the bores and pedants. Religious controversy, educational reform and politics tested the quality of his mind, revealing its capacity, its breadth, its precision, but also its ponderous gravity. Those who only came into contact with the political Prince Albert may be pardoned for thinking him wise but heavy, sound but portentous. For such people it must have been incomprehensible that the same mind which could marshal all the intricacies of the Schleswig-Holstein question and which could only grapple with the Oxford Movement after a deep immersion in the Nicaean Creed or the Councils of Trent, could yet produce the gay phantasia of the Great Exhibition — the most romantic episode in the prosaic age of mid-Victorian England. Masters, artisans, labourers steeped in the dull, solid round of heavy commercial manufacture were to gaze spellbound at the beauty, variety and oddity collected for them, till they could say with Thackeray's Irishman :

Amazed I pass
From glass to glass,
Deloighted I survey 'em ;

[1] *Queen Victoria*, p. 212.

Fresh wondthers grows,
Before me nose,
In this sublime Musayum.

How could the " sublime Musayum " have sprung from the mind which produced those memoranda over which Victorian statesmen sighed and groaned but never tittered? The answer is that politics revealed only a part, and not the most interesting part, of the Prince's intellect.

The Great Exhibition was primarily the product of that artistic side to the Prince which softened and illumined his nature. For music and pictures his mind had a natural bent, turning easily to what was most congenial to it. In politics and affairs he did his best, but, as Stockmar noticed early on, not readily, and largely from a sense of duty.

Several interests of the Prince and several sides to his character led him on to the Great Exhibition, but the idea made a particular appeal to one of his romantic mind. No one except the Queen and a handful of intimates about the Court appreciated the true quality of the Prince's nature. Lady Lyttelton once came upon him unawares at Osborne when he was thundering on the organ. She noticed that through all the cadences of the music his playing was marked by a vein of melancholy, fine but constant. No one — she reflected — would ever guess the depths in his character " except sometimes from the expression in his eyes ".[1]

Music was the absorbing relaxation of the Prince's life. Not only was he an accomplished singer and player — so much so that his aristocratic enemies used to call him " the operatic tenor " — but his own compositions were by no means contemptible for a man much occupied in the world. His best work was the tune for the chorale " In Life's gay morn " which was sung by Jenny Lind at King Edward VII's marriage. He also composed a Te Deum in C which was sung by 300 voices at the Queen's Jubilee service in Westminster Abbey in 1887.

[1] Martin, i, 86.

The Prince did much to enhance the musical taste of his generation in England. During the early years of the Queen's reign interest in music was largely confined to women and clergymen. This interest did not extend much beyond Handel and Haydn, though there was a growing taste for Mozart, especially for the operas. England produced at this time only two composers of any merit — Field and Sterndale Bennett, but during the middle years of the century musical appreciation widened and spread to larger sections of the population, thereby preparing the ground for the rebirth of English music which coincided with the later years of the Queen's reign.[1]

In this enrichment of the musical taste of the public the Prince played an important part. The two principal organisations for concerts at this period were the Philharmonic Society and the Antient Concerts. The latter was a conservative body, generally with a Royal Duke or Archbishop as its Director, who chose the programme, which was mostly confined to Haydn and Mozart. On many occasions during the 1840's the Prince was Director and selected the music. He was, for example, responsible for persuading Mendelssohn in 1847 to play a prelude and fugue of Bach on the organ at one of these concerts. He also frequently chose the programmes at the Philharmonic Society, arranging in 1855 for Wagner to conduct the overture to *Tannhauser*.

The Prince's friendship with Mendelssohn was close, and after the first public performance of *Elijah* in England, at which he was present, he gave his copy of the words to Mendelssohn with this inscription :

> To the Noble Artist, who, surrounded by the Baal worship of debased art, has been able, by his genius and science, like another Elijah, faithfully to preserve the worship of true art, and once more to accustom our ear, amid the whirl of empty frivolous sounds, to the pure tones of sympathetic feeling and legitimate harmony ; to the Great Master who brings home to us the unity of his conception

[1] *Early Victorian England* (Oxford, 1934), ii, 251 ff.

through the whole maze of his creation from the soft whispering to the mighty raging of the elements.

Inscribed in grateful remembrance by

ALBERT.[1]

In private the Queen and Prince both sang to Mendelssohn's accompaniment on the organ, and in describing the Prince's playing of the organ he said that it was "charming, clear and correct."[2]

The Prince took great pains in reorganising the Queen's private band, changing it from wind to strings. He himself invariably chose the programme for the state and semi-private parties where the band performed. Through his choice the first performance of Schubert's C major Symphony in England was given by this band, and Wagner's *Lohengrin* was likewise first heard in this country in the drawing-room of Windsor Castle. Beethoven, Mozart and Mendelssohn were his favourite composers, and while the private band was playing some of their works he was to be seen standing slightly apart from the gay and fashionable company. Rapt in reverie, he showed by the look on his face, which the Queen was quick to notice, that he was far away in a world of rich and mellow beauty from which the cares and preoccupations of government, which fatigued his brain, were strictly barred. Sterndale Bennett who studied the Prince at a performance of Bach's Passion Music, which he was following from a full score, said that his face revealed "so fascinating, so individual an expression of interest and enjoyment" as to justify his being regarded as "the ideal amateur of music".[3]

Next to music he found his chief enjoyment and his greatest relaxation in the study of art. Both he and the Queen took considerable trouble to have themselves taught to draw, to paint in water-colours and in oils, to etch and to lithograph. Examples of their work in these various media abound at Windsor. They

[1] Martin. Appendix to vol. i. [2] Martin, i, 486.
[3] *Life of Sterndale Bennett.* Cambridge Press, 1907.

all show a certain standard of prettiness and accomplishment but they were not remarkably different from the kind of lively sketch which adorned the album of many a Victorian miss. Certainly the Prince — and for that matter the Queen — never made any extravagant claims as to the value of their artistic labours. In conversation with a member of the Court the Prince explained that " persons in our position of life can never be distinguished artists ". He went on to say, " Our business is not so much to create as to learn to appreciate and understand the work of others, and we can never do this till we have realised the difficulties to be overcome ". After setting out all the lessons he had taken both in art and music he emphasised that he had had these lessons, " not, of course, with a view of doing anything worth looking at or hearing, but simply to enable me to judge and appreciate the work of others ".[1]

He quickly won the confidence of English artists both by his habit of going to see them in their studios and by his knowledge of pictures. This confidence was not even disturbed by an alarming sharp instrument which he used to carry in his pocket and with which he used to point out suggested alterations and improvements, at some peril to the canvas.

When Frith exhibited " Derby Day " in the Academy he notes:

> the Prince Consort surprised me exceedingly by his intimate knowledge of what I may call *the conduct* of a picture. He told me why I had done certain things and how, if a certain change had been made, my object would have been assisted. How the masses of light and shade might still be more evenly balanced, and how some parts of the picture might receive still more completion. I put many of the Prince's suggestions to the proof after the close of the Exhibition, and I improved my picture in every instance.[2]

He was a frequent visitor to the studios of that wild imaginative artist, John Martin, whose paintings he greatly admired.

[1] Martin, iv, 15, 16.
[2] *My Autobiography*, by W. P. Frith. Bentley, 1887.

On one occasion Martin startled his Chelsea neighbours by receiving the Prince in his dressing-gown. He thought Martin's picture, " The Deluge ", was outstandingly original and successful, and he suggested that Martin should paint a series of three, " The Eve of the Deluge ", " The Deluge ", and " The Assuaging of the Waters ". The first he commissioned for the royal collection, and it now hangs in Buckingham Palace.[1]

He was never afraid to express his views in public and at an exhibition of the New Water-Colour Society he strongly advocated white mounts instead of gold ones. On his advice the Queen arranged for Millais' " Carpenter's Shop " — the most controversial picture exhibited in the Academy in 1850 — to be sent down to her at Windsor when she was recovering from the birth of her third son. At the Academy banquet in the following year, and it was the only one which he ever attended, he deprecated newspaper criticisms of artists' work. (Art critics in those days were invariably harsh and often venal.) Contrasting the circumstances of modern artists with those of their forerunners who, undisturbed by criticism, could paint, as he said, " Madonnas in the seclusion of convents," he went on, " an unkind word of criticism passes like a cold blast over their tender shoots and shrivels them up, checking the flow of their sap, which was rising to produce, perhaps, multitudes of flowers and fruit." [2]

King Leopold was somewhat scandalised by the way in which the Prince mingled with artists, and writing to the Queen he said, " the dealings with artists require great prudence ; they are acquainted with all classes of society and for that very reason dangerous ; they are hardly *ever satisfied*, and when you have too much to do with them you are sure to have *des ennuis* ".[3]

Though he may have lacked the flamboyant good taste of King George IV (and the capacity of that king for spending

[1] *John Martin*, by Mary Pendered. Hurst and Blackett, 1923.

[2] *Speeches*, p. 128.

[3] It seems more probable that King Leopold really wrote " *des ennemis* ". *Letters*, ii, 46.

money which he had not got), he ranks with him as a careful and inspired custodian of the royal treasures. For example, he was personally responsible for the discovery that some hundreds of pictures were stacked downstairs at Hampton Court : he arranged for these to be cleaned and hung in the various royal palaces. At a time when the National Gallery contained no Italian pictures of the fourteenth century, only two of the fifteenth century and only one early Flemish picture the Prince was buying such pictures with great judgment and discrimination. Among this collection were the "Duccio Triptych", "The Gentile da Fabriano Madonna", two paintings by Fra Angelico, and a Benozzo Gozzoli, a Memling Madonna (now in the the National Gallery), the Cranach "Apollo and Diana" and a very interesting Madonna of the Moravian School. That he had a deep and genuine feeling for those early paintings is suggested by the fact that they were almost all hung in his private rooms at Osborne — his dressing-room and the room in which he worked.

Anyone familiar with the royal collection of pictures will realise the absurdity of Strachey's gibe that he skied the Gainsboroughs so that the Winterhalters might be the better displayed. In fact the Gainsboroughs at Windsor are still hanging just as they were arranged by him : though the room in which they hang is small, they are given the most prominent place in it, and all except three are hanging at eye level.

His taste and judgment were again shown by his care for the royal collection of drawings. These he found in great disorder and he decided that they ought to be properly arranged for the benefit of students. He weeded out the indecent prints collected by King George IV, telling the Queen, "there are quantities of the most dreadfully obscene character."[1] The collection was too large for him to tackle all at once so he decided to concentrate on the Raphael drawings. He broke up the albums of drawings, mounting them on sunk mounts for the preservation of the

[1] Royal Archives.

drawings. He collected engravings and photographs of every known fragment of Raphael's work, and he was in fact a pioneer of the employment of photography for comparative studies. To the end of his life the collection was an object of never-failing interest and pleasure.

He was always anxious that the royal collections should be available for serious students, and one of the first people to benefit from this was Carlyle, who saw for himself how completely the Prince had become familiar with the contents of the royal collection. When he was at Windsor, with the Librarian, examining prints of Frederick the Great for his history, the Prince was announced. At once Carlyle was impressed with his knowledge and modesty ; he has left for posterity one of the best accounts of the appearance of the Prince as he was at this time, which was just before he was thirty.

> There in truth was the handsome young gentleman, very jolly and handsome in his loose greyish clothes . . . well built figure of near my own height, florid blond face with fair hair [1] but the eyes were much better than I had fancied ; a pair of strong steady eyes with a good healthy briskness in them. He was civility itself in a fine simple fashion.[2]

But as with music the Prince's interest in painting was not confined to a gratification of his own enjoyment. He made great efforts to enlighten and enlarge the artistic appreciation of the contemporary Englishman. Certainly during the early years of the Queen's reign English Art was in the doldrums. A writer in the *Daily Telegraph* with justice pointed out that public taste in England in 1840 was " of the coarsest and most uncouth order ", adding that even in the most genteel families the drawing-master took his place " with the fiddler and the French Cook ".[3]

There were two reasons for the plight of English Art during the early Victorian Era ; the first was the virtual disappearance

[1] In fact, as the paintings of the Prince show, his hair was dark brown.
[2] *Letters of Carlyle*, edited by Alexander Carlyle. John Lane, 1924.
[3] *Daily Telegraph*, December 20th, 1861.

of the intelligent patron and the second was the debauchery of public taste by commerce.

The death of Lord Egremont in 1837 — the last person in England to patronise the arts on a princely scale — marked the end of that open-handed, aristocratic patronage which had sustained and encouraged artists throughout the eighteenth century. A new class had become interested in pictures. This was realised when it was known that the finest private collection of Landseer was owned by a ship's captain, that the largest buyers of Turner were a carriage maker and an oil merchant and that the chief patron of Etty — the great master of the nude — was appropriately enough a tailor. Many of these and other patrons of the new type undoubtedly had a real knowledge of pictures but some " went in " for pictures with the same sort of motives as they " went in " for cloth, ships, oil or (in the case of Ruskin's father) sherry wine. This broadening of the demand for pictures led inevitably to the importation, on a large scale, of inferior copies of old masters. Many a man, after a lucky speculation in railway shares, had a quick dabble in pictures on the profits. The shrill vituperation of Ruskin no less than the tortured outpourings of Haydon in his diary show how parlous was the plight into which the arts had fallen.

Some artists began to think that the only hope of restoring the fallen fortunes of British art was for the state to enter the field in place of the old private patron. For example, the splendid collection of Old Master drawings made by Lawrence was offered for sale to the state and it was of this offer that Talleyrand observed, " Si vous n'achetez pas ces choses-là vous êtes des barbares." The purchase was not made partly because of the great fear of jobbery if the Government was to undertake transactions of that kind.

The Prince was able to render English art a great service by helping to rouse government interest in the arts. He saw clearly, as did many enlightened painters, that in the long run government or the state would have to fill the gap created by the extinction of the private patron.

His chance came in 1841 when Peel offered him the chairmanship of the Royal Commission on the Fine Arts. This was set up with the object of deciding whether the rebuilding of the Houses of Parliament did not afford an opportunity for encouraging artists and developing British taste. Lord Melbourne, himself a member of the Commission, at once warned the Queen against "spending the public money in the encouragement of the Fine Arts".[1] The Prince was, however, determined that this should be done and that an experiment should be made with painting frescoes on the walls of the new Houses of Parliament — a type of painting which, at this time, was popular on the Continent. At once the cry went up from many an indigent English painter that the Prince intended to use foreign artists. These fears he was able to soothe in conversation with Eastlake, the Secretary of the Commission. They had a frank talk — the Prince standing with one knee on a chair, the light showing "his beautiful face to great advantage", and Eastlake was immediately impressed by his sense and modesty.

The Royal Commission was a distinguished one, including all the leading politicians, Hallam the historian, Sam Rogers and later Macaulay. But the Prince by his knowledge and enthusiasm dominated the Commission, and it was his suggestion that the frescoes for the walls of the House of Commons should be thrown open to public competition with prizes ranging in value from £300 to £100. No less than 141 entries were sent in and the Prince was delighted. "The Realization of my wishes and prophecies cannot fail to be most gratifying to me", he wrote.[2] G. F. Watts won one of the £300 prizes with a picture of "Caractacus led in triumph through the streets of Rome".

Ruskin, who certainly shared all the Prince's indignation at the depression of artistic taste in England in the 1840's, said of the

[1] *Letters*, i, 334. [2] Royal Archives.

fresco experiment, "it is a splendid sea for the strong swimmer, but you might as well throw a covey of chickens into the Atlantic as our R.A.'s into fresco." [1]

On the whole the experiment was a failure, dragging on for year after year until the public interest was exhausted. Watts, in spite of his initial success, was only commissioned to paint one fresco, that of St. George and the Dragon which was skied in an upper waiting-room. In 1850 the House of Commons became restive over the delays and reduced the vote for the Fine Arts Commission by £1050 — the chief complaint being that Landseer's picture of "The Monarch of the Glen" was to be hung in the peers' refreshment room where it would only be of permanent use to the waiters. The Prince was furious at this vote and observed to the Chancellor of the Exchequer that the peers' refreshment room was just the apartment "for deer and game". [2]

When the Prince died the work on the frescoes was hurried through and somewhat skimped. In the result the pictures are more curious than successful, more historical than artistic. It may, however, be hoped that enshrining, as they do, the greatest events in English history, they occasionally remind members of Parliament, bustling past them, of something a trifle less humdrum than their local newspapers and grumbling letters from their constituents. Probably those who enjoy them most are visitors whose listless gaze is caught by the frescoes as it might be caught by an illustrated magazine in a dentist's waiting-room.

Although the results of this experiment in fresco-painting were not all that the Prince had hoped, the preparations for them unquestionably stimulated public taste and, to that extent, amply justified his exertions. During the eight weeks in which the fresco cartoons for competition were exhibited in Westminster Hall in 1845, over 500,000 people saw them.

However, by personal experiment the Prince proved that

[1] Works of Ruskin (Library Edition), vol. iv, p. 393.

[2] Royal Archives.

fresco could be successfully carried out in England. In 1843 he arranged for the walls of the summer-house in the gardens of Buckingham Palace to be decorated with eight lunettes illustrating Milton's *Comus*. Among the artists chosen to do this were Landseer, Maclise and Eastlake, and the pictures were reproduced in a handsome book with an introduction by Mrs. Jameson — a noted bluestocking of the day and a repository of much of the cheeping malice of Lady Byron. This form of decoration was driven forward by the Prince with great energy and as the Queen expressed it, " the whole was dearest Albert's own idea ".[1] The results were handsome and generally admired.

The Prince was ever pressing that the public should be given increased facilities for seeing pictures and that the public galleries should be made more attractive. For example, in 1848 he arranged for an important collection of early paintings to be shown to the public in Kensington Palace. This collection had originally been formed by Prince Oettingen-Wallerstein, and when this Prince fell into financial troubles the Prince Consort acquired them. After trying in vain to interest the National Gallery in the collection he kept them himself. At his death twenty-two of the pictures, in accordance with his wishes, were given to the National Gallery.

On all matters connected with art the politicians were very sluggish, and the Prince made it his business to bring forward questions of taste for the attention of the Cabinet. He was, for example, responsible for the erection of Cleopatra's Needle as the following letter to Lord John Russell shows.

January 20th, 1847

My dear Lord John

The famous Obelisk called " Cleopatra's Needle " which has been [*sic*] given to George III after the expulsion of the French out of Egypt is now lying on the sandbeach near Alexandria. I hear that

[1] Journal.

the French Government are trying to get possession of it and to move it to Paris. This would be a real disgrace to our Government, moreover we possess absolutely nothing of the kind in England. The removal of the Obelisk originally was abandoned from a want of machinery. This plea can hardly be brought forward now-a-days.

Would not you undertake to have this national trophy and universally renowned work of Art brought to London? And have it erected as a principle ornament to the Metropolis?

Ever yours truly,

ALBERT.[1]

His efforts were not always encouraged and he can hardly have had more unpromising material than Lord John Manners who was First Commissioner of Works in the Conservative Government of 1852. The Prince sent for him and suggested certain ways in which a Commissioner of Works could help the national taste. Describing the interview, Lord John wrote, "Being entirely ignorant of the very first principles of Art and knowing nothing of the subjects on which he was discoursing, I maintained a discreet, respectful silence".[2]

Such ignorance well became the author of the familiar lines

Let wealth and commerce, laws and learning die,
But leave us still our old nobility.

On occasions he could speak his mind to the professional experts and he once startled Gilbert Scott — the prosperous architect of the Gothic revival — by a tirade against the lack of architectural education in England. He called this "contemptible in the extreme" and he shocked Scott by contrasting the aesthetic sensibilities of architects unfavourably with those of builders and military engineers.[3]

Although it is easy to make the cheap point that the Prince's taste was not always centred on objects which the twentieth

[1] Royal Archives.

[2] *Lord John Manners*, by C. Whibley. Blackwood, 1924.

[3] *Personal and Professional Recollections*, by Sir George Gilbert Scott. Sampson, 1879.

century would applaud, no one could deny that his taste was wide and enlightened, and that he derived from his study of pictures an enjoyment which was sincerely and deeply felt. To the Prince Consort might well be applied some words which Ruskin wrote in *The Stones of Venice*, " the purest and most thoughtful minds are those which love colour the most ".

Thus the Prince's natural concern at the state of public taste predisposed him for the great venture of the Exhibition. But one other factor was immensely important in driving him forward to the brilliant bazaar in Hyde Park. Under the lash of Ruskin's stinging prose, flying and cracking round them, the Prince's English contemporaries had begun their long search for moral purpose in art. " Every great composition in the world," Ruskin wrote, " every great piece of painting or literature, without any exception, from the birth of man to this hour, is an assertion of moral law."[1] Under the influence of these fashionable doctrines, the Prince sought a moral justification for his own sensual enjoyment of painting and music by striving to spread the same enjoyment throughout all classes. He felt that the dinginess of men's homes, the squalor of their work, the ugliness of their manufactured products could all be relieved and dignified by familiarising them with things of beauty. By these means mankind was to progress to a higher, nobler order of life. He had caught the brave echoes of the thinkers of mid-Victorian England. Browning was writing

Progress is
The law of life, man is not Man as yet.[2]

At the same time Tennyson was arguing that the bestial in man must gradually give place to the celestial. Mankind must

Move upward, working out the beast,
And let the ape and tiger die.[3]

[1] Ruskin, xxix, 265. [2] *Paracelsus.* [3] *In Memoriam.*

Carlyle was trumpeting, " Close thy Byron; open thy Goethe . . . there is in man a HIGHER than love of happiness."[1]

The Prince himself, in a speech in 1850, voiced the optimism of his age when he said, " So man is approaching a more complete fulfilment of that great and sacred mission which he has to perform in the world."[2]

On the strong wings of science and of art mankind was to soar to a nobler, fuller life. Such was the Prince's roaming fancy under the influence of which the idea of the Exhibition was conceived.

Some would argue that the idea of a great International Exhibition was not really his, but that it sprang, somewhat unexpectedly, from the resourceful genius of the Civil Service. An Assistant Keepership in the Public Record Office — a rather undistinguished perch in the Government service — was at this time filled by a Mr. Henry Cole, whose labours at his office desk left him plenty of time for foreign travel and even to win a prize for the design of a tea-service. Mr. Cole visited the *Exposition* in Paris in 1849 and returned to England imbued with the idea of enlarging one of the annual Exhibitions of Art Manufacture, sponsored by the Society of Arts into a great International Exhibition on the lines of the Paris *Exposition*.

The Queen, on the other hand, through Sir Theodore Martin, makes it clear that she believed the Prince to have been meditating something of this kind long before, inspired thereto by youthful recollections of the old Frankfurt Fairs. Whether the credit for being the first to think of the Exhibition belongs to the Prince or to Cole — and arguing over these things is rather like a squabble in the nursery — is immaterial. Without the encouragement and unflagging support of the Prince the idea could never have been executed. For this reason alone the Queen was perfectly justified in saying, " Albert's dearest name is immortalised with this great conception."[3]

[1] *Sartor Resartus*, Book II, chap. ix.

[2] *Speeches*, p. 111.

[3] *Letters*, ii, 318.

So far as any public body was responsible for the Exhibition, the credit for this must go to the Royal Society of Arts. Of this body the Prince had been President since 1843 and, as he explained, he had always taken a personal interest in its objective — the application of science and art to industry. In 1847, 1848 and 1849 Exhibitions were held in the Society's house of "Select Specimens of British Manufacture and Decorative Art". Cole — a prominent member of the Royal Society of Arts — had played an important part in these Exhibitions, coaxing industrialists to exhibit.

In June 1849 the Prince, Cole and the Secretary of the Royal Society of Arts were discussing the possibility of an International Exhibition in 1851. By the following month matters were sufficiently advanced for the Prince to broach the subject to the Government, and also to Sir Robert Peel. Even in these early days the authors of the project were looking to Hyde Park as a large central place suited to house the building for the Exhibition. The Prince called in to the discussions two practical men — Thomas Cubitt the architect, who was also an active member of the Society of Arts, and Playfair the distinguished chemist. The Prince, Playfair and Cubitt had been jointly responsible for some rather disagreeable experiments at Osborne to convert the sewage from the house into manure for the farms.

Playfair was the type of Englishman or Scot who instinctively appealed to the Prince. He was accomplished, practical and serious, and later on the Prince appointed him as a gentleman usher. This appointment shows how the Prince was hedged in and how difficult it was for him to mix easily with people outside that narrow oligarchic circle on which the Court depended. One of the Prince's secretaries immediately complained at the appointment, saying that Dr. Playfair was "a man of low birth, ordinary appearance and uncouth manners."[1] The Prince may be pardoned for having sought to break down the appointments

[1] Royal Archives.

of those handsome, polished, aristocratic nullities with which the Court abounded — those husks of men as they were once cruelly called.

The first task of those interested in the project of the Exhibition was to make certain that British manufacturers would support it and that they did not echo the sentiments of the Clitheroe calico manufacturer who, when approached, said that the bankruptcy gazette and the grave left him no time for Exhibitions.

Consequently, during August and September 1849, Cole was sent all over Great Britain to sound the manufacturers, and the result was highly encouraging. Though expressly against orders he could not resist the temptation of slipping in the words, "Prince Albert is behind this", and many a stolid Victorian business man, whose vision was limited by the counting-house on week-days and the chapel on Sundays, was inspired to promise his support for this daring sally into the unknown.

The Prince now saw that money would have to be quickly raised and he realised that at least £100,000 would be needed. Himself he could contribute virtually nothing because his income which, after income tax, was not more than £29,000 was absorbed by the expenses of Balmoral, Osborne and his farms at Windsor. He set down on paper at this time the injustice of that reduced allowance which he had been voted on first marrying the Queen, emphasising the claims on his liberality of Literature, Science, Art and Industry, adding, "I have felt very painfully that I was crippled in my means of usefulness to the country and to the throne".[1]

However, those responsible for the project of the Exhibition were relieved of the need for private bounty by the appointment of a Royal Commission, under the chairmanship of the Prince, to arrange for subscriptions, to secure the co-operation of local bodies and to work out all the details. To all the problems of the Exhibition the Prince addressed himself with meticulous care and

[1] Royal Archives.

the manufacturers, the foreigners and the colonists would never have rallied to the support of the scheme without his skilful shepherding. The pressure of work was enormous and under the strain of it the Queen noticed that he slept badly and "looks very ill of an evening".[1] The Vice-President of the Royal Commission did not exaggerate when he wrote that, without the Prince, "the whole thing would fall to pieces".[2]

There were two problems, the one arising from the other, which were especially vexatious. The Prince was, from the first, determined that the only setting for the Exhibition sufficiently dignified, central and expansive was Hyde Park. To this the *soi-disant* fashionables, as the Queen called them, who were presumably the canterers in the Row, took violent exception and, supported by extreme reactionaries, they concentrated objection on the building which they argued would permanently gash and disfigure the Park.

In the House of Commons a conservative colonel could solemnly say that "people living near Hyde Park would be well advised to keep a sharp look out after their silver spoons and forks", adding as something rather less valuable than these solid hall-marks of respectability "and their maidservants".[3]

In the House of Lords, Brougham, in his very best slap-stick style, espoused the cause of the residents near the Park whose rights were to be destroyed by the Prince and his venal body of advisers. He referred to "the absolute prostration of the understanding which takes place even in the minds of the bravest men when the word prince is mentioned in this country".[4] He estimated that 400 carts a day would pass through the fashionable residential quarters off the Kensington Road disturbing the solemn peace of the inhabitants, many of whom were judges.

Consequently, when Paxton designed an Exhibition hall of glass, which could be easily moved and comparatively easily put up, the Prince turned to it "as a drowning mariner turns to his

[1] Martin, ii, 243. [2] Martin, ii, 244. [3] Hansard. [4] Hansard.

cork belt ".[1] The glass house or, as Ruskin rudely called it, " the cucumber frame between two chimneys ", was not conceived by the Prince but his enthusiastic support for the design made its adoption certain.

Baulked of their main grievance the enemies of the Exhibition sought more fantastic objections. Foreign trash was to flood the country. The chastity of agricultural labourers was to be debauched by the temptations of London. Socialists and " men of the Red Colour ", as Brougham called them, would congregate in subversive masses round Hyde Park.

The Prince battled manfully with these absurd criticisms, meeting them with firmness and humour. The King of Prussia grew so alarmed at these imaginary dangers that he wished to stop his relations from coming to the Exhibition. To him Prince Albert wrote :

Mathematicians have calculated that the Crystal Palace will blow down in the first strong gale, Engineers that the galleries would crash in and destroy the visitors ; Political Economists have prophecied a scarcity of food in London owing to the vast concourse of people ; Doctors that owing to so many races coming into contact with each other the Black Death of the Middle Ages would make its appearance as it did after the Crusades ; Moralists that England would be infected by all the scourges of the civilised and uncivilised world ; Theologians that this second Tower of Babel would draw upon it the vengeance of an offended God.

I can give no guarantee against these perils, nor am I in a position to assume responsibility for the possibly menaced lives of your Royal relatives.[2]

Inevitable fears that the Roman Catholics would use the Exhibition for their own nefarious propaganda purposes were forthcoming. The Prime Minister wrote to the Prince that complaints had been expressed that Pugin, the distinguished architect, who was a Roman Catholic, had turned his Mediaeval Court into

[1] *1851 and the Crystal Palace*, by Christopher Hobhouse. John Murray, 1937.

[2] Jagow, *Letters*, p. 176.

a kind of advertising booth for Popery. The Prince replied that he had successfully prevented the Belgians from sending over a positive Madame Tussaud's Exhibition of the Pope and twelve cardinals (including Cardinal Wiseman) as an excuse for setting off the splendid intricacies of Brussels lace. He added, " but I cannot prevent crucifixes, *rosiers*, altar plate etc. etc. which form legitimate articles of trade. Those who object to their idolatrous character must be relieved to find Indian Pagodas and Chinese Idols in other parts of the Exhibition." [1]

But on May Day 1851 all the anxious preparations, the tribulations and the sneering were forgotten in the gorgeous and spectacular triumph of the opening ceremony. " Quite satisfactory " was the Prince's terse description of that day which the Queen, in her flamboyant style said, " made my heart swell with pride and glory and thankfulness." [2] The Prince, in the full-dress uniform of a Field-Marshal, and the Queen in a dress of pink watered silk, with their two eldest children, drove out from Buckingham Palace soon after half-past eleven. It was estimated by the police that there were 700,000 people between Buckingham Palace and the glass house, while inside the latter were over 30,000 people. The opening ceremony took place in the main transept, which was largely filled with rich hangings, statuary and coloured porcelain. The size of the building was emphasised by the large elm beneath whose ample shade the Royal Party was grouped. After the Prince, as Chairman of the Commissioners, had welcomed the Queen, the Royal Family processed round the building, though they noticed that in most of the bays the foreign exhibits were not unpacked. With the music of Handel and the voices of a vast choir ringing in their ears the Queen and Prince were deeply and strangely moved. Back at the Palace they came out on the balcony, which would appear to be the first occasion on which this was done by an English sovereign.

[1] Royal Archives. [2] Martin, ii, 364.

Against a solid background of machinery and raw materials were the inevitable oddities of every exhibition, the garden-seat for Osborne made out of coal, champagne made from rhubarb, the safety swimming swan for shipwrecks, the " char-volant " — a carriage drawn by kites, — a pulpit connected by gutta-percha tubes to the pews of the deaf, a doctor's walking-stick which contained an enema, a knife with 300 blades, Lord Eldon and his brother, in their judicial robes, carved from a single block of 20 tons of marble, a statue of Queen Victoria in zinc and a group of stuffed frogs, one holding up an umbrella, from Wurtemberg.

But it was none of these things which moved that stern and stolid generation to tears, which gave them the feeling, only magnified a thousandfold, of being in church. The Home Secretary, Charles Kingsley and many others were all in tears as they crossed the threshold of the glass house. The Prime Minister, as became a politician, shivered slightly as he entered for fear that the Conservatives might get back to power and break this prosperity from which the Exhibition sprang. A foreign friend of the Prince reflected with some sense that these Exhibitions were really the tournaments of the Middle Ages in modern dress. The Exhibition was above all a festival of peace — a proof of international friendship — and it was this which drew the tears to many a hardened old reprobate's eyes.

In sober language the Prince echoed these high hopes in a letter to the Prime Minister.

May 2, 1851

My dear Lord John

Many thanks for your letter and congratulations upon the wonderful success of yesterday. The sight was ample repaiment [*sic*] for any trouble during the last two years, but most I hope from the beneficial effects which the contemplation of the works brought together will have upon the different nations who contributed them.[1]

[1] Royal Archives.

A little later he wrote to Lord John that the sight of the Exhibition alone was " elevating to the national mind ".[1]

As is well known, the particular dream of brotherhood and universal peace which the Exhibition was to mark was rudely dispelled by the outbreak of the Crimean War three years later.

It is not, however, fanciful to suggest that the more lasting effects of the Exhibition lay not so much in the elevation of the national mind as in the aggrandisement of the national character. The Exhibition drove home to the public, in a way which was beyond the capacity of newspapers at that time, the character of their far-flung Empire, and the extent of the riches which could be drawn from it. The awe-inspiring majesty of the Crystal Palace in 1851 was the first step along the road of imperialist expansion — from Rotten Row to Majuba Hill, Omdurman and Mafeking.

Indeed, Thackeray, in the May Day ode with which he marked the Exhibition, seems to have caught something of that imperial ranting which was later to inspire Kipling :

Oh, awful is that crown of yours,
Queen of innumerable realms
Sitting beneath the budding elms
Of English May !

A wondrous sceptre 'tis to bear :
Strange mystery of God which set
Upon her brow yon coronet, —
The foremost crown

Of all the world, on one so fair !
That chose her to it from her birth,
And bade the sons of all the earth,
To her bow down.

After five months, during which just over six million people visited the Exhibition, the curtain was rung down, leaving the Commissioners with a handsome profit of £180,000. Yet the

[1] Royal Archives.

Exhibition was not the success on the intellectual side for which its promoters had hoped.[1] Nothing daunted, the Prince determined to carry on, with the surplus from the Exhibition, the ideals for which it had been promoted. When it was clear that there would be a substantial surplus he drew up a memorandum urging that four institutions for raw materials, machinery, manufacture and plastic art should be built in South Kensington. Each building was to have a library, a lecture room, a room for *conversaziones* and a miniature crystal palace for exhibitions. He also urged that public societies like the Geological, Botanical, Linnaean, Zoological, Royal Agricultural, Civil Engineers and Royal Societies should be housed on this site. As an indication of the strength of the Prince's feelings for the scheme, it is revealing that he noted down when a representative of the Government went to bid for the site, " May God speed him, that he may not have to pay too much ".[2]

The land was bought but the scheme did not thrive. In the emasculated version of the Prince's splendid plans with which the twentieth century is familiar, the site is covered with a sad jumble of museums and institutions. In South Kensington where much is dim and all is ugly, they are perhaps not out of place, but they should not be regarded as indicative of either the Prince's ideals or of his aspirations for an enlightened public taste. If something indicative of those is sought it will be found in the Crystal Palace, gay with the flags of all nations on that bright May morning in 1851, the inside relieved and diversified with countless examples of industry, ingenuity and ornament, and the whole fairy building vibrant as

> the people hum from floor to roof
> with Babel tongue.

[1] " As for the importance of the Great Exhibition it had none." This bold assertion by Mr. Christopher Hobhouse in his gay and sparkling book on the Exhibition might not command general support, but it is based on truth.

[2] Royal Archives.

CHAPTER X

CLIMAX OF HIS POWERS

As the Prince's life unwound to its sudden and unexpected ending his preoccupation with affairs and business became ever closer and more absorbing. In the last year of his life the Queen complained that he was so busy that she saw him " but very little in the day ".[1] As has already been explained — and as Stockmar had always foretold — he had become a European personality. Not only did the British Government avail itself of his guidance on all important issues of foreign politics, but his advice was sought and followed by the courts of Prussia, Belgium and Portugal, and his views did not fall on wholly deaf ears when they were unfolded before that bemused and sombre sovereign — the Emperor Napoleon III.

In private conversation with the Emperor he gave it as his opinion that the destinies of nations did not depend on armies and rulers but were really controlled by philosophers. The Emperor, more realistic, thought that dynasties and glory were all that the average citizen was capable of absorbing, and he illustrated this by recalling that the Empress Eugénie had been greeted in the South of France with cries of " Vive *Marie-Louise* ". Increasingly it became clear to the Prince that the Emperor, deaf to the prosaic lessons of philosophy, was bent on walking the crimson path of dynastic glory.

Frequent visits to France impressed on the Prince the scale of Napoleon's preparations for war. When he and the Queen were at Cherbourg in 1858 he sent for the Ministers in attendance and

[1] *Letters*, iii, 436.

pointed out to them the strength of the Cherbourg fortifications which had been revealed, in part, by the *feu de joie* with which the royal yacht had been welcomed. He added that this bristling fortress was a very great peril to England (*höchst verderblich*) demanding immediate counter-measures. At the end of the visit he said, "I am conscious of a change in the Emperor," [1] and he spoke of "the enormous crimes which he is meditating against Europe." [2]

This sense of an impending onslaught by the French coloured his entire outlook on European affairs. He felt in particular that the English Government was dangerously supine on the question of rearmament and, as he wrote to Stockmar, "we are constantly digging our spurs into their sides".[3] The very range of the Prince's knowledge gave him authority as is shown by the following letter written only eight weeks before he died.

BALMORAL
12th October 1861

MY DEAR LORD PALMERSTON

I am glad to see from your letter of the 7th instant that you keep up the steam about our defences. . . . With regard to the Enfield rifle, I do not know what the objection taken to it is. A greater strength in the barrel is all that I thought might be required; for, as regards range and accuracy of shooting, it goes far beyond the possible requirements of military service. If a change be contemplated, it will be worth considering whether we should not at once go to the breech-loaders. They are sure to carry the day eventually, and there are plenty of patents out which answer admirably. The breech-loading carbine of the cavalry is a most excellent weapon (it is W. Richards). We have tried it here after deer and found it very good. I have been shooting this year exclusively with Lancaster's breech loaders [4] and found the advantage in a hundred ways so great over the muzzle loading rifles that I shall quite abandon these. . . .

The simplification of the ammunition, dispensing with a separate

[1] Martin, iv, 275.
[2] *Paris Embassy during the Second Empire*, Wellesley. Butterworth, 1928.
[3] Martin, iv, 85.
[4] A gift from the Queen.

cap is another great advantage ; so is the power of loading in any position, without exposing oneself (stretched out in the heather, for instance).

The question of altering the bore of our muskets is, on the other hand, a most serious one, leading to mixture of ammunition, which would be fatal in military operations. We must have 220,000 Enfield rifle muskets out in the Army, 120,000 in the Militia and near 100,000 among the Volunteers — together somewhere about 400,000, and we have got about 300,000 in store, and must have several millions of cartridges made up.

One decided superiority *Whitworth's* rifle has over all others, and that is the more horizontal trajectory. All other long-range rifles throw their balls at high elevations so that the men are sure to miss by shooting over or under the object aimed at. . . .[1]

Richard Cobden, who was virtually a pacifist, said of the Prince's preoccupations with rearmament, "As for Prince Albert's rifle mania, that is pure Germanism in the disguise of British patriotism."[2] He was hinting that the Prince only wished to see England strong so that she could fall in behind the anti-French policy of Prussia, playing the part of a sturdy pawn in the Hohenzollern gambits. Certainly the Prince was on intimate terms with the Prussian Court, and strongly supported the idea of a united Germany under the lead of Prussia. He saw in Prussia a Liberal state — and this was of course before the rise of Bismarck — which had the power to influence the petty principalities and kingdoms of Germany away from the Catholic absolutism of Austria.

At the same time Napoleon was an obstacle to the unification of Germany. His lack-lustre gaze had long rested steadily on the Rhine as the desirable eastern frontier for his Empire. Consequently the idea of Germany unified into a strong single state was in opposition to his policy. To this extent an anti-French policy was automatically pro-German.

But the Prince was always justifiably indignant when he was

[1] Martin, v, 404. [2] Martin, v, 173.

accused of harnessing German policy to England. Certainly he was meticulous in trying to avoid this impression. He was apprehensive of Napoleon not for fear of the danger to Germany but because he knew, from many discussions with the Emperor, that he was allowing his mind to play with the bustle and glory of a general European war.

As early as 1857 the Emperor had broached to the Prince the possibility of a revision of the Treaties of 1815 by which the frontiers and peace of Europe were still bound. Most solemnly the Prince warned him of the dangers of any such policy. He pointed out that history proved that the objects with which a European war was started were never achieved and that the terms of peace with which such a war was ended were invariably far removed from the proclamations with which the belligerents had accompanied the unsheathing of their swords. In recording this interview the Prince wrote, " I begged him to open the book of history which lay before him ".[1] The intrigues of the Emperor, of which the Prince became increasingly conscious, saddened and alarmed him. " He has been born and bred a conspirator ", he wrote,[2] and to his brother he commented, " May God forgive the man who wantonly between sleep and waking is bringing so much unhappiness into the world ".[3] With the poet the Prince would have found it in his heart of hearts to say, " We love not this French God — this child of Hell ".

Against these apprehensions about Napoleon which, not without justification, loomed large in the Prince's mind, must be judged his last encounter with his old enemy Palmerston. This final combat centred round the prickly issue of Italian unity, a question which came to the boil in 1859 just as Palmerston, after a short conservative interregnum, returned to Downing Street. Lord John was his Foreign Secretary. At this time Palmerston was seventy-five, Russell was sixty-seven and this pair of elderly gentlemen proceeded to fasten on the Italian problem with gusto.

[1] Martin, iv, 104. [2] Martin, iv, 355. [3] Jagow, p. 323.

After fifteen years of squabbling and bickering between themselves, the two statesmen were able to bury the hatchet in the flesh and blood of the Risorgimento. "Those two dreadful old men",[1] as Queen Victoria called them, looked on Italy rather as a vivisectionist looks greedily on a rabbit's entrails. That country was to prove the truth of everything which Whiggery had thought, and wrought and taught. Poets took up the glory of the theme, and historians, glancing back with nepotic affection to Lord Macaulay, sought to prove that Italian revolutions all redounded to the greater glory of England in 1688. The Prince, who lacked the insular Whiggery of Lord John and the Macaulay family, may, therefore, be pardoned, and should not be indiscriminately blamed, for looking at this question without ideological bias but as a question of practical politics.

By the end of the 1850's it was tolerably clear that without foreign help the Italians were insufficiently strong to expel the Austrians from Northern Italy. That expulsion was plainly the first preliminary step to the unification of the independent principalities and kingdoms of which Italy was composed. The strongest of these kingdoms was Piedmont, ruled by a clever but sensual sovereign — Victor Emmanuel — who was advised by a statesman of great ability and penetration — Cavour. By 1859 Napoleon — not unmindful that the first laurels of his uncle had been won in Italy — showed by wanton insults to the Austrians that he was ready to take a hand in driving them from Italy by force of arms. In this he was partially successful by the two bloody battles of Solferino and Magenta which were fought in the summer of 1859. At this juncture Palmerston and Russell took office, and they at once sought to push the whole weight of English influence behind Napoleon and the Italians. Trenchantly, but fairly, the Prince explained to the Prince of Prussia how the Italian issue was viewed by himself and English public opinion.

[1] E. L. Woodward, *Age of Reform*.

I personally still fail to believe that the Corporate State in Italy, brought into being by revolution, civil war, treachery and invasion, can prove a success. Here, however, enthusiasm is so high that such a view is regarded as high treason. . . . The deep horror at the long misgovernment of Rome and Naples, which Austrian pressure alone has made possible since 1816, is the thing which causes the nation to shout aloud for Liberty, and dulls every other feeling or consideration.[1]

Almost immediately the Court began to titivate Lord John's despatches and even to reject them outright. A few weeks after the formation of Palmerston's Government, the Prince took the remarkable step of asking Lord Granville, who was a member of the Cabinet as Lord President, to keep him informed of all discussions in the Cabinet on the Italian question.[2] This, which might be called the highest form of espionage, was a step of very doubtful propriety and prudence. The length to which these confidential reports went is illustrated by an event later in the year. The " two old ringleaders ", as Clarendon called Russell and Palmerston, were determined to appoint Sir James Hudson as the British plenipotentiary to the Congress in Paris which was to settle the Italian issue. As a young man Hudson had been assistant private secretary to King William IV and was the messenger who dashed across Europe in 1834 to call back Sir Robert Peel when the King unexpectedly dismissed the Whig Government. As minister to the court of King Victor Emmanuel he had betrayed violent sympathy with the unity of Italy. The Queen and Prince absolutely refused to countenance his appointment. In describing the meeting of the Cabinet which discussed this imbroglio, Lord Granville wrote to the Prince that Lord John asked—

whether he was to inform Her Majesty that the Cabinet were of opinion that Sir James Hudson was the fittest person . . . or whether he should acquiesce in Her Majesty's commands, reserving his own

[1] Jagow, p. 352.
[2] *Life of Lord Granville*, by Fitzmaurice. Longmans, 1905.

opinion as to the fitness of Sir James. The chancellor answered " undoubtedly the second course will be the best ". I then stated my reasons, or rather repeated them, for objecting to Sir James Hudson. Mr. Gladstone made a hesitating remark. Sir G. Lewis and the Duke of Argyle, Sir Charles Wood and Sir George Grey — the latter very strongly — supported the second course. . . . Lord Palmerston spoke with some temper and dogmatically as to who were right and who were wrong, but advised Lord John to take the second course.[1]

Considering that no official record of Cabinet discussions was then kept this letter is astonishing in its disregard for that secrecy with which the doctrine of collective Cabinet responsibility was invested. The only possible excuse for such a correspondence was the fear of the Prince that Palmerston and Russell were leading the country towards war and the knowledge that a majority of their Cabinet colleagues were opposed to their policy.

Certainly Lord John was outrageously difficult. In one of his letters to the Queen he suddenly introduced a paean of praise for the doctrines of the Revolution of 1688 in reply to a question from the Queen whether Sardinia was to be asked to refrain from interference in the affairs of central Italy. With some warmth the Queen replied, thanking him for his note in which " she is not able to find any answer to her letter. . . . The Queen cannot make out what the doctrines of the Revolution of 1688 can have to do with this."[2] From this high-falutin nonsense Lord John passed to positive rudeness, telling the Queen flatly that he was unwilling to obtrude his advice on her, and that " the liberation of the Italian people from a foreign yoke is, in the eyes of Lord Palmerston and Lord John Russell, an increase of freedom and happiness at which as well-wishers to mankind they cannot but rejoice ". This letter, with a touch of Elizabethan spirit, Queen Victoria refused to accept, sending it back to Lord Palmerston with the remark that it lacked " the respect which is due from a Minister to his sovereign ".[3] Lord John grumbled and groused but gave

[1] *Letters*, iii, 377. [2] *Letters*, iii, 383, 384. [3] *Letters*, iii, 388.

way. To Sidney Herbert he had said a few weeks previously, " we might as well live under a despotism." [1] At the end of the year the Prince Consort summed up the position.

All his [Lord Palmerston's] old tricks of 1848 and the previous period are revived again. Having Lord John Russell at the Foreign Office, whose inefficiency in the office (save for Italy) and fear of Lord Palmerston, makes him a ready tool and convenient ally ; he [Palmerston] tries to carry on a policy of revenge against Austria and to bind us to the Emperor Napoleon more than ever, regardless of all the interests of England or Europe, and if impeded by the Cabinet or the Queen he is violent and overbearing, and if this be of no avail cheats and tricks. He has taken towards the Crown quite his old position of 1851 before he was dismissed by Lord John, has again pamphlets written against me and the Coburg influence in order to bear down all opposition.[2]

In spite of this, most of the thunder of the Court rolled round the head of the unhappy Lord John. Only once was there an open breach between Queen and Prime Minister. In the summer of 1861 Palmerston was anxious to appoint Sir Henry Layard as Under-Secretary at the Foreign Office. Layard, by training a solicitor, deserted that honourable calling for some much publicised excavations at Nineveh and in his public career was greatly assisted by the friendship of the editor of *The Times*. In reply to Palmerston's suggestion the Queen simply wrote, " In the contact with foreign countries we should be represented only by thorough gentlemen ", adding that if Palmerston would otherwise resign she would accept Layard as " the lesser of two evils ".[3]

Writing back to the Queen, Palmerston described this as " Your Majesty's gracious and condescending acquiescence ". He continued in his best sarcastic style to refer to the " most sincere pain " which he always felt when differing from the Queen and that he always distrusted " the value of his own conclusions when they differ from those to which your Majesty has

[1] Granville, i, 357. [2] Royal Archives. [3] Royal Archives.

arrived ".[1] The Prince sent the whole correspondence to Lord Granville with the comment that " Lord Palmerston's flattery is uncalled for and offensive to delicate feelings ".[2]

Nonetheless, it is characteristic of the generosity of Palmerston's temperament and of his capacity for desensitising the pricks and rubs of public life that a few weeks after this, when the Prince was lying mortally ill, he insisted on the very best medical advice being sought, adding, " This is a matter of the most momentous national importance, and all considerations of personal feeling and susceptibilities must absolutely give way to the public interest." [3] The Prince would have highly valued this tribute from his redoubtable antagonist and, in particular, the suggestion that his work for the Queen was of " momentous national importance ".

Certainly his labour was unremitting and the Queen has enshrined for posterity her recollections of him at work. In the morning they were called at 7 by a wardrobe-maid. The Prince got up almost at once, put on a dressing-gown and went straight to his sitting-room where a green lamp was lighted on his desk, the quills were sharpened and all inanimate objects beckoned the labourer to toil. Unlike the Queen he felt the cold, and latterly he wore a wig indoors. He generally worked with a fire of which — except in winter — the Queen disapproved.[4] Writing to his eldest daughter one September he said, " Mama will be much hurt when she gets up and finds that I have had a fire lit ".[5] During what he called " this golden morning hour " [6] he wrote his letters and most of the drafts for the Queen which he would bring to her saying, " Here is a draft I have done for you. Read it. I should think it would do." [7] Having dressed — and he always wore the ribband of the Garter under his waistcoat — he would have breakfast at 9, during which he would read *The Times*.

[1] *Letters*, iii, 446.
[2] Royal Archives.
[3] Martin, v, 435.
[4] Royal Archives.
[5] Martin, iv, 303.
[6] Martin, iv, 303.
[7] Martin, v, 273.

Like thousands of Victorian *paterfamiliases* he would call out to the Queen or his children, "Don't disturb me — I am busy reading".[1]

Thus fortified he would discuss with his secretarial staff the business of the day and the Queen would hear him striding down the corridor or running upstairs. The lethargic corpulence, to which some writers have attributed his early death, was never in evidence in his movements which to the last betrayed the hurry and bustle of his nervous temperament.

One characteristic of the Prince which perhaps most sharply distinguished him from those nurtured in the English tradition was that he sought work. Englishmen of that period — and particularly the politicians — were inclined to leave a knotty problem to sort itself out, or to the dissolving charms of a glass of port wine sipped round the dinner-table by candle-light. Not so the Prince. He liked all problems to be caught within the orderly media of drafts and memoranda and formal discussions. When the English Cabinet took over the Government of India he set out very clearly what he expected as the following letter, based on his draft, shows.

All despatches, when received and perused by the Secretary of State, to be sent to the Queen. They may be merely forwarded in boxes from the Office without being accompanied by any letter from the Secretary of State, unless he should think an explanation necessary. No draft of instructions or orders to be sent out without having been previously submitted to the Queen. The label on the boxes of the office containing such drafts to be marked "For Approval".

In the cases of Civil appointments the Secretary of State will himself take the Queen's pleasure before communicating with the gentlemen to be appointed.

Copies or a précis of the Minutes of the Council to be regularly transmitted to the Queen.

The Secretary of State to obtain the Queen's sanction to important measures previously to his bringing them before the Council for discussion.[2]

[1] Martin, iv, 274. [2] *Letters*, iii, 299.

A little later, in a letter to the Secretary of State for India, he evolved the surprising doctrine that " the Civil Servants are the Queen's servants and not the servants of the Government ".[1]

One result of the Prince's anxiety that the Queen should be fully apprised of what was going on in all branches of the Government was that the volume of work flowing in to palace and castle was prodigious. Only a man of the first ability could have usefully tackled this work. Anyone with the mentality of a clerk could have scanned the papers, but only a man of the keenest intellect could have maintained, on an infinite variety of subjects, the steady jet of comment, deletion and criticism to which the papers were subjected. No doubt on many subjects the Prince's judgment was awry. In trivial matters, for example, he was capable of believing that Disraeli had bribed *The Times*,[2] and he seriously proposed that after the Indian Mutiny the Queen should be called " The Great Mogul ".[3] On graver topics he was too ready to attribute the darkest motives to men like Napoleon and Palmerston whom he had never understood. Too frequently such figures as these became to him " Gorgons and Hydras, and Chimaeras dire ".

Yet all who came under the force of his mind were compelled — often in spite of tenacious prejudices — to admire his intellect and to agree with its reasoning. Those who persist in regarding the Prince as a species of hard-working clerk only do so by flouting the evidence. In private conversation with a friend, Lord Granville — and few men knew the working of the Government machine better than he — said of the Prince :

His knowledge and information are astonishing, and there is not a Department of the Government regarding all the details and management of which he is not much better informed and more capable than the Minister at the head of it. In foreign affairs particularly he has prevented a great deal of mischief and kept the Government out of innumerable scrapes.[4]

[1] *Letters*, iii, 399.
[2] Royal Archives.
[3] Granville, i, 260.
[4] Greville, vii, 304, 305.

Similar sentiments, though expressed with the more glittering language of his race, were uttered by Disraeli.

> With Prince Albert — he told the Russian Ambassador — we have buried our sovereign. This German Prince has governed England for twenty-one years with a wisdom and energy such as none of our Kings have ever shown. . . . If he had outlived some of our "old stagers" he would have given us, while retaining all constitutional guarantees, the blessings of absolute government.[1]

The reasoning of the last sentence is facile but dubious. It ranks with the *cliché* (beloved by the professional historian) that if the Prince Consort had lived there must have developed a clash between Crown and Cabinet. The tides of history have drawn the English monarchy far from the deep waters of political power and it is a mistake — at once easy and prevailing — to judge the events of 1840 to 1860 in the light of that knowledge. There were, in fact, two important influences, apart from the character of either the Prince or the Queen, which combined during those two decades to magnify the political influence of the English Crown. The first was the weakness and confusion of parties during the period and the lack of any really lively party issue. The second was the importance of foreign politics at a time when the new dynasties of the Teutonic system of Monarchy were becoming firmly established. As Palmerston once expressed it, the advantage of royalty dealing with royalty on questions of foreign policy was that "The Prince can say many things which we can not". "Very naturally", was Queen Victoria's laconic comment on this remark.[2] The old Catholic sovereigns still clung precariously to the southern fringes of Europe: otherwise the new dynasties were everywhere. "This amazing breed of idols", to revert to Mr. H. G. Wells's trenchant phrase, were not the less amazing because they had the power to move and chat, filling the European stage with a divine company splendid in affluence,

[1] Moneypenny and Buckle, *Life of Disraeli*, 1929, vol. ii, 117.

[2] Martin, iv, 95.

deportment and mutual adulation. In that magic circle Great Britain had to find a place, and it was fortunate for her and vital for the political importance of the monarchy that the Queen and Prince were virtually the centre of the throng. The change which had come over monarchy is illustrated by recalling that King George III never left England in his life and, apart from family intimates, scarcely entertained visiting foreigners. Greville — ever a sensitive observer — noticed the change at once. " We are overrun with visiting royalties present and prospective ", he wrote in 1857. " It is a new feature of the present day, the flitting about of royal personages." [1]

The celebration of the Princess Royal's marriage further showed the family and dynastic ties by which Europe was linked. *The Times* set out the names of royal persons attending the Ball at Buckingham Palace, held in honour of this event. Apart from thirteen members of the English Royal Family, those present consisted of

> The King of the Belgians, the Duke of Brabant, the Count of Flanders, the Prince and Princess Frederick William of Prussia, the Prince and Princess of Prussia, Prince Albert of Prussia, Prince Frederick Charles of Prussia, Prince Frederick Albert of Prussia, Prince Adalbert of Prussia, the Prince of Hohenzollern Sigmaringen, the Duke of Saxe-Coburg-Gotha, the Duchess of Orleans, the Comte de Paris, the Duc de Chartres, the Princess of Salerno, the Duke and Duchess d'Aumale, Prince Edward of Saxe-Weimar, the Prince of Leiningen, Prince Victor of Hohenlohe Langenburg and Prince Julius of Holstein Glücksburg.

Against this contemporary background, and not in relation to future developments, the political influence of the Crown under the Prince must be set and judged. Then it will be seen that the events of European history ineluctably magnified the political stature of the English sovereign. To argue from these premises that the ability of the Prince was guiding the monarchy

[1] Greville, vii, 292 and 294.

into absolutism or into a position where a clash with politicians was certain is to ignore the facts. Admittedly he was determined that the sovereign, as represented by Queen Victoria, should not become, in Stockmar's phrase, " a mandarin figure, which has to nod its head in assent, or shake it in denial, as its Minister pleases ".[1] His object was to increase the prestige and popularity of the Crown by lifting it above the squabbles of party and by investing it with the glamour of morality — a virtue which still retained something of its stern attractions. Stockmar, ever the master of a stylish phrase, described this as " moral oil for the driving wheels of the constitutional machine ".[2] The Prince was not aiming at autocracy or absolutism : he rather saw the sovereign as a partner with the Cabinet — a partner whose special province was vigilance and cautionary advice.

The following letter, prepared by the Prince for the Queen to send to the Foreign Secretary, is a characteristic example of how the principle worked.

BUCKINGHAM PALACE
May 1st 1858

The Queen has received a draft from Lord Cowley on the Danish question which she cannot sanction as submitted to her. The question is a most important one and a false step on our part may produce a war between France and Germany. The Queen would wish Lord Malmesbury to call on her in the course of to-morrow when the Prince could discuss the matter with him more fully.[3]

He did not hesitate to express disagreement with the Government but as he always gave sound reasons to back his opinion he did not, with most men, incur hostility. For example, he wrote to the Prime Minister in the last year of his life :

There is no doubt in my mind, as to the future immense value of the interior of Africa, and it is on that account amongst others that I regret so much the policy followed by the Government in establishing free Republics in rear of our Colony of the Cape, which cut it off

[1] Martin, ii, 547. [2] Martin, ii, 550. [3] *Letters*, iii, 280.

entirely from the interior, and place between us and it a foreign race bent on exterminating the natives rather than civilizing them.[1]

There was to be no obtrusion of the Crown, still less a clash with the politicians, for as the Prince himself expressed it, "*silent* influence is precisely that which operates the greatest and widest good".[2]

One faithful heart at least was beating in loyal gratitude for all that her lord and master had achieved. Writing to her uncle in 1858 the Queen said:

> To-morrow is the eighteenth anniversary of my blessed marriage which has brought such universal blessings on the country and Europe! For what has not my beloved and perfect Albert done? Raised monarchy to the *highest* pinnacle of respect, and rendered it popular beyond what it *ever* was in this country.[3]

Yet one of the oddest and most persistent legends about the Prince is that he was miserably unhappy and that he drifted into death with a kind of contented abandon as a happy release from the toil and miseries of the world. Strachey set the pace for this romance by saying that the Prince "believed that he was a failure and he began to despair".[4] For this there is no evidence whatever. King Leopold wrote to the Queen after the Prince's death a letter which, making every allowance for the King's constitutional capacity for suave exaggeration, is revealing. He says:

> He certainly had all that England can give, and on this globe it is the most complete; he had reached the difficult point of being fully acknowledged what he was — the superior man of all. He told me when my old friend the Duke was still alive, how fond they are in England to have an authority to quote. . . . He had become that authority, and for a mind like his it was a real satisfaction. Few human beings could be said to have been in possession of so much.[5]

Admittedly, like all who engage in politics and seek to follow the flickering light of ideals, he suffered searing disappointments.

[1] Royal Archives. [2] Martin, ii, 469.
[3] *Letters*, iii, 264. [4] Strachey, p. 209. [5] Royal Archives.

"Immorality"—he once observed—"is everywhere in the ascendant and, therefore, nothing can come right."[1] He was irritated by the antics of Napoleon, and he gave free rein to his irritation in writing to his intimates, but these are counter-balanced by references to the satisfactory state of home politics and to his happiness in his family circle.

Admittedly, too, he was prone to complain of ill health and overwork. An attack of toothache was described in a letter to Stockmar as "my sufferings are frightful".[2] During these closing years there are constant references in his letters to the Princess Royal and to Stockmar to the unrelenting pressure of work. Writing from Osborne in the early summer of 1860 to the Princess Royal he says:

> Your letter has found me in the enjoyment of the most glorious air, the most fragrant odours, the merriest choirs of birds and the most luxuriant verdure; and were there not so many things that reminded one of the so called World (that is to say of miserable men) one might abandon oneself wholly to the enjoyment of the real world. There is no such good fortune, however, for poor me; and this being so one's feelings remain under the influence of the treadmill of never-ending business. The donkey in Carisbrooke, which you will remember, is my true counterpart. He too, would rather munch thistles in the Castle Moat than turn round in the wheel at the Castle Well; and small are the thanks he gets for his labour.[3]

A very human letter—such as scores of public men might write without drawing on their heads the implication that they were in despair. As he himself was never tired of saying, "Genuine happiness is only to be found in work." Indeed it is ludicrous to label a man miserable who in the closing months of his life could write of his twenty-one years in England: "We have only to thank God that he has vouchsafed so much happiness to us".[4] John Brown, whose comments on his royal employers were always expressed with Highland frankness, said of the Prince to

[1] Martin, ii, 323.
[2] Martin, v, 295.
[3] Martin, v, 109.
[4] Jagow, p. 359.

the Queen, " Its very pleasant to walk with a person who is always content." [1]

Nor are there any grounds for supposing that he was depressed because he was a failure or, as is frequently argued, because he was not appreciated in England, though it is easy to see how this particular legend took root. The Queen with her generous, chivalrous nature was heart-broken — especially after the Prince's death — that the public was ignorant of all that he had done to help her and to stablish the monarchy. He had always contrived to let her have the credit for everything he did ; he had always acted in the sense of his memorandum to the Duke of Wellington that his position required that " the husband should sink his *own individual* existence in that of his wife ".[2] With poignancy she grieved that not only was his work unappreciated but that he had been consistently underrated and misunderstood. But those feelings were hers, not his. The good graces of the multitude he never sought : indeed he deliberately shunned them. Nor was he depressed by the attacks on himself in the newspapers. When he was made Prince Consort in 1857 *The Times* had a most offensive leading article saying that it was hoped that the new dignity might lead to increased respect for its illustrious holder " on the banks of the Spree and the Danube ". The Prince merely observed that this sneering article was a poor return for the generosity of the Court in giving the news exclusively to *The Times*.[3] He was amused by the caricatures and lampoons about himself of which he made a fine collection for, as the Queen noticed, he enjoyed a joke nonetheless for being the subject of it.[4] Nor did he ever betray any sign that he was embittered by the savage attacks on him in 1854, for, as he observed to Stockmar, he felt " no spirit of petty complaint over what I am quite able to bear calmly." [5]

[1] *Leaves from the Journal of our Life in the Highlands*, p. 132.
[2] Martin, ii, 260.
[3] Martin, iv, 65.
[4] Martin, ii, 298.
[5] Martin, ii, 541.

Those writers who persist in portraying the Prince Consort as broken-hearted by the indifference of the public, as a mature specimen of the hero of *Misunderstood*, have never asked themselves the reason for the Prince's unpopularity. The reason is not far to seek. His English contemporaries suspected — and they were perfectly right — that the Prince never liked them. They recognised all his virtues but they saw that the man who served them so well had — apart from his own family — left his heart with his own people.[1]

As a young man his reserve and coldness had made an unfavourable impression, and advancing years did little to soften those feelings. Discreet, dogmatic and a doctrinaire, he lacked the lightness of touch and inconsequence which even in the solemnity of the mid-Victorian Age an Englishman liked and understood. Bagehot — one of the shrewdest minds of the nineteenth century, — who had an unqualified admiration for the Prince, and in particular for the balance of his political judgment, put his finger on the flaw in the Prince's make-up which was peculiarly damaging in English eyes when he said, " He had not the knack of dropping seed without appearing to sow it." [2]

Possibly more serious for his good standing with the English was his sense of humour. He had, said one of his equerries, " Unmistakeable marks of the snark." [3] That creature, it will be recalled, was remarkable for its slowness in taking a jest and it always looked grave at a pun. This is not quite true of the Prince because it has with sorrow to be confessed that he particularly enjoyed evolving a pun — that mirthless manifestation of Victorian humour. When there was some discussion about putting up a statue of King Richard I, the Prince observed that English people had transferred their affection from Richard Cœur de Lion to Richard Cœur de Cotton (Richard Cobden).

1 This argument is well developed in the *Spectator* for December 12th, 1874.

2 The *Economist*, November 4th, 1878.

3 *Henry Ponsonby*, by Arthur Ponsonby. Macmillan, 1942.

Certainly he was not without humour and, being an admirable mimic, he used to keep the family circle in fits of laughter by copying the mannerisms of Highlanders or people he had known as a boy at Coburg. Nor was he lacking in a spark of malicious humour, as when he announced at a family luncheon, "I have just been looking at the Queen without any clothes." Everybody, including the Queen, who was swathed in the ample garb of Victorian womanhood, was slightly startled till he explained that he had been to see a statue of the Queen in its preliminary stages.[1] Of the same order of humour was his remark when the Emperor Napoleon came to Windsor, "I shall have to have precautions taken in the crypt of St. George's Chapel to see that George III does not turn in his grave."[2] Lord Malmesbury, a frequent minister in attendance at Court, who had ample opportunity to judge, said that the Prince had "a great fund of humour *quand il se déboutonne* ".[3] But where his humour was defective, in English opinion, was that he kept it absolutely distinct from his work. To his work he brought one side of his personality — the grave, laborious, patient, solemn thinker to whom wit was anathema — the characteristic of that flippancy in the English temperament which he detested. This elevation of business into the realm of high endeavour — this habit of approaching the writing-table as if it were the pew in church, was characteristically German, and made him appear snark-like to all with whom he worked. Nonetheless, to appraise the Prince fairly it is important not to judge him by the standards of an Englishman's foibles and prejudices. Above all it is important not to argue as Lytton Strachey does, that because he lacked a certain lightness of touch he was "miserable", and because he was solemn he was "sick at heart".[4] Judgments of that type — though it is easy to see how antipathetic the Prince was to a man of Strachey's stimulating

[1] Royal Archives. [2] Jagow, p. 230.
[3] Malmesbury, *Memoirs of an Ex-Minister.* Longmans, 1884.
[4] Lytton Strachey, p. 208.

PHOTOGRAPH AFTER THE MARRIAGE OF THE PRINCESS ROYAL, WHO IS STANDING BY THE QUEEN

In the back row, from left to right, are Prince Frederick of Prussia, Prince Consort, Prince Alfred, Prince of Wales, King Leopold

wit and brilliant subtlety of character — are as misleading as the golden haze of adoration with which the Queen has blurred the outlines of his personality, through which we see him dimly as a cross between King Arthur and an Admirable Crichton.

Even in private life he was capable of somewhat pompous moralisings. For example, it has been whispered that he fell slightly in love with the Empress Eugénie and the Queen wrote in her Journal, " Albert who is seldom much pleased with ladies or princesses, is very fond of her and her great ally ".[1] Yet in writing to Stockmar of the friendship between the two Courts, which enshrined this perfectly innocent attachment, he used the portentous phrase, " Our relation rests upon an honourable, moral basis ".[2] Few men can have had a greater command of the bromide than had the Prince ; the obvious fell from his pen in soporific profusion. Of his son-in-law at the time of his marriage he could write, " Many of the books of life lie open to him which before were closed ",[3] and to his daughter he could write, " Thus you can both consciously work for good, and what can mankind desire more ? "[4] Reading these sentences and countless others like them the reader is almost impelled to the conclusion that the Prince Consort must have been rather like a Victorian Archdeacon at the luncheon-table on Sunday. Yet this would leave out of account the personality and character which lay behind these expressions of the obvious and which cannot now be recaptured. An example from more modern times may serve to illustrate this point. To read a speech of Lord Grey of Fallodon was not dissimilar from conning the pages of a child's copy-book : to hear the speech was to be transported into a world rich with dignity and common sense, strong with principle and integrity. Such also was the experience of the Queen and her family, who knew the character which lay behind the preacher. Though she may be deemed excessively partial, the Queen was

[1] Quoted in Martin, iv, 95.
[2] Martin, iv, 99.
[3] Jagow, p. 341.
[4] Jagow, p. 358.

not far from the truth when she wrote of him to the mentor of the Coburg family, " He is very very great. . . . His greatness is wonderfully combined with abnegation of self, with humility, with great courage — with such kindness too, and goodness. . . ." [1] But perhaps most convincing of all is the verdict of Lady Ponsonby, who, through her husband's position at Court, had ample opportunities for judging. A woman of almost masculine clarity of mind, an advanced Radical with the fearlessness and originality of her Grey ancestry, she was the first person to write with perfect frankness about Queen Victoria.[2] Flattery or adulation was not in her composition. With shrewdness she observed,

> the qualities of the Prince's character would place him, I think, on a far higher level than those of his mind. Unselfish, patient, kind-hearted, truthful and just, one felt it was possible to rely upon him as upon a strong rock.[3]

She goes on to say that his manner was " the least pleasing thing about him ", and that the typical smart Englishman could not shake off the feeling that he was talking to a foreign professor. This was exacerbated by the shyness of the Prince, and it is recorded that when he met a distinguished American writer — Motley, the author of *The Rise of the Dutch Republic* — he could not get on terms of equality but kept on discussing humdrum affairs, till the poor American decided that never in the long history of mankind had more been made of the weather.[4] Nervousness also made the Prince speak with a much more marked foreign accent when talking to strangers.[5]

He found his recreation not in conventional pleasures — not in the club-house, the spirit bottle or the excitements of feminine friendships — not even in reading, but in the indulgence of his

[1] Martin, ii, 390. [2] See *Quarterly Review*, vol. 193.

[3] *Mary Ponsonby*, by M. Ponsonby. Murray, 1927.

[4] *Correspondence of J. L. Motley*, edited by G. W. Curtis. John Murray, 1889. [5] Martin, iv, 10.

aesthetic sense and in the company of his wife and family. Here the true measure of the Prince's character and greatness is to be found, because his home life did not run so smoothly as those reading the Queen's description of it might imagine.

The Queen, though she was, as he expressed it, " a delightful companion ", was not always easy. The conventional portrait of the Queen as a clinging, adoring wife, bowed in abject submission to the slightest whim and gesture of her lord and master, is derived more from her imagination than from the facts. Human beings are not capable of suddenly altering their character, of levelling flat the hills and valleys of individuality in response to the wishes of another. Although the Prince smoothed out the narrowness and prejudice of the Queen's mind, the vigour and tenacity of her character remained. Though it would be an exaggeration to say of Queen Victoria, as old Mrs. Carlyle said of her son, " thou's gey ill to live wi' ", her temperament, which was anxious, nervous and emotional, did not create a placid background for domestic life. She was inclined to fasten with her whole being on any project which she wanted to carry out to an extent which was almost unbalanced. For example, she once wrote to a member of the royal secretariat about something she wanted done, " She has been thinking of it continually, day and night ".[1]

The Prince made a tactful reference to this side of the Queen's temperament in a letter to his eldest daughter when he wrote :

> For your Mama, who lives much in the past and future, perhaps more than in the present, it is a spiritual necessity to cling to moments that are flown and to recollections, and to form plans for the future. . . . This carries her, of course, into the realm of hopes and apprehensions.[2]

When her hopes were disappointed or her apprehensions loomed large she was inclined to break out with lamentations which were petulant and exaggerated.

[1] Martin, v, 218. [2] Royal Archives.

Like all women of spirit and character she found it almost impossible to argue with him she loved. Starting to complain of something which provoked her, she would suddenly be convulsed in a paroxysm of tears. In order to get round this difficulty the Prince urged that she should put down on paper anything that was bothering her. " When you have causes of complaint, uneasiness, distresses etc. etc. don't keep them to yourself—afraid to bring them out, and if you cannot speak upon them write." [1] Not the least touching of the characteristics of the Queen was her appreciation of her own temperament. " My nature is too passionate, my emotions are too fervent ", she wrote to an intimate friend, " he guided and protected me, he comforted and encouraged me." [2]

Never was this guidance and comfort shown to better advantage than in the spring of 1861 when the Queen had the misfortune to lose her mother, the Duchess of Kent. This amiable Duchess — for such in old age she became — died at the age of seventy-four, peacefully and without prolonged suffering. Her death was naturally an occasion for sorrow, for the lingering memories of former days, but not for abandoned grief. Yet the Queen indulged her sorrow to an extent which was almost hysterical. A fortnight after her mother's death she was writing with morbid gusto of " the *weeping*, which day after day is my welcome friend ".[3] King Leopold, to whom this was written, was not the soul of discretion and either through him or through Stockmar the rumour flashed through the Courts of Europe that, like her grandfather, King George III, the Queen had become unhinged in her mind. The Queen never knew this scandal, but the Prince did and naturally he was distressed beyond measure.[4]

[1] Memorandum of the Prince to the Queen. Royal Archives. For the practice of the Queen and Prince in exchanging memoranda on personal matters, see also *The Queen thanks Sir Howard*, by McClintock. John Murray.

[2] Bolitho, *Further Letters of Queen Victoria*, p. 127.

[3] *Letters*, iii, 437.

[4] Bolitho, *Victoria and Albert*, p. 160.

Never did he show himself more patient and understanding than in his efforts to assuage the Queen's grief. Months later, when the Court was at Balmoral and about to set out for Windsor, where the Duchess had died, the Queen sent across a memorandum to the Prince grieving over the prospect of a return to Windsor. He replied :

BALMORAL
Oct. 22nd 1861

I can give you a very good certificate this time and am pleased to witness with you your own improvement.

What I can do to contribute to your getting over the painful sensations which a return to Windsor under such sadly altered circumstances will be readily and cheerfully done. My advice to be less occupied with yourself and your own feelings is really the kindest I can give, for pain is felt chiefly by dwelling on it and can thereby be heightened to an *unbearable extent*. This is not hard philosophy, but common sense supported by common and general experience. If you will take increased interest in things unconnected with personal feelings, you will find the task much lightened of governing those feelings in general which you state to be your great difficulty in life. God's assistance and support will not fail you in your endeavour.[1]

Not even the stilted English of this paper can hide the sympathy, the devotion and the deep understanding of character which obtrude themselves in every line. Indeed, in the far greater sorrow to which the Queen was unsuspectingly advancing these words brought her abiding comfort and solace, fortifying her to fight against the self-indulgence of grief.

This sombre side of their relationship only serves to set off the gaiety and happiness which bound them together. While it may be considered slightly mawkish of the Queen to have revealed as fully as she did the domestic bliss of her married life, she did this because she saw that the key to a full understanding of the Prince's character was his complete unselfishness and his consideration for her. One example from the many revelations of the Queen may

[1] Royal Archives.

suffice. When the Princess Royal was married and was saying farewell to her parents they were — as is the hard lot of parents on such occasions — profoundly moved. The Prince perhaps felt it more than did the Queen. He was accompanying the bride and bridegroom on part of their journey and as he was starting he went up to the Queen and whispered, "I grieve so much to leave you." [1]

In dedicating to his memory her "Journal of Our Life in the Highlands" the Queen refers to his having made her life "bright and happy". Indeed all the slightly unconventional things which the Queen most enjoyed — the Christmas parties for staff and family, the excursions abroad, the expeditions incognita and the easy familiarity with the Highlanders — sprang from the Prince. In the superb language of Lytton Strachey, "a kind of glory, a radiance as of an unearthly holiness, seemed to glow about these golden hours".[2] Queen and Prince were in truth abundantly happy and they even contrived to squeeze some warmth and enjoyment out of the cold formalities of their official life. On one occasion when a new Russian Ambassador was presented to the Queen on appointment he mistook the Prince, who was present, for a lord-in-waiting. Suddenly realising his blunder he spun round to the Prince saying, "Comment, c'est vous." The Queen and Prince were convulsed with laughing.[3] When the Prince, resplendent in his robes as Chancellor of Cambridge University, delivered a formal address of congratulation to the Queen on the marriage of the Princess Royal, the Queen received his address standing and the onlookers were quick to note the look of amusement which passed between them. At a levee they abandoned all attempt at self-control when a clergyman, overcome with fright, passed them without obeisance. The Lord Chamberlain tried to make him go back and do it properly, but the poor man, thoroughly flustered, stood copying the Lord

[1] Martin, iv, 168. [2] Strachey, p. 194.
[3] Lord Malmesbury, *Memoirs of an Ex-Minister*.

Chamberlain's gestures, which he thought were in some way a necessary part of the formalities.[1]

Although it does not accord with the popular conception of the Prince Consort, he was most at his ease and most relaxed in the company of his children. We see him in the closing months of his life playing with the infant Princess Beatrice ; he would envelop her in one of those vast, well laundered, Victorian dinner-napkins, lift her up as if she were in a hammock and swing her through his legs ; the child would shout with glee, while the Duchess of Kent stood by chuckling in her rich guttural German laughter. Always on New Year's Eve there was a children's dance at Windsor and the Prince joined in with the activity of a boy. Although in the words of the Queen " he danced lightly and beautifully ", she goes on to say that " he disliked it in general " but on these occasions he capered and pirouetted with a zest which inspired them all.[2] At the country dance, which was the prelude to the playing in of the New Year, he would skip down the middle and then with twinkling feet dance Poussette. He would then run back to help the children and his amused laughter at their awkward fixes could be heard above the music.

At Christmas, which was invariably spent at Windsor, the children were given their presents on Christmas Eve in the Queen's private sitting-rooms. The chandeliers in these rooms were taken down and huge Christmas trees, with coloured wax lights and adorned with bonbons, were lighted up. The whole scene resembled a superb and brilliant bazaar, and Princess Louise — a girl of twelve — was once heard to remark on entering, " Vraiment, c'est un peu trop extravagant." [3] Courtiers, princes and princesses jostled one another, talked and jested without fear that they might be " giving the back " to royalty. On the last Christmas of the Prince's life people were amused to notice Prince Arthur, who had been given a splendid pop-gun, taking a quick pot-shot at his father and then by way of amends ceremoniously

[1] Royal Archives. [2] Royal Archives. [3] Royal Archives.

presenting arms.[1] The Queen's sister, recalling the delightful terms which bound the children to their father, observed that in their company " he was so like a child ".[2]

On the elder children his influence was abiding and their affection for him was unbounded — perhaps in excess of what they felt for the Queen. They seem to have been able to pierce through the shyness which veiled his intensely affectionate nature and to appreciate not only the loving-kindness of his heart but the quality of his character. When the Princess Royal married she confided to the Queen, " I think it will kill me to take leave of dear Papa ".[3] On the day after they parted, when they had driven together through heavy snow and cheering crowds to the terminus of the North Kent Railway, he wrote :

> I am not of a demonstrative nature and therefore you can hardly know how dear you have always been to me, and what a void you have left behind in my heart : yet not in my heart for there assuredly you will abide henceforth, as till now you have done, but in my daily life, which is evermore reminding my heart of your absence.[4]

The conventional picture of the Prince as a stern, unbending Victorian paterfamilias has no foundation save in imagination and prejudice. Those who believe this particular fairy-tale seek to explain away the relations between the Prince and his eldest daughter by implying that she was his favourite child and that there was some peculiar affinity between their two characters. In fact, Stockmar noticed that the Princess was the most like the English Royal Family of all the Queen's children.[5] He did not, of course, mean that the Princess had inherited the weaknesses of the flesh for which that family had won some notoriety, but that she had inherited their talents and versatility.

Had the Prince lived, it would seem likely that his relations with his next daughter — the Princess Alice — would have been

[1] *J. T. Delane*, by Arthur Dasent. Murray, 1908.
[2] *Letters and Verses of A. T. Stanley*, edited by R. E. Prothero, 1895.
[3] Martin, iv, 167.
[4] Martin, iv, 169.
[5] *Life of Wilberforce*, ii, 280.

on much the same footing as his relations with the Crown Princess. Certainly Princess Alice adored him, basing her whole life on his teaching and on what she imagined he would have wished. When in 1878 she came to die, those gathered round her bed caught her dying words, " dear Papa ". It is significant proof of the understanding between father and daughter that during his last illness he seems to have relied entirely on her, even telling her things about his illness, and in particular his conviction that he was dying, which he hesitated to reveal to the Queen.

The relations of the Prince Consort with his eldest son are perhaps more revealing of his character than anything else. Through the mists of pathos which roll heavily round this subject — for it is sad rather than funny — the observer can see the glad confidence of the Victorian turning to disappointment. Moreover, it shows the Prince's belief, which again is typical of men of his generation, that man should never give way to failure, that disappointments were merely a bugle-call to fresh exertions, to more careful provision against human foibles, to stouter barriers against the boundless surprises of human nature.

Both the Prince and the Queen started from the premise, which was perfectly sound, that the training of the Prince of Wales was their inescapable duty to the country. The child was just as much *l'Infant d'Angleterre* — to use a phrase of Lady Lyttelton's — as he was their own. Accordingly, Ministers of the Crown, bishops, scientists and foreigners were called in to advise, and sound sense with some high-falutin nonsense were flung into a vast hodge-podge of educational memoranda.

Stockmar set the ball rolling with a prodigious memorandum which began with the comfortable truism — " the child is born with natural dispositions to good and evil ". The Baron was writing at the Pavilion and, gazing on the splendid Chinese extravagance, he allowed his mind to rest on the man who had planned it all and lavished the British taxpayers' money in constructing it. He then solemnly set down on paper that the follies of George IV were due to a faulty education. He ended by saying that the Prince of Wales should be given an education " truly moral and truly English ", and that the Prince and Queen were too young to guide the education of the royal infants and that it became " their sacred duty " to consult more experienced persons and " to follow their advice ".[1]

This was written while the Prince of Wales was still an infant and for the time being the problem was solved by the appointment of Lady Lyttelton — a woman of charm and sensibility — to the post of governess. However, two years later memoranda were again beginning to fly to and fro. The Queen wrote, " I wish that he should grow up entirely under *his Father's eye*, and every step be guided by him, so that when he has attained the age of sixteen or seventeen he may be a real companion to his father ".[2] Stockmar followed suit and pointed out, with some shrewdness, that Prince Albert's own interests, " political, moral, mental and national ", were inseparably bound up with those of the Prince of Wales and that any shortcomings in his training would be " certain to be avenged upon his father ".[3] With the bland optimism of a prelate the Bishop of Oxford pronounced that " the great object in view is to make him the most perfect man ".[4] The Baron Bunsen, who was consulted, strongly urged that the Prince of Wales's tutor should be a clergyman and named, in this connexion, Arthur Stanley, son of the Bishop of Norwich, and afterwards Dean of Westminster. That this suggestion did not bear fruit was a thousand pities, for if anyone could have guided the Prince of Wales aright, it would have been this man imbued with

> Goodness warm and truth without alloy,
> And temper sweet, and love of all things pure,
> And joy in light, and power to spread the joy.[5]

[1] Martin, ii, 175, and Royal Archives. [2] Royal Archives.
[3] Martin, i, 193. [4] Royal Archives.
[5] Matthew Arnold. The Prince and Queen would have liked to appoint Bishop Wilberforce but they did not wish to interfere with his chances of promotion in the Church. This was while the Bishop was still in favour at Court and before the disagreements over the Hampden appointment.

Unluckily, Stockmar argued strongly against a clerical tutor because he felt that a clergyman was bound to prejudice the boy against science, which was certain " to influence *society* far more generally and powerfully than it has ever done before ".[1] This advice was sufficient to rule out Stanley but not to exclude all clergy, and in the result the Reverend Henry Birch was appointed — an Eton master. He had all the uninspired amiability of his kind — not a whole-time clergyman, nor yet a whole-time schoolmaster, but always the perfect gentleman. His pupil, of course, loved him.

Before Mr. Birch started his duties the Prince drew up a time-table for each day's work.

Religion	half an hour at a stretch
English	one hour
Writing	half an hour
French	one hour
Music	half an hour
Calculating	half an hour
German	one hour
Drawing	half an hour
Geography	half an hour

This was in 1849 when the Prince was seven and a half and the programme was severe. The Prince added :

It will be well to let mental and more mechanical exertion alternate in order not to strain the intellect or wear out the patience of the child.

Immediately after the meal in the middle of the day it will be well not to work the mind of the child.

The Prince will not go to church till he has passed his eighth birthday but the Tutor might on Sunday have a short doctrinal exercise with him . . . the Prince ought to say his prayers morning and evening before the Tutor.[2]

Among the piles of memoranda, the pages of instruction to tutors and the compilation of time-tables, was one shred of advice

[1] Royal Archives. [2] Royal Archives.

which the Prince would have done well to ponder. This came from the flippant but wise mind of that exhausted man of the world, Lord Melbourne, whose vital powers, crippled by paralysis, were slowly running down at Brocket. He had written, "Be not over solicitous about education. It may be able to do much. . . . It may mould and direct character, but it rarely alters it."[1]

For in the case of the Prince of Wales his parents made the mistake of expecting too much from education. The child's good qualities were obvious — a great charm of manner (even as a boy) and a confiding, deeply affectionate nature. "We agreed that he was such a dear little boy", wrote the Queen in her Journal. But as he grew older his good qualities were increasingly vitiated by obstinacy, passion, a great capacity for exaggeration and a complete inability to learn. He showed no improvement under Mr. Birch and it was decided to try the effects of a whipping from his father.[2] Evidently this did no good and in the following year the famous phrenologist, George Combe, was called in to examine the boy. He reported on the nervous excitability, extreme obstinacy and passionate nature of the Prince of Wales, adding, with some shrewdness, that his self-esteem was very markedly developed and that this should be played upon to correct his other faults.[3]

Against this very unfavourable picture of the boy formed by his parents should be set the opinion of Lady Lyttelton, who, while admitting that he was not clever, said that he was truthful and possessed of "very good principles".[4] No doubt her picture was, broadly speaking, correct, but the very fact that he was not clever, or as his parents would have expressed it, perversely stupid, was the cause of all the trouble. The Prince and Queen made the great and elementary mistake of most parents in

[1] *Letters*, i, 365.
[2] Diary of Sir James Clark. Royal Archives.
[3] Royal Archives.
[4] Greville, vi, 418.

expecting their children to be replicas of themselves. The Prince used to refer in early days to his two elder children as "the improved edition"[1] and he told the Queen that "parents lived their lives over again in their children".[2] The Queen, with all the vehemence of her nature, was determined that her sons should take after their father. At the same time there was in the case of the Queen and Prince some excuse for the mistake of expecting their heir to be themselves in replica. By them monarchy was based on intelligence and application to business and they could not conceive how it could survive if the sovereign was indolent and flighty. The fate which overtook some of the sovereigns of Europe in 1848 — just at the moment they were planning the Prince's education — sharpened their apprehensions on this score.

In 1852 Birch departed and was succeeded by Frederick Waymouth Gibbs. This gentleman, a fellow of Trinity College, Cambridge, and the intimate friend of the illustrious Cambridge family of Stephen (to whom he owed his appointment, and from whom he had caught some of their stark intellectuality), was first sent abroad by the Prince to rub up his learning before taking charge of the child of ten, who cordially detested him. After leaving royal circles Mr. Gibbs won some notoriety by writing an open letter to the Bishop of London called, "Once a clergyman — always a clergyman". Tutors might come and tutors might go but the curriculum of the unlucky child went on for ever.

When the Prince of Wales was seventeen he was given a measure of independence on passing from the hands of tutors to the care of a governor. This was accompanied by a memorandum in which it was pointed out to him that life is composed of duties and that in their discharge "the true Christian, true soldier and true gentleman" can be recognised. The youth was told with depressing emphasis that he was starting the most difficult study

[1] *Leaves from a Journal of Our Life in the Highlands*, p. 31.
[2] Lord Esher, *Influence of King Edward*. John Murray, 1915.

of his life, " how to become a good man and a thorough gentleman". He was likewise warned against the thraldom of depending for everything on servants. It was signed " V.R. and A." but the style betrays the authorship as " A."[1] According to Greville, this grave and formidable document so touched the youth that he showed it to the Dean of Windsor to the accompaniment of floods of tears.

At the same time the greatest care was taken by the Prince Consort to choose appropriate young men who were to be attached to his son. He took particular pride in his choice of Lord Valletort, who, as he says, " has been much on the continent, is a thoroughly good, moral and accomplished man, draws well and plays, and never was at a public school, but passed his youth in attendance on an invalid father." [2] This saintly male nurse can hardly have been stimulating company for the lively young Prince.

In a long memorandum to these young gentlemen the Prince went at enormous length into the qualities distinguishing a gentleman, and particularly warned them against encouraging the Prince of Wales to ridicule people or to take part " in anything approaching a practical joke ". They were to steer him clear of " mere games of cards and billiards, and idle gossiping talk ", but they were to try to induce him " to devote some of his leisure time to music, to the fine arts, either drawing or looking over drawings, engravings etc. to hearing poetry, amusing books or good plays read aloud, in short, to anything that whilst it amuses may gently exercise the mind ".[3]

Now that the Prince was older, the plans of his father were redoubled. As the young man showed ever more emphatically that he had no disposition for learning, the Prince worked out a meticulous curriculum appropriate for one who aimed at spending his life in the amply billowing gown of a don, but quite unsuited

[1] Greville, vii, 383. [2] Martin, iv, 206.

[3] Lord Esher, *Influence of King Edward*.

for one destined by the gods to wear a crown rather than a mortar-board. Tutors, professors, scientists, historians, mathematicians and preachers — marionettes dancing to the manipulation of the Prince Consort — tortured the boy's intelligence like the morbid spectres in a nightmare provoked by a surfeit of plum-cake. Entire Universities — Edinburgh, Oxford and Cambridge — swam before his startled gaze when he passed a few terms as an undergraduate of these seats of learning. He was there just long enough to be bored — not quite long enough to get to know the horse-copers, dog-fanciers and rat-catchers who formed the best undergraduate society of the day. His companions were a handful of clergymen and port-drenched dons carefully chosen by his tutors.

Even with his son in these safe hands the Prince never relaxed, and as the alluring dangers of Commem. at Oxford drew near he wrote, " I trust you understand that the Balls etc. etc. which you visit are not visited by you for your amusement but to give pleasure to others by your presence ".[1] Almost pathetic by its remoteness from reality was the following letter from the Prince to his son at Oxford : " I hope you have begun your little dinner parties again and are seeing the chief men of the University at your table. . . . Is Professor Walker's lecture interesting ? I never heard him lecture." [2] Hardly less pathetic was his comment to his son when he heard that he did his work cheerfully, " This is the only road to happiness and I want to see you happy ".[3]

No one would attempt to justify the educational austerities of Prince Albert. They illustrate a characteristic which is marked and constant in the Teutonic race — an infinite capacity for planning without any power to vary the plan when circumstances demand it. Nonetheless, admirers of King Edward VII have on occasion made almost too much of their case against the Prince. For example, Lord Redesdale — resplendent in silk hat and *pince-nez* — indignantly writes, " What would not the boy have given

[1] Royal Archives. [2] Royal Archives. [3] Royal Archives.

for a game of football? How he would have loved to drive a cricket ball over the boundary!"[1] Would he? In fact plenty of companions and plenty of games were provided for him, but as he developed an agreeable habit of ill-treating his companions the games were not exactly instructive in the team spirit. In fact, Mamas used to tremble lest their sons should be chosen for an afternoon's bullying at Windsor Castle.[2] This was no doubt all rather harmless and boyish and the sensible way of dealing with it was shown by Lady Lyttelton's eldest grandson, who when he was summoned to play cricket with the Prince always directed the ball with unerring skill and some speed at the royal legs.

Sympathisers with King Edward likewise allow their hearts to gallop off with their judgment when they condemn the Prince Consort's educational arrangements without viewing them against their contemporary background, because to judge the curriculum by modern standards is to fall into a very obvious trap inviting disaster. Yet into that trap commentators on this subject monotonously tumble. Writers of the present day, accustomed to private schools where the Matron is far more important than the Headmaster, and to public schools where the dust sits thickly on the rod and chastisement takes the form of a fireside-chat freely interspersed with the soothing tinkle of Christian names, naturally find it difficult to appreciate the stern efficiency of Victorian education. If Mr. Wackford Squeers be deemed a shade grotesque, a study of Dr. Arnold or a glance at *Tom Brown's Schooldays* shows the Victorian curriculum in the full starkness of its glory. Even a gentle governess opened a vast storehouse of knowledge before the weary gaze of her charges.

> The total chronicles of man, the mind,
> The morals, something of the frame, the rock,
> The star, the bird, the fish, the shell, the flower,
> Electric, chemic laws, and all the rest,
> And whatsoever can be taught or known.[3]

[1] *Memories*, by Lord Redesdale, Hutchinson, 1916, i, p. 164.

[2] *The Queen thanks Sir Howard*, p. 43.

[3] *The Princess*.

" That very eccentric Lord Brougham ", as Queen Victoria described him, once electrified a public meeting by crying, " Look out, gentlemen, the schoolmaster is abroad ! " In the nineteenth century, enlightened thinkers from Lord Brougham downwards felt that the schoolmaster, trailing clouds of light and learning, was to transmogrify the mind of man. Inspired by this prevailing optimism the Prince planned the education of his children and against that background should his efforts be judged. He himself said that education was the finest legacy which a father could bequeath to his children,[1] although in a moment of irritation when his second son was caught smoking he admitted to Stockmar, " Really, education can do nothing for children." [2]

In a very private conversation with Lord Clarendon, which it was indiscreet of Lord Clarendon to repeat, the Prince confessed that perhaps the aggressive treatment of the Prince of Wales which he and the Queen had employed had been a mistake. He said that the disagreeable task of punishment had always fallen on him, and that he hesitated to resist the harshness of the Queen towards the children because of the fear of exciting her if she were thwarted.[3] Greville had some grounds for saying of the Queen's feelings for the Prince of Wales that she " does not much like the child ".[4] The events leading up to the death of the Prince Consort, as will be explained in the next chapter, turned the feeling into what Lord Palmerston called " unconquerable aversion ".[5]

The relations of the Prince Consort with his eldest son are easily distorted by exaggerating the differences between them. While no one could possibly gloss over the irksomeness of the educational treadmill arranged by the father, this must be set against a background of family life which was friendly, affection-

[1] *Adolphe Quetelet et le Prince Albert de Saxe-Coburg-Gotha.* Brussels, 1919.
[2] Royal Archives. [3] Greville, vii, 388, 389. [4] Greville, vi, 9.
[5] George Villiers, *A Vanished Victorian.* Eyre and Spottiswoode, 1938.

ate and normal. The Princess Royal was not exaggerating when she alluded in a letter to her brother to the happiness of their childhood and youth.[1]

Certainly there is no evidence either in the Royal Archives or in the printed authorities to justify the belief that the relations between the Prince and his eldest son were other than deeply affectionate. "Bertie is much improved" is a constant refrain in his letters to Stockmar, and he was always quick to give him the credit for anything he did well. In 1860 he wrote to Stockmar:

> That you see so many signs of improvement in the young gentleman is a great joy and comfort to us; for parents who watch their son with anxiety and set their hopes for him high are in some measure incapable of forming a clear estimate, and are at the same time apt to be impatient if their hopes are not fulfilled.[2]

For his part the Prince of Wales valued his father's advice, always sought it (though he may not have always followed it) and felt for him an abiding respect and affection. At the Royal Academy Banquet, some years after his father's death, he attempted to speak of him but broke down in a burst of sobbing. Nor is it without significance that in his first speech as King he made a touching reference to "my father — ever to be lamented, good and wise".

[1] Royal Archives. [2] Martin, v, 87.

CHAPTER XI

TYPHOID FEVER

YET by an odd tweak of fortune the conduct of the Prince of Wales was not without its influence when that sombre shadow lowered over the Castle in the winter of 1861. For the first ten months of that year the Prince, though excessively busy, was not ailing. He had in fact rather enjoyed the freedom from court functions following the death of the Duchess of Kent, since a period of Court mourning, though productive of great sartorial inconvenience for judges, guards officers and courtiers, can have — for the central figures of the Court — some of the solace and pleasure of an unexpected holiday. The summer visit to Osborne had been prolonged, and the Prince had bathed daily with his son-in-law the Crown Prince. At Balmoral he had shot well, and the Queen's paroxysms of grief over her mother were beginning to subside under the influence of those Highland expeditions which she enjoyed with such intensity. By the end of October the Court was back at Windsor ready once more to shoulder the burdens of formality and routine. On November 9th something of its old gaiety returned when the Prince of Wales came over from Cambridge for the celebration of his twentieth birthday. At his father's request he led in the Queen to dinner and she noted in her Journal that " the band played for the first time since our sad loss ".

One family cloud oppressed the Prince. His youngest son, the Prince Leopold, who was eight, had developed the scourge of haemophilia which had manifested itself in a severe attack of bleeding at Osborne in the summer, and the doctors had decided that he ought not to spend the winter in England. The Prince was much occupied in the arrangements for this journey and selected for the boy's travelling-companion General Bowater, a Waterloo veteran of seventy-four. When this somewhat melancholy combination of ailing youth and halting age arrived at Cannes the old gentleman went straight to his bed and shortly afterwards died. This was particularly awkward because the boy was stranded in a strange land and the Prince was much engrossed in finding an adequate substitute who could go out at once. During the closing weeks of his life the Prince was haunted by anxiety for the child's health — hardly able to bring himself to open his letters, " because they may contain bad news about Leopold ".

At the beginning of November a further anxiety loomed on the horizon. At Lisbon typhoid fever was knocking down the members of the Portuguese Royal Family like Stockmar among the skittles. Two of the King's brothers died of the fever, and the King himself was known to be critically ill. King Pedro — a young man of twenty-five, amiable, accomplished and clever — was a specially favourite cousin of the Prince and Queen. On November 12th came the news that he had died. The Queen went so far as to say, " My Albert loved him like a son."[1] Apart from his own personal feelings the Prince, as he explained to his eldest daughter, deplored the loss of one who would have upheld with integrity the monarchical principle and might have done much for what he called " a degraded country and people ".[2]

However, worse was to come. On the evening after he received the telegram announcing King Pedro's death, he was told a piece of news which, according to Queen Victoria, " broke my Angel's heart ".[3] A letter in the Royal Archives makes it plain that this news concerned an escapade with a woman on the part of the Prince of Wales, and that it caused his father the deepest pain and anxiety.

[1] Journal. [2] Martin, v, 411. [3] *Letters*, November 12th, 1863.

If the Prince Consort's vexation seems a shade exaggerated to modern tastes, it should be remembered that the typical Victorian father, when his son got into a scrape or his daughter formed an undesirable attachment, was capable of unsuspected flights of histrionics. Nor were such escapades in any way uncommon among Victorian youths who enjoyed discovering those unlawful amusements outlined by Dr. Johnson :

> Call the Betsies, Kates and Jennies,
> All the names that banish care ;
> Lavish of your grandsire's guineas,
> Show the spirit of an heir.

But the spirit of an heir, as the novels of the nineteenth century repeatedly remind us, was extremely dangerous to paternal bank balances and paternal acres, and this explains why fathers often went to great lengths to extinguish that spirit. Anger sprang as much from prudence as from morality. These conventional feelings of his generation no doubt coloured the Prince Consort's outlook, but in his case they were magnified by two considerations.

The first was the appreciation of the damage which might be done to the whole monarchical structure. That easy-going, self-indulgence which he had watched with horror in his own brother was the dry-rot which could destroy the high ideals of monarchy from within. Were he and the Queen to watch their own life's work being slowly undermined before their eyes from the same cause ?

The second consideration which helps to explain the strength of the Prince's feelings is more personal. Long ago, as a youth, he had told his secretary that he did not fear temptation with women because that species of vice disgusted him.[1] The years of maturity had done nothing to shake that distaste, and it is significant that in an important appreciation of the Prince's character, based on material provided by the Queen, the way in

[1] Royal Archives.

which vice "depressed him, grieved him, horrified him" is emphasised.[1] On November 20th he wrote to the Prince of Wales assuring him that all the people round him would do everything to help him, "but they will be powerless unless they be met on your part with that openness and honesty which must characterize the dealings of gentlemen towards each other".[2] Five days later he travelled by special train to Cambridge, spending the night at Madingley Hall with the Prince of Wales. He returned the next day "much relieved" according to the Queen.[3]

Though the Prince was a large man his constitution was not robust and, as his letters to Stockmar show, anxieties were always apt to draw upon his stock of nervous energy. The cumulative effect of his anxiety over Prince Leopold and his grief for King Pedro, crowned by his alarm about the Prince of Wales, was immediately serious. From the middle of November he virtually ceased to sleep and on his return from Cambridge on November 26th he was plainly ill. Three days later he went out to watch the Queen reviewing the Eton Volunteers. Although the day was warm it was noticed that the Prince was muffled up in a fur coat, and he remarked that he felt as if cold water was being poured down his back. On Sunday, December 1st, he got up, as usual, at 7 and modified a despatch which the Foreign Office was sending to the American Government over the Trent affair. These modifications were not without their influence in relieving the very serious tension between the two countries. As he handed the draft to the Queen he said, "I could scarcely hold my pen."[4]

He went to church that morning and attended luncheon with a large party of guests but he ate nothing and was plainly seriously ill. On the following morning he did not dress, and he was handed over to the Court physicians and the full discipline of illness.

[1] *Speeches* — the Introduction.
[2] Royal Archives.
[3] Royal Archives.
[4] Martin, v, 421.

At that time private nurses were unknown and the Prince was tended by his personal servants, his private secretaries and the Princess Alice. His doctors seem to have decided that the restlessness of fever must be given full indulgence, and they allowed him to wander through the Castle as fancy dictated. Wearing a dressing-gown he moved by day or night from his bedroom to his dressing-room and then on to his sitting-room. On December 6th the Queen, without apparent surprise, noted that " he changed his room two or three times during the night ". On the following day the doctors had to admit that the Prince was suffering from " gastric or low fever ".[1] He was now more regularly confined to bed, though he was allowed to be wheeled about the Castle. The range of his wanderings was extended to include the Blue Room, in which King William IV and King George IV had died. He himself expired in this room exactly a week after the doctors had diagnosed his illness.

The Prince seems to have collapsed under the quick blows of fever into a stupor of complaint and distress — a mere hulk of the splendid personality who had led and enlightened his family. Occasionally his mind would struggle through the fog of confusion and shine as of old. Once he asked for a chorale to be played at a distance, but instead of turning to his daughter, as was his practice in health, and saying " Es ist doch gar zu schön " (It is really quite too lovely), he merely murmured, " Das reicht hin " (That is enough). One morning, with the sun shining and the birds piping a feeble winter ditty, he thought he was back in the Rosenau listening to the dawn chorus in that Paradise. Once he attempted a joke and when his private secretary handed him a loathsome draught of physic, he raised the glass, saying, " Your very good health, Grey ". Yet as was true of so much of the married life of the Queen and Prince, its final moments on December 14th were not to be private. The room was filled with doctors, valets and secretaries, and occasionally the Prince

[1] Gastric fever was the old-fashioned euphemism for typhoid fever.

would drag himself from the mists of unconsciousness to murmur in German some words of comfort to the Queen. Towards the end he was heard to say, "Gutes Frauchen," accompanied by a piteous moan, and the Queen fancied that he was trying to express the words of comfort which he had once whispered to her, "I grieve so much to leave you." At 5 o'clock on December 14th his children passed by the bed to say farewell, and six hours later, peacefully but without any clear recognition of the Queen, he died.

An hour later the citizens of London, who still lived thickly clustered round their work, were startled to hear the great bell of St. Paul's Cathedral crashing on the midnight air. On the following morning — a day of peerless winter beauty — the news was chalked up on the walls, announced by the clergy in church and whispered by the sidesmen as they collected the offertory. The bland optimism of royal bulletins had done nothing to prepare the public for a shock which was felt as keenly and widely as that of the death of the Princess Charlotte in childbirth forty years back. The words "favourable" and "unfavourable" slipped in and out of the bulletins, but it was not until six hours before his death that the critical nature of the illness was admitted.

On December 6th the Queen had written to her uncle that she was "*very very* anxious"[1] and yet no word was breathed to the public. On the following Sunday it was necessary to put off a party of guests at the Castle and a statement was issued — though not a bulletin — to the effect that the Prince was suffering from "a feverish cold". Considering that when this announcement was issued the Prince was suffering from periods of delirium (although the doctors assured the Queen that they were "of no moment") it must rank as one of the great masterpieces of understatement.

The public pardonably felt — and this feeling found expression in the newspapers — that the Prince's illness had been grossly

[1] *Letters*, iii, 471.

mishandled. They argued that there must have been laxness for the Prince, at the age of forty-two, in the full vigour of manhood, to succumb to a brief attack of fever. Nor were they comforted when they surveyed the team of doctors responsible for the case. At their head was Sir James Clark, aged seventy-three, who was largely remembered for his mistaken diagnosis in the case of Lady Flora Hastings. He was assisted by another septuagenarian, Sir Henry Holland, who had made his name as the medical attendant on King George IV's wife during her questionable junketings round the Mediterranean. Few would have disagreed with Lord Clarendon who said of these eminent practitioners, "They are not fit to attend a sick cat."[1]

Yet it would plainly be silly to condemn the doctors by contrasting their treatment with the medical fal-lals of the modern world. They no doubt did their utmost and Sir James Clark wrote some years after :

> On looking back I have the satisfaction, after viewing the case in all its bearings, of feeling that everything was done to save him that human art, as far as at present known, could do. . . . For years he had worked his brain so much that the nervous system sank sadly under the influence of the febrile poison.[2]

Sir William Jenner, who established the difference between typhoid and typhus fevers, was in charge of the case under Sir James Clark. Writing afterwards to a friend he said :

> You can have no idea of the excellence of the man — he was the finest specimen of intellectual and moral greatness and religious excellence I have ever known — so great, so good did I think him that when sitting at his bedhead in the stillness of night, fearing the result, I have longed and longed that I might die in his place.[3]

The doctors do, however, appear to have been obstinately optimistic. "Good, kind, old Sir James", as the Queen called him, constantly assured her that "there is no cause for alarm

[1] *Paris Embassy during Second Empire.*
[2] Royal Archives. [3] Royal Archives.

either present or future". On the fatal 14th another of the doctors brightly said to the Queen, "I never despair with fever, my own son was left for dead and recovered."[1]

The question really turns on whether the doctors should not have diagnosed the illness more quickly. The *Lancet*, no doubt with this criticism in mind, defined the cause of the Prince's death as "typhoid fever not very severe in its early stages". When the Prince of Wales went to register his father's death in Windsor he certified that he had died from typhoid fever lasting for twenty-one days, which would take the origin of the illness back to the visit to Madingley. From the very start Palmerston, well aware of the menacing capabilities of the royal doctors, was insistent that outside opinion should be sought. As early as December 1st, when he was one of the guests at the Castle, he expressed a wish that another physician should be consulted. Subsequently, almost all the members of the Cabinet wrote to either Phipps or Grey urging a change of doctors, and on December 7th Palmerston wrote:

> If it is unavoidable that the highest interests of the nation must be sacrificed to personal and professional jealousy, there is no help for it and so it must be. I could say much about the past, but my thoughts are wholly engrossed with the future.[2]

From the first the Prince seems to have convinced himself that his illness was mortal. On the Wednesday before he died he asked the Princess Alice whether she had written to the Crown Princess. She said, "Yes, I told her that you are very ill." "You did wrong," he replied, "you should have told her that I am dying. Yes, I am dying." It seems probable that in order to combat the Prince's conviction that he was dying the doctors and the Queen assumed an optimism that they did not feel. Certainly there is no evidence to show that the Queen ever blamed the doctors. She rather believed that his untimely death was provoked by worry over the conduct of the Prince of Wales.

[1] Journal. [2] Royal Archives.

Whether this caused the Prince's death in the sense of predisposing him to the germ, or whether it prevented a recovery from what had already lodged in the system, is one of those medical disputations which are apt to disturb the solemnities of many a deathbed. In this case the views of the doctors are of less importance than those of the Queen. She believed, with all the tenacity of her nature, that her husband died from worry over the Prince of Wales — a belief in which she was fortified when the doctors assured her in the early days of the illness that her husband was only suffering from " worry and overwork ". In his review of the case, already quoted, Sir James Clark says in a clear reference to this aspect of the illness, " There was excessive mental excitement on one very recent occasion ".[1] This manifested itself by the Prince constantly calling for the Prince of Wales's governor, General Bruce, when he was delirious. This explains why the Queen resolutely refused to summon the Prince of Wales to Windsor when his father was plainly dying — a step which was taken by the Princess Alice without her mother's knowledge. This likewise explains her dislike for the Prince of Wales in his young manhood which has puzzled posterity and which she made not the least effort to hide. She startled Lord Clarendon shortly after her husband's death by saying to him of the Prince of Wales, " It quite irritates me to see him in the room."[2]

Irrational as the Queen's attitude to the Prince of Wales may have been, it was characteristic of someone of her intense nature who, in the face of misfortune, was always prone to vent her feelings on individuals. Her own daughter at the time of the Emperor Frederick's death displayed very similar feelings (though

[1] Royal Archives.

[2] *A Vanished Victorian*. It should be added that in the face of his mother's treatment — always unsympathetic and at times harsh — the Prince of Wales showed admirable loyalty and magnanimity. He never allowed the slightest whisper against his mother, and historians must accord him and the Princess of Wales full credit for refusing to foster those silly rivalries which disgraced the English Royal Family in the eighteenth century.

the reason for them was very much more obvious) for her eldest son. Certainly nobody in possession of all the facts would venture to criticise the Queen, for in the untimely death of the Prince Consort she was confronted by a disaster of imponderable magnitude. In felicitous language Palmerston, in the House of Commons, referring to the isolation of the Queen's position, said that she " is left in a solitude of grief which could hardly befall any other person in the realm."

Yet there were no hysterics and there is no truth in Lytton Strachey's assertion that the widowed Queen emitted " one long wild shriek that rang through the terror-stricken castle ". Indeed, a moment's reflection shows that the human voice, without the aid of myriads of amplifiers, is not capable of piercing the stone solidity of castle walls. On December 14th the ordered momentum of Court life — naturally enough — completely collapsed. Ladies-in-waiting and gentlemen of the Household gathered in apprehensive groups, oppressed with forebodings but clutching at any portent which seemed to give rise to hope. At 11 o'clock a footman, in scarlet livery, came running along the corridor with a request that the Duchess of Atholl, who was lady-in-waiting, would go to the Queen at once. She met the Queen coming out of the room in which the Prince had just died, sobbing, " Oh, Duchess, he is dead ! He is dead ! " She then saw all her children, spoke to them of their father and dedicated herself to continue his work. After this she lay down on a sofa in a room opening out of the Blue Room where the Prince lay, and the members of the Household trooped past her to pay their last respects to their master. One by one they filed past and, making a violent effort to compose herself, she said to each, " You will not desert me ? You will all help me ? " [1]

Her family sought to comfort her. The Prince of Wales embraced her and said, " I will become everything you wish." [2] From Berlin her eldest daughter wrote, " In doing Papa's will I

[1] Royal Archives and *The Queen thanks Sir Howard.* [2] Eleanor Stanley.

shall be doing God's will ".[1] A few days later she added, "I looked to Papa's advice for educating William which is such a difficult task ".[2] And that kindly uncle, still living, the sole survivor of his generation, the honest broker who had brought them together, maintaining his original, incisive style and despising conventional words of sympathy, wrote to the Queen of the dead Prince "whom I loved more than my own children ".[3]

The funeral took place in St. George's Chapel on Monday, December 23rd, and in accordance with the wishes of the Prince it was as simple as fashion and tradition allowed. The morbid accompaniments of royal funerals of former times — nightfall, massed bands of the Guards, flambeaux and sweeping mourning-cloaks — were accorded no place. The service was held at midday and was dignified but not dramatic. When the coffin, resplendent in crimson velvet, adorned with a gold coronet and bearing the words, " Augustissimae et potentissimae Victoriae reginae conjugis percarissimi ", had been lowered to the vault, Garter King at Arms was too moved to pronounce with any comprehension the style and dignities of the Prince. When the choir sang the chorale which contained the lines

> So fall asleep in slumber deep,
> Slumber that knows no ending,

and which was set to one of the Prince's own compositions, even " old dry political eyes which seemed as if they had long forgotten how to weep " melted in sympathy.[4]

Yet the plain pageantry of the Prince's funeral was not in keeping with that gloating over the portents of death which was characteristic of the nineteenth century. A Victorian funeral sermon — wallowing in every detail of physical disintegration — was one of the goads with which the clergy drove their palpitating congregations to their knees. " Can thy terrors, death, appal

[1] Royal Archives.
[2] Royal Archives.
[3] Royal Archives.
[4] Wilberforce, iii, 44.

us?" these unhappy victims bravely sang. A rich chorus of archdeacons, canons and divines boomed back,

> Soon will you and I be lying
> Each within our narrow bed.

The Prince was spared nothing. The pace was set by the Bishop of Gloucester who, preaching in the cathedral at Gloucester, started his sermon with obvious relish. "It is not often, my friends, that we witness the grand spectacle of a national sorrow." Up and down the country preachers thundered out their sermons invoking the awful majesty of death. With scant regard for the facts they pictured to their congregations the blazing stars and golden crowns of the Prince lying in the dusty darkness of the vaults of St. George's, and with glee they shouted that the companion of earth's greatest sovereign was from henceforth the companion of worms.

Thus stimulated, the country gave itself over to an orgy of mourning. The shops were festooned with black. In the ribbon and bonnet emporiums which lent gaiety and style to the streets of Victorian England all the coloured stuffs and ribbons were tucked away. In London it was observed that not a soul of any class was without mourning clothes.

Here and there a discordant note crept in. Birkbeck Hill, the accomplished editor of Johnson, thought that praise of the Prince and his virtues ought to have been made a felony, and that the nation should recover from its amazement "at the astonishing discovery that even princes can die".[1] Dickens — vexed at having to abandon his series of very profitable but vainglorious declamations from his own books — wrote with characteristic waspishness, "What Jackasses people are making of themselves over this death!"[2] And far away in the icy flats of Norfolk, Lord Orford, eccentric as only a Norfolk nobleman can be, on hearing that the Prince had died, immediately changed into his

[1] *Letters of George Birkbeck Hill.* Arnold, 1906.
[2] Dame Una Pope-Hennessy, *Charles Dickens.*

brightest clothes to express his pleasure that at least one foreigner was safely out of the way.

It is, however, clear, and it was even felt at the time, that the public sentiment was one of grief for the Queen, not of grief with her. When the public read how, on the insistent advice of her Government and uncle, she had torn herself from her husband's coffin to travel to Osborne, through stations swept of every vestige of humanity, their hearts were wrung. Yet the only sympathy which she valued or desired was that which stressed what she had lost. She was, for example, pleased by the letter from Palmerston who, having broken down in convulsive sobbing when he heard the news, wrote of the Prince as " that perfect Being ".[1] On the other hand, she was not pleased when a distinguished churchman wrote to her, " Henceforth you must remember that Christ himself will be your husband ". This unlucky phrase aways stuck in her mind, and in later years she said when repeating it, " That is what I call twaddle ".[2]

In estimating the character and influence of eminent men or women, writers are sometimes prone to wander in the airy realms of imagination — to consider what might have happened if their lives had been prolonged, or to attempt to calculate what might have been the effect if people with other temperaments and characters had occupied their place. Strachey, for example, draws a brilliant portrait of the Prince Consort in old age. If as a young man in the twenties he had been able to do battle with the doughty Palmerston, of what might he not have been capable in old age ? As Strachey pertinently asks, " What Minister could have withstood the wisdom of the venerable Prince ? " Nor is it fanciful to argue that his influence and friendship with the first Emperor of Germany might have made the ruthless triumph of Bismarck less easy and possibly less complete. Equally fascinating is the picture of Victorian England if Queen Victoria's

[1] Royal Archives.

[2] *Randall Davidson*, by the Bishop of Chichester. Oxford Press, 1935.

husband had possessed the vices of the Prince's brother or the circumscribed intelligence and healthy bluster of the Duke of Cambridge. Contemplating such a picture we can only say that having regard to the pliability of the Queen's character in youth, it would have been totally, alarmingly different from that which we know.

For undeniably the Prince's claim to greatness rests on his services to monarchy. While he did not create the Coburg conception of monarchy, which sprang from the genius of his uncle Leopold guided by Stockmar, he seized the torch from them and sped it on its way with amazing verve and strength. Indeed it may well be argued that by statecraft King Leopold lifted monarchy from the abyss, but that the Prince reinforced his work by investing it with integrity and nobility. He can certainly claim to be the creator of the modern English monarchical tradition. The establishment of business on an orderly, impartial foundation, with the fostering of those aspects of the nation's life which spring from something higher than mere material pursuits, was the torch brightly burning which he handed on to his successors.

Of necessity some of his services to the monarchy died with him, and this is particularly true of his political work. Lord John Russell once remarked of the Prince that "he was an informal but potent member of all Cabinets". The widowed Queen clung with great tenacity to that position, but by the end of the century the march of events had made great inroads on it. Nonetheless, the political influence of the Crown from 1840 to 1860 — perhaps insufficiently appreciated by historians — cut deep into that epoch, with consequences on public affairs of great significance.

Yet the observant reader will not have failed to remark that in spite of the bustle of business to which he applied himself with energy, and in spite of the diversity of his accomplishments, the Prince moves across the pages of history with a lack of ostentation which is curious. To the mid-Victorian the sign of respectability

THE PRINCE AND THE QUEEN, 1860
From a photograph

and success was the amount of splash in the world which the prosperous were capable of making. Large houses, rich solid furnishings, endless courses at dinner, countless servants — these were the marks of a gentleman. In its good, solid way the age was showy, extravagant, luxurious. That prevailing characteristic the Prince never displayed. In an era of splendour the Court was frugal. The blazing extravagance of the Court of the Second Empire, which had exactly caught the spirit of the age, found no reflection at Buckingham Palace or at Windsor Castle. The Prince governed all with a prudent simplicity which was at once something new in the annals of the English monarchy, and was also revealing of the indifference of the Prince's character to the foibles and fashions of his contemporaries.

Bacon once observed — doubtless with an eye to Queen Elizabeth — that female reigns are generally eclipsed by marriage. Fundamentally this was true of Queen Victoria's reign, but it was certainly not appreciated by the public at the time. The ship of monarchy sailed with a natural splendour through which the watchers failed to see the hands which were on the helm. Not the smallest of the Prince's achievements was to carry out unflinchingly the primary duty of his position which he set himself and once defined as " sinking his own *individual existence* in that of his wife ".

But the Prince's influence and his claim to the interest of posterity rest on something broader than his contribution to the structure of monarchy. Disraeli in a telling phrase wrote of him, " he formed and guided his generation with benignant power ". That was profoundly true, for in its most marked characteristics the age was Albertian rather than Victorian. The years from 1840 to 1860 reveal a heightened interest in art, in music, in finer manufactured goods, and they likewise show a growing tolerance in religious matters, a more general understanding of the charms of domestic felicity and a vague striving after higher things. While it would be an exaggeration to argue that the

Prince was solely responsible for these developments, he undoubtedly gave them a decided impetus. Of the average middle-class citizen it could be said that on all these questions — whether consciously or not is beside the mark — " in his master's steps he trod ". The very success of nineteenth-century England laid it open to the besetting sin of self-idolatry. The Prince was ever seeking to set before the people something worthier of worship than their own commercial and material triumphs. In spite of everything which can be said against nineteenth-century England — its cruelty, its grossness, its complacency, its selfishness — these vices cannot wholly smother that nobility which shines through them all. It fortified the fibres of the people, excusing their follies and absurdities. While that side of Victorian character was fostered by poets and writers it also gained strength from the example of the Prince. Though this instance may seem petty, it is significant that when he was asked to give a prize to Wellington College he asked that it should be allotted to the noblest boy. Nobility of character is of course a large quality to which mankind is rightly chary of laying claim. But that was the quality which the Prince most admired and by the light of which he sought to guide his own life,

> Ennobling this dull pomp — the life of Kings
> By contemplation of diviner things.

To exaggerate the virtues of princes is a vanity which dates far back in history — at any rate to the days when David exulted over Saul. Disraeli was no doubt guilty of this human foible when he told the Queen that the Prince was the only man he had known " who achieved the Ideal ". The outlook of the Prince was too practical, too robust for tinsel tributes of this kind. But those who seek without sycophancy to gauge the Prince's character would do well to ponder one portent. Byron, as is well known, could find no higher praise for a man than to say that he was a hero to his valet. Even more searching of a man's heroic qualities is his reputation with his private secretaries, for temper is apt to fray more easily at the desk than at the dressing-table. From this exacting test — the verdict of his private secretaries — the Prince escapes unscathed. Anson, Grey and Phipps with no ulterior motive, often writing with no idea that the Queen or posterity would see their words, are uniform in considered eulogy. Sir Charles Phipps — judicious, unruffled and loathing frothy exaggeration — wrote of his master that he was " the best man that I ever met with in my life ". The justification for this verdict is borne out by an examination of the Prince's public speeches, of his official communications with ministers, of his private correspondence, of his exertions to lift the public mind out of the trough of material things ; all are marked by the same largeness of view and a complete absence of selfishness.

Rolling back the mists of sentiment and the clouds of eulogy which still perhaps hide the true Prince Consort, we, from the vantage-point of eighty years on, can see him as he was — the embodiment of character and goodness. At these qualities later generations may have tittered, may have sought to mock them as redolent of governesses and public-school masters, but the laughter they have raised has been somewhat half-hearted. The personality of the Prince was " shy to illumine " his virtues, but as he stands out more clearly from history they shine with a glowing grace which, in spite of the fustian of twentieth-century morality, compels alike our understanding and admiration.

INDEX

THE END

PRINTED BY R. & R. CLARK, LTD., EDINBURGH

KING ALFRED'S COLLEGE
LIBRARY